Psychology Revivals

Culture and Early Interactions

In the late 1960s, after a period of intense acceleration of the pace of research on human infancy, a number of investigators – some anthropologists, some psychologists, some psychiatrists and paediatricians, and even a few ethologists – developed the conviction that certain contributions to the understanding of infancy would come from, and perhaps only come from, cross-cultural and cross-population studies.

This book, originally published in 1981, represents part of the first fruit of that conviction, and its impressive range of chapters justifies not only the belief itself but also the several rationales behind it.

Culture and Early Interactions

Edited by
Tiffany M. Field
Anita Miller Sostek
Peter Vietze
P. Herbert Leiderman

LONDON AND NEW YORK

First published in 1981
by Lawrence Erlbaum Associates, Inc.

This edition first published in 2014 by Psychology Press
27 Church Road, Hove, BN3 2FA

and by Psychology Press
711 Third Avenue, New York, NY 10017

Psychology Press is an imprint of the Taylor & Francis Group, an informa business

Copyright © 1981 by Lawrence Erlbaum Associates, Inc.

The right of Tiffany Field, Anita Miller Sostek, Peter Vietze, P. Herbert Leiderman to be identified as author of this work has been asserted by them in accordance with sections 77 and 78 of the Copyright, Designs and Patents Act 1988.

All rights reserved. No part of this book may be reprinted or reproduced or utilised in any form or by any electronic, mechanical, or other means, now known or hereafter invented, including photocopying and recording, or in any information storage or retrieval system, without permission in writing from the publishers.

Publisher's Note
The publisher has gone to great lengths to ensure the quality of this reprint but points out that some imperfections in the original copies may be apparent.

Disclaimer
The publisher has made every effort to trace copyright holders and welcomes correspondence from those they have been unable to contact.

A Library of Congress record exists under ISBN: 0898590973

ISBN: 978-1-84872-457-0 (hbk)
ISBN: 978-1-315-76565-5 (ebk)
ISBN: 978-1-84872-458-7 (pbk)

CULTURE AND EARLY INTERACTIONS

Edited by
TIFFANY M. FIELD
University of Miami Medical School

ANITA M. SOSTEK
Georgetown University School of Medicine

PETER VIETZE
National Institute of Child Health and Human Development

P. HERBERT LEIDERMAN
Stanford University

LAWRENCE ERLBAUM ASSOCIATES, PUBLISHERS
1981   Hillsdale, New Jersey

Copyright © 1981 by Lawrence Erlbaum Associates, Inc.
All rights reserved. No part of this book may be reproduced in
any form, by photostat, microform, retrieval system, or any other
means, without the prior written permission of the publisher.

Lawrence Erlbaum Associates, Inc., Publishers
365 Broadway
Hillsdale, New Jersey 07642

Library of Congress Cataloging in Publication Data
Main entry under title:

Culture and early interactions.

Includes bibliographies and indexes.
1. Mother and child—Cross-cultural studies.
I. Field, Tiffany.
HQ755.85.C84   306.8'7   81-9805
ISBN 0-89859-097-3   AACR2

Printed in the United States of America

Contents

Foreword *Melvin Konner*   xi
Preface   xv

I CULTURAL CONTEXTS

1. **Residence Patterns and the Environment of Mother-Infant Interaction Among the Navajo**   3
   James S. Chisholm

   Introduction   3
   Methodological Issues in Assessing the Effect
      of the Social Context on Early Interactions   5
   Assessing the Effect of the Social Context on
      Mother-Infant Interaction Among the Navajo   6
   The Social Context of Navajo and Anglo-American
      Residence Patterns   7
   Effect of the Social Context on Navajo and
      Anglo Mother-Infant Interaction   11
   The Effect of the Social Context on Navajo Nuclear
      and Extended Family Children's Fear of Strangers   14
   Summary and Conclusions   16
   References   18

2. **Social Context in Caregiver-Infant Interaction: A Film Study of Fais and the United States** 21
Anita Miller Sostek, Peter Vietze, Martha Zaslow, Laura Kreiss, Fransje van der Waals, and *Donald Rubinstein*

Introduction 21
Physical Geography of Fais Island 22
Demography 23
Childbirth, Childrearing, and Adoption 25
Aims and Methods 27
Cross-Cultural Comparisons 29
Social Context Analyses 29
Discussion 33
Use of Existing Ethnographic Film 35
References 36

II CULTURAL AND SOCIOECONOMIC STATUS

3. **Mother-Infant Interactions Among Lower SES Black, Cuban, Puerto Rican and South American Immigrants** 41
Tiffany M. Field and *Susan M. Widmayer*

Introduction 41
Historical Background and Cultural Values 43
Method of Study 51
Discussion 56
References 60

4. **Middle Class Differences in the Mother-Child Interaction and the Child's Cognitive Development** 63
Candice Feiring and Michael Lewis

Method 67
Results Age Level Analyses 74
Developmental Changes 78
Discussion 85
References 89

III CULTURAL VALUES

5. **Father-Mother-Infant Interaction in the Newborn Period: A German-American Comparison**   95
   Ross D. Parke, Karin Grossmann, and Barbara R. Tinsley

   Method   *102*
   Procedure   *103*
   Results   *104*
   Discussion   *109*
   References   *111*

6. **A Comparison of Anglo, Hopi, and Navajo Mothers and Infants**   115
   John W. Callaghan

   Method   *115*
   Results   *119*
   Discussion   *127*
   Conclusion   *130*
   References   *131*

7. **Maternal Rhythmicity in Three American Cultures**   133
   Barbara Fourcher Fajardo and Daniel G. Freedman

   Group Differences in Maternal Rhythmicity   *135*
   Relationships Between Infant Averting and Maternal Rhythmicity   *140*
   References   *146*

8. **Mother-Infant Interaction Among the Gusii of Kenya**   149
   Suzanne Dixon, Edward Tronick, Constance Keefer, and T. Berry Brazelton

   Introduction   *149*
   Method of Study   *154*
   Results   *157*
   Discussion   *163*
   References   *167*

IV GROWTH AND DEVELOPMENTAL STATUS OF INFANTS

9. **Infant and Caretaker Behavior as Mediators of Nutritional and Social Intervention in the Barrios of Bogota** *171*
   Charles M. Super, John Clement, Lea Vuori, Niels Christiansen, Jose O. Mora, and M. Guillermo Herrera

   Design of the Bogata Study *173*
   The Effects of Intervention *178*
   Discussion *186*
   Conclusion *187*
   References *188*

10. **Early Interactions in the Marquesas Islands** *189*
    Mary Martini and John Kirkpatrick

    Introduction *189*
    Ethnographic Background *189*
    Marquesan Views of Development *191*
    Descriptions of Infancy *192*
    Film Study Methodology *195*
    Patterns of Interaction *196*
    Discussion *207*
    Conclusion *212*
    References *213*

11. **Age-Related Changes in Attachment Behavior in Polymatrically Reared Infants: The Kenyan Gusii** *215*
    Guy Reed and P. Herbert Leiderman

    Introduction *215*
    Selection of Attachment Behavioral Indices *216*
    Social and Cultural Context *218*
    Discussion *230*
    References *234*

V METHODOLOGICAL CONSIDERATIONS

12. The Cross-Cultural Study of Early Interaction: Implications from Research on Culture and Cognition *237*
Martha Zaslow and *Barbara Rogoff*

Methodological Issues in Cross-Cultural Studies of Cognition *238*
Comparable Issues in Cross-Cultural Studies of Early Interaction *242*
Conclusion *252*
References *253*

Author Index *257*
Subject Index *263*

Foreword

In the late 1960s, after a period of intense acceleration of the pace of research on human infancy, a number of investigators—some anthropologists, some psychologists, some psychiatrists and pediatricians, and even a few ethologists—developed the conviction that certain contributions to the understanding of infancy would come from, and perhaps only from, cross-cultural and cross-population studies.

This book represents part of the first fruit of that conviction, and its impressive range of chapters justifies not only the belief itself but also the several rationales behind it. For example, it was argued at the time that the cross-cultural range of variation would include environments for infants and young children that would be impossible to find in the mainstream of American culture or to reproduce in ethical experiments. The chapter by Chisholm documents a setting among the Navajo which, although within the geographic borders of the continental United States, preserves in some cases the extended family in the traditional Navajo *hogan,* unchanged for centuries, and in many cases the use of the cradleboard for the tight swaddling of infants—a practice unknown to the American middle class but widespread in Native American cultures. The chapter by Dixon and colleagues and that by Reed and Leiderman focus on infant care in a tropical African community, the Gusii, where traditionally all infants have been subject to the influence of multiple caretakers, an option the American middle class has been aloof from until recently, and which it has approached with apprehension. Other chapters detail infant care and mother-infant interaction on Fais, a remote island in the western Pacific, one square mile in area, where most of infant life takes place in a dense social context, and in the Marquesas Islands, where the diffusion of nurturance of infants among various adults is traditionally greater than in most of the societies in the ethnographic record—a circumstance thought in the past to relate to Marquesan women's exceptional concern for the beauty of their breasts. The child psychologist or other child development professional who is uncurious about how infants and children behave and grow in these exotic settings must have a narrow focus of interest indeed.

Another conviction of the early days of cross-cultural research on infancy and childhood was that not all things would vary, and that a byproduct of research on cultural and population differences would be the elucidation of universal features of infant and child behavior and its development, as well as of caretaking behavior. The chapter by Zaslow and Rogoff, even while it focuses on differences due to cultural context, exposes similarities which are the basis for the comparisons of all the many different cultures mentioned. Indeed the volume taken as a whole has a common set of themes, expressed in a common language, which really constitute a thread woven together from the universal features of the behavior of infants and children and their caretakers.

The 1960s were also the heyday of studies of social class differences in infants and children, but anthropologists such as Beatrice Whiting criticized social class as a "package" variable which, like most psychological constructs, continued to ignore cultural complexities. The chapters here by Field and Widmayer and by Feiring and Lewis, together with much other evidence, show decisively how much cultural variation has been overlooked in the "packaging," and how much may be gained by investigating that variation, even within a single socioeconomic stratum—whether high or low—in the United States.

One of the great questions of mother-infant research has been whether individual and even group variation in behavior patterns and their development could be attributed in part to causes independent of the environment. This question has now been answered in the affirmative, certainly for individuals, probably, to a lesser extent, for certain groups. Far from immediately evoking the pessimism that was predicted by the warnings of extreme environmentalists, these findings promised, and continue to promise, a greater appreciation of the possibilities for intervention, based on a clearer understanding of the effect of the infant on its caregiver; not to mention that they show a greater respect for intrinsic individuality than does the *tabula rasa* view of individual differences. The chapters by Fajardo and Freedman and by Callaghan show that the known differences, both individual and group, in the behavioral equipment with which we enter the world, are not without consequences for the details of mother-infant interaction; and further, that some of the features of caretaking that we consider most cultural may be in part responses on the part of adults to intergroup and interindividual variation in intrinsically determined neonatal and infant behavior.

I would like to close with special mention of the chapter by Super and colleagues. Most of the chapters in this book, and indeed most of the literature of mother-infant interaction, carry implicit or explicit speculations about the later effects of early variations. I say "speculations" rather than "conclusions" because virtually all such statements (my own included) are motivated by the wishful fallacy of *post hoc ergo propter hoc*. No matter how you squeeze a correlation, it will never yield you a cause; but one good intervention experiment—and this one is on an exceptionally large sample for studies of the kind—can give a quasicausal significance to a thousand correlations, while suggesting the need to reinterpret some others. Frequently there are ethical objections to intervention studies, but these, it seems to me, are often based on convictions about the effects of varying the early environment which are unwarranted on the basis of present knowledge. Indeed such studies are imperative components in the apparatus for generating such knowledge. They must form the basis for future ethical and policy judgements, and for a science of early experience effects which will be convincing to skeptical investigators both within and outside of child development research. In the meanwhile, as we think about what is advisable in the design of early environments, it will surely help to understand what is possible, and the latter category must henceforth take into account the rapidly growing body of information on what is done in different cultures; without it we will blindly narrow all our possibilities. We must remember, too, that this is quite urgent research, since the range of worldwide variation is rapidly narrowing. We have a lot to do and not much time in which to do it, but this impressive book makes a fine beginning.

Melvin Konner
Department of Anthropology
Harvard University

Preface

Over the last decade a number of researchers have studied the early social interactions of infants in an attempt to understand the origins of social communication and attachment. While many of the patterns and processes of early interactions have been ascribed to the nature of human infants interacting with their mothers, these patterns and processes do not appear to be universal. Just as the recent volume *Culture and infancy* presented evidence for cultural variability in childrearing patterns, this volume provides data on the variable effects of cultural values and contexts on early social interaction patterns.

Culture and early interactions is a collection of studies conducted by psychologists, anthropologists, pediatricians and psychiatrists among Hispanic, Hopi, and Navajo cultures within the U.S., as well as cultures of other continents, Europe, Africa, South America and islands of the South Pacific. These investigators have closely analyzed filmed observations of face-to-face, feeding and play interactions, and interpreted their findings in light of varying cultural contexts, such as the public/private context of early interactions, or varying cultural values regarding the roles of interaction partners such as mothers, fathers and siblings and social behaviors such as eye contact. In some cultures, for example, face-to-face interactions with the mother rarely occur, since the infant is typically placed outward to relate to other members of the social group or because the sibling is considered the primary social interaction partner. In others, social behaviors such as eye contact and smiling are not salient features of early interactions as they are in our own culture.

While each of the chapters in this volume addresses several cultural considerations, the volume has been organized in sections according to the major variables studied including: cultural contexts, cultural and socioeconomic status, cultural values, growth and developmental status of infants, and methodological considerations.

The volume offers a body of research, a comprehensive source of references and a methodology for considering the cultural contexts within which early social interactions occur. For those who are interested in early interactions or cultural influences, these studies provide a multidimensional approach to understanding early social communication behaviors which are common to and unique to different cultures.

Tiffany Field

CULTURAL CONTEXTS

1 Residence Patterns and the Environment of Mother-Infant Interaction Among the Navajo

James S. Chisholm
University of New Mexico,
Albuquerque

INTRODUCTION

Most child development researchers, especially those studying attachment, have been concerned with mother–infant interaction per se. However, a number of cross-cultural studies have observed that the nature of mother–infant interaction is at least partially a function of variables that cannot be observed in their interaction itself. Paramount among these variables are the availability and identity of all other potential caretakers or interactors. Most notable of these studies are those by John and Bea Whiting and their students and colleagues. For example, in their summary analysis of socialization data from each of the Six Cultures studies, Whiting and Whiting (1975) report that a major determinant of child behavior was the "status of the target," i.e., the age/sex/kinship identity of the person with whom the child was interacting. They found that fully 80% of children's interactions in all six cultures were with parents (11%), peers (54%) and infants (15%). Types of interaction were lumped as: nurturant, prosocial aggressive, sociable, intimate-dependent and dominant-dependent. There was a strong, cross-cultural correlation between the status of the target (age/sex/kinship identity) and certain types of interaction (e.g., interaction with infants was nurturant, those with parents was intimate-dependent and nonaggressive). From these and other findings, the Whitings argue that the primary socializing effect of parents and other caretakers is not so much in their direct, face-to-face effect on the child, but rather in their power to assign the child certain tasks, or otherwise place him/her in certain social settings where the child will be surrounded by others of certain age/sex/kinship identities and where the child will thus tend to have a preponderance of certain types of interactions.

In a more recent formulation of their approach, B. Whiting (1980) argues that knowing the age/sex/kinship identities of potential interactors in the social settings that occupy most of the child's time will allow one to predict characteristic patterns of interpersonal behavior. She further argues that there are a limited number of types of behavior that are satisfying in any interaction with certain age/sex/kinship statuses and that these patterns of interactive behavior are readily learned—more by trial and error than by external reward and punishment. Fundamental to the Whitings' (1975) approach is that their data clearly demonstrate that the major determinants of the child's social setting, and thus his/her most characteristic types of interaction, are the subsistence ecological variables that determine group size and composition and daily activities.

In addition to the age/sex/kinship identity of potential interactors, the simple number of others available for interaction may also be expected to affect the nature of early interactions, not only because the number may affect the age/sex/kinship distribution, but also because the number determines the child's opportunity for any interaction at all. In a study of infant development among the Logoli of Kenya, for example. Munroe and Munroe (1971) found that in large households infants were held significantly more often than in smaller, less dense households. Also, the larger the household, the more quickly someone (not necessarily the mother) responded to the child's cries (even when he/she was being held). Making the point that household size will affect the nature of early interactions in more global ways than holding and responding to cries, the Munroes reanalyzed Ainsworth's (1967) data on Ganda infant attachment behaviors and showed that the rated level of mother–infant attachment was inversely related to household density.

Much of the significance of the Whitings's approach for assessing the developmental impact of the larger social context on early interactions depends on the degree to which types of interaction learned in one setting may generalize to other settings with potential interactors of different age/sex/kinship identities. To some extent this generalization depends on the number of different social settings available to the child, the frequency with which the child moves from one setting to the next, and the relative constancy of each setting throughout development. In any case, there is good evidence that types of interactive behavior learned in one setting do generalize to other settings. For example, the Whitings (1975) found that an average of 26% of the variance in "intimate-dependent" behavior was accounted for by the age/sex/kinship identity of the interactor, as was 25% of the variance in "nurturant" behavior, 25% of the variance in "aggressive" behavior and as much as 31% of the variance in "sociable" behavior. In a specific study of this sort of generalization, Ember (1973) found that in Kenya Oyugis boys who were child nurses (because of a unique sex ratio in their families; girls are preferred) were also significantly more nurturant to noninfants than other boys who did not have to act as child nurses to their siblings.

METHODOLOGICAL ISSUES IN ASSESSING THE EFFECT OF THE SOCIAL CONTEXT ON EARLY INTERACTIONS

There are two important methodological issues that must be addressed when setting out to examine the effect of the social context on early interactions. They are defining and measuring the social context and the interactions themselves. For most field projects it is impossible to identify all the social settings that a child encounters, let alone the age/sex/kinship identities of the child's companions and caretakers in each one, but it has been shown that by far the major determinant of the number and age/sex/kinship identities of a child's most common interactive partners is the type, size and composition of his/her residence group (Leiderman & Leiderman 1977; Minturn & Lambert 1964; Weisner & Gallimore 1977; Whiting & Whiting 1975). Only in industrial Europe and North America does the isolated neolocal, nuclear family unit predominate, while in the rest of the world there is a very great variety of marriage and postmarital residence rules and customs, for which there exists in anthropology a complete taxonomic system.

The second problem, defining and measuring interactions, is more thorny. Briefly, the Whitings and their colleagues have approached this problem with a time/event-sampling technique in which interactive behaviors observed during a 5-minute time sample were classified as: seeks help, seeks attention, seeks dominance, suggests responsibly, offers support, offers help, acts sociably, touches, reprimands, assaults sociably, assaults, or symbolic aggression (Whiting & Whiting, 1975, p. 40). Like any observation technique, this one presents advantages and disadvantages. Among its disadvantages is the short time period sampled. Observation for only 5 minutes means it is impossible to examine the social contextual correlates of length of interaction, which may often last longer than 5-minutes and may show variation depending on the identity of the interactor. The small number of events sampled means information will be lost and the relatively subjective nature of the event definitions require a certain degree of intuitive decision-making by the observer, especially when a behavior might reasonably be classified into more than one category (e.g., when is a touch a "touch," or "acts sociably," or "offers help," or "offers support"?).

On the other hand, the advantages of this sort of observation technique are precisely where its more objective ethological alternate technique is weakest: in the realm of "meaning." The items in an ethologist's behavior catalogue are derived from observation and defined in terms of observable behavior. Thus these catalogues do not include items that are subjective, inferential or even partially defined in terms of motivation (Blurton Jones & Woodson, 1979). But because the acts observed in the Whiting approach are derived from previous cross-cultural research and a specific theory of social interaction (Sears, Maccoby & Levin, 1957; Whiting & Child, 1953) and because each field worker is thoroughly familiar with the culture in which he or she works, this approach yields data that can be interpreted in terms of widely-held psychological constructs largely unavailable to the ethologist.

Much has been written about the problems of reliability and validity in both ethology and psychological anthropology, and they are issues that cannot be ignored. However, one can focus on reliability and validity to such an extent that theory becomes impoverished. Further, the cornerstone of the scientific method does not rest so much on reliability and validity as it does on productive and replicable results. The central finding of the Whitings and their colleagues is that knowing the age/sex/kinship identities of potential interactors in the social settings that occupy most of a child's time will allow one to predict characteristic patterns of that child's interpersonal behavior. This is a productive finding that has been replicated in the several cultures studied by the Whitings and their colleagues. One purpose of this chapter is to show that this central finding has been replicated in yet another culture, but with younger children, and by using widely different, ethological observation techniques.

ASSESSING THE EFFECT OF THE SOCIAL CONTEXT ON MOTHER-INFANT INTERACTION AMONG THE NAVAJO

In an attempt to describe the effects of cradleboard use on Navajo mother-infant interaction, I conducted an ethological/anthropological study of child development in an isolated and traditional community on the Navajo reservation (which I will call Cottonwood Springs) where all but two of the 38 children in the sample were using, or had used, the cradleboard. In addition, I was able to also observe 11 Anglo-American mother-infant pairs in Flagstaff, Arizona, six of whom were using the cradleboard.

The ethological observation techniques used were based on those developed by Blurton Jones (Blurton Jones, 1972; Blurton Jones & Woodson, 1979). Over 150 carefully predefined mother and infant behaviors and aspects of their interaction and its setting were recorded continuously during observation sessions that totaled 1 hour every 2 months. All observations were made during daylight hours, largely at the convenience of each family, in the child's home with his or her mother present, under completely naturalistic conditions. There were wide variations in the number of other people present during observations, but they, like the child's mother, were asked to carry on with their activities as if I were not present. Data were not recorded in the first two or three meetings with each family, and my impressions were that if my presence disrupted family routine at all, this disruption over the 30-40 minutes of my presence was small. More important, I had no indication that my presence affected the actual interactive behavior of mother or infant. To some extent this may have been due to the dictates of Navajo etiquette, which call for the polite ignoring of strangers (cf. Basso, 1970).

In addition to the ethological observation data, extensive background data on each family provided information on patterns of caretaking, developmental milestones, family configuration, kinship, and residence patterns. More than 1100 spot observations also provided a more macroscopic view of the infants' activities, state, whereabouts and social settings on a day-to-day basis over the 20 months of fieldwork.

Using a series of bivariate and multivariate analytic procedures, I was able to show that the cradleboard did have the effects that had been predicted, but that these effects were transient and essentially unrelated to either the major dimensions of Navajo mother–infant interaction or to the major dimensions of differences between Navajo and Anglo patterns of mother–infant interaction. Instead, within- and between-culture differences in patterns of mother–infant interaction were best accounted for by individual differences in each child's opportunity for interaction with others besides mother (Chisholm, 1978, 1980; Chisholm & Richards, 1978). These differences, in turn, were a function of the composition of each child's residence group and these data provide a good illustration of how the wider social context of early interactions may influence specific aspects of mother–infant and infant–other interaction.

THE SOCIAL CONTEXT OF NAVAJO AND ANGLO-AMERICAN RESIDENCE PATTERNS

The "typical" residence group among the Navajo has long been said to be the matrilocal extended family camp, which consists of two to about six hogans in a cluster, each one ordinarily housing a nuclear family related to the others through matrilineal kinship ties. With a sheepherding subsistence base and range land that is marginal at best, these camps have been widely dispersed to best maximize suitable land for grazing. Each camp is at least a mile from its nearest neighbor, and often further.

In the Cottonwood Springs area, however, the typical residence pattern did not prevail. The 38 children in the sample were found in 27 separate households in 26 separate camps. Of the 27 households, 14 (51.9%) were separate, neolocal, nuclear family camps in which the couple had left the natal camp of both husband and wife and had set off on their own. Of the 13 households found in large extended family camps, only six were matrilocal, six were patrilocal, and in one the couple resided with other kinds of relatives. This atypically high rate of neolocal, nuclear family residence is a function of the continuing deterioration of the grazing land coupled with a steady increase in both human and sheep population. These factors have made it adaptive for even greater dispersal over the range for smaller groups with smaller flocks of sheep. In addition, the opportunity for wage work is slowly increasing on the reservation as is nuclear family residence, in part, because people wish to live closer to their jobs, which are almost exclusively near the local trading posts. The increase in cash income from these jobs and from unemployment compensation, social security benefits, and other forms of welfare have led in turn to an increase in the purchase of pickup trucks. With more pickup trucks it is possible to maintain more camps and small flocks that are widely dispersed, and families living away from their relatives near the trading post can help with sheepherding and other cooperative family tasks on weekends. Thus, the change in Navajo residence patterns is due mainly to large scale economic–technological and ecological factors (Chisholm, 1978).

My total Cottonwood Springs sample consisted of 19 children living in neolocal, nuclear family camps and 19 living in the larger and more traditional matri- and patrilocal extended family camps. Table 1.1 provides a summary of the similarities and differences in some of the major dimensions of the social contexts of these two residence types.

For the purposes of this discussion, the most significant dimension of differences is the extended family camp child's greater potential for interaction with more people of both sexes of a wider age range who are also related and/or very familiar. By the same token, the extended family camp child may have a greater potential for interaction with his or her mother because there are more people to

TABLE 1.1
Characteristics of the Navajo Nuclear and Extended Families

	Nuclear	Extended	$(p<)$[a]
age of father	40.8	31.4	.05
age of mother	32.2	30.7	
mother's age at marriage	21.1	18.9	
number of children	5.9	4.4	
birth interval (weeks)	102.0	128.0	.05
months of breast-feeding	4.1	13.8	.05
camp population	7.9	15.0	.001
household population	7.9	6.9	
rooms per household	2.4	1.5	
miles to trading post[b]	7.5	10.2	
miles to nearest neighbor[c]	.3	1.3	.05

[a] Two-tailed t-test.

[b] The spatial distribution of nuclear family camps was bi-modal. Most were located even farther from the trading post than the extended family camps but the ones right in the trading post complex lowered the mean distance significantly.

[c] The nearest neighbor *outside* of camp. The figures here are somewhat misleading for both groups, as there are usually three or four camps in an area where there is good grazing, but it is often ten or more miles to the next such favored area. The nuclear families in the trading post complex significantly lowered the mean for all nuclear family camps.

help the mother with siblings and with her other duties about the camp. This is true because the extended family camps have significantly more people in all age categories; in addition to his or her own siblings, the extended family camp child has another 1.6 peers (aged 0-3 years), another 2.9 potential child caretakers/playmates (aged 3-12 years) and another 3.6 teenaged or adult caretakers. Excluding the 1.6 infants besides her own (for whom she would have to help care for to some extent), the extended family camp mother has an additional 6.5 people over the age of three who may not only help her with her own children, but with many of her other duties.

The significantly greater mean birth interval of the extended family camp mothers was unexpected. The reason for this greater birth interval can only be guessed at, but it might be related to the longer period of breast-feeding reported by the extended family camp mothers. Because lactation is known to at least partially suppress ovulation (Crosignani & Robyn, 1977), the factors that reduce breast-feeding or the frequency/duration of breast-feeding bouts (Konner & Worthman, 1980) might also help reduce the birth interval. One of these factors could be the relative dearth of close emotional support provided to the nuclear camp mother because she does not live with her own or her husband's family (cf. Raphael, 1974). A more likely, and related, explanation might be the practical difficulties of breast-feeding frequently and/or for long periods where there are not only more children who need care, but fewer older children and adults to provide assistance. The shorter birth interval in the nuclear family camps may also narrow the age range of the nuclear family camp child's potential familiar interactors.

Except for the few nuclear families who live near their jobs in the trading post area, most children in nuclear family camps will also have less experience with strangers than will extended family camp children. This is so because there exists greater potential for movement and travel in the larger extended family camps where there are more pickup trucks and more potential drivers. In the nuclear family camps there are not only fewer trucks and drivers but fewer potential babysitters to mind the other children if the parents wish to make a trip to the trading post.

All of the above points were corroborated by data from the 1100 spot observations. Comparing nuclear and extended family camp children, the nuclear family children were observed at home more often than the extended family camp children ($p < .001$); they were observed actually inside their house or hogan more than the extended family camp children ($p < .001$); their mothers were observed with them more often ($p < .01$) but they were less likely to be held or carried by mother ($p < .001$), and, as expected, the nuclear family camp children were observed in the presence of fewer other people than the extended family camp children ($p < .001$).

Differences in children's opportunity for interaction with others, and with others of different age/sex/kinship-familiarity identities proved to be as powerful a determinant of Navajo-Anglo differences in the social context of infancy as it was for the nuclear-extended family differences within the Navajo sample. Table 1.2 provides a summary of the major differences between the Navajo and Anglo samples in the social contexts of their residence groups.

Of the 11 Anglo-American families, 10 lived right in the city of Flagstaff in typical Anglo single family units. One family lived for part of the time in a large communal farm just on the outskirts of town. In this commune, the child was surrounded by a large but widely variable number of others who were not related in any formal way. Despite the fact that this family lived in a sort of "extended family," all 11 Anglo families were treated as a group for most purposes of comparison.

Further, despite the fact that the Anglo families and half the Navajo families were formally classified as having neolocal, nuclear family residence, it must be stressed that the social context of Navajo nuclear family residence was widely different from that of the Anglo nuclear families. First, all but two of the Anglo children were first-born, only children, whereas the Navajo nuclear family children had an average of 4.9 older siblings. Second, the Anglo families lived in an urban center, usually no more than a few yards from several other families who were not related in any way and with whom there was a minimal social interaction or mutual aid. Third, the Anglo children, unlike all the Navajo children, were exposed to a constant stream of their parents' friends, strangers on the street in front of their houses and at the local shopping centers, postmen, repairmen, and a multitude of others of all age and sex categories (and many racial/ethnic groups as well).

On the other hand, the Anglo child was almost never exposed to any relatives other than his or her parents. Anglo children saw and met many more people of a much wider variety than did Navajo children but were actually familiar with a much smaller percentage of the total population than were the Navajo children.

TABLE 1.2
Characteristics of the Navajo and Anglo Families

	Navajo	*Anglo*	$(p<)$[a]
age of father	36.8	26.1	.001
age of mother	31.5	25.9	.001
mother's age at marriage	20.0	22.2	.01
number of children	5.2	1.2	.001
birth interval (weeks)	112.4	(all but two first-born)	
months of breast-feeding	8.7	13.7	.10
household population[b]	7.4	3.2	.01
rooms per household	2.0	5.6	.001
miles to nearest neighbor	.8	<.1	.001

[a] Two-tailed t-test.
[b] One Anglo family living in a communal house excluded.

The Navajo children saw and met fewer people but were familiar (and/or actually related) with a much higher percentage of these people than the Anglo children. Some of the more isolated Navajo children, for example, might never meet an actual stranger until they went away to school at age five.

One of the most obvious ways in which these differences in the social context of residence groups may affect mother–infant interaction is through their direct affect on mothers' time and attention. With her own family typically living in another state, with her own friends typically living several blocks away, and with no older children to act as substitute caretakers, Anglo mothers were forced into a much more exclusive and constant proximity to their children. Spot observation data showed that although there was no difference in the frequency with which Navajo and Anglo children were left alone (out of sight of anybody), Navajo mothers were more likely ($p < .05$), when absent, to leave their children in the care of a grandmother, aunt or older sibling.

A final aspect of Navajo–Anglo differences in the social context of early interactions is related as much to the physical qualities of the residence itself as it is to the number and identity of its inhabitants. The Anglo homes in Flagstaff had more rooms than the Navajo homes ($p < .05$; most Navajos lived in one-room hogans, but a few lived in 3–4 room cinder block houses), more stairs, more doors, more furniture, and many more dishwashers, toasters, telephones, TV sets, etc. These differences mean that there are more, and more varied, physical environments for Anglo mother–infant interaction and a greater likelihood that the Anglo mother and infant will be separated or out of sight all together in separate rooms. The electrical appliances and TV sets, telephones, etc. also mean that the Anglo mother will be called away from interaction with her child more often to attend to the demands of the doorbell, telephone, burning toast, etc. On the other hand, Navajo mothers cannot use TV sets as babysitters—or to occupy their own attention while their infants are seeking companionship.

EFFECTS OF THE SOCIAL CONTEXT ON NAVAJO AND ANGLO MOTHER–INFANT INTERACTION

In order to examine the effects of the larger social context on within- and between-culture differences in patterns of mother–infant interaction, multiple regression techniques were used. The dependent variables were those mother and infant behaviors during interaction, and global measurements of their interaction as a whole, which showed the most significant and/or consistent differences over the child's first year of life. These are listed in Table 1.3.

Not all of these within- and between-group differences are significant, but most were significant for at least two of the four quarters of the first year. The most striking aspect of these differences, however, is not so much the degree, but the fact that they were consistent throughout the year, i.e., the rank-ordering of

TABLE 1.3.
Within- and Between-culture Comparisons of Aspects of
Mother-infant Interaction[a]

	Navajo nuclear	Navajo extended	Anglo
mutual gaze	.12	.13	.18
mother talk to child	.10	.17	.33
mother touch, pat child	.07	.11	.12
mother approach, leave child	.07	.09	.12
child vocalize	.13	.19	.23
child vocalize and look at mother	.03	.04	.05
child approach, leave mother	.01	.04	.06
mean interaction length (mins.)	1.68	2.60	4.63

[a] Expressed as the rate of occurrence per 15 seconds of interaction, averaged across all interactions observed.

the three groups was the same on each variable at each quarter. In every instance, Navajo nuclear family patterns of interaction were less like Anglo nuclear family patterns than those of the Navajo extended families. The three groups did not differ significantly on all of the nearly 80 behavior items that occurred with enough frequency to be analyzed, nor was the pattern of differences identical for some of the more rare behaviors, but the behaviors listed here represent fundamental and theoretically highly significant dimensions of interaction.

The independent variables entered into the regression equations as predictors of mother and infant interactive behaviors were those that were expected to influence the behavior of mother, infant, or both. They were: the mother's rate of behavior to her child, the child's rate of behavior to mother, the rate at which all other people present during interaction directed behavior toward the infant, the percentage of the interaction during which the child was on the cradleboard, the percentage of the interaction during which the child was held on mother's lap, the percentage of the interaction devoted to caretaking (nursing, feeding, dressing, cleaning, etc.) and whether the mother or the infant initiated the interaction. In the end, four of these independent variables proved to be significantly related to the mother and infant behaviors on which the three groups differed most. These variables are listed in Table 1.4.

The same pattern of within- and between-group differences is as evident in these independent variables as it was in the dependent variables. Again, the Navajo extended family pattern is more like the Anglo pattern than is the Navajo nuclear family pattern.

Together, these four variables accounted for far more of the variance in the mother and infant interactive behavior variables than any combination of all of the other independent variables. For example, they accounted for as much as 47% of the variance in *mutual gazing*, 40% of the variance in *mother approach*,

TABLE 1.4.
Within- and Between-culture Comparisons of Aspects of the
Social Environment of Mother-infant Interaction[a]

	Navajo nuclear	Navajo extended	Anglo
mother rate of behavior	1.28	1.61	1.80
child rate of behavior	.46	.50	.74
all others rate of behavior	.43	.32	.15
% interaction on lap	23.32	33.52	38.05

[a] Expressed as rate of occurrence per 15 sec of interaction, averaged across all interactions observed, except for "% interaction on lap" variable.

leave child, and 37% of *mother talk to child*. In the first quarter they accounted for 49% of the variance in mean interaction length, 35% in the second quarter and fully 60% in the second half of the first year.

Furthermore, another series of analyses showed that of these four variables, the single most powerful was the rate at which all others present directed behavior toward the infant. This variable accounted for 39% of the variance in the mother's rate of behavior to her child and nearly 30% of the variance in the child's rate of behavior to mother. During the first quarter of the year, this variable also accounted for 34% of the variance in proportion of all interaction time during which the child was held on the mother's lap (but this figure dropped to 21% in the second quarter and was negligible in the second half of the first year).

In sum, the nature of mother–infant interaction differed within and between cultures according to the composition of the residence groups, and these analyses show that these differences are best explained in terms of the impact of the behavior of the other people present in these groups on the behavior of mother and infant. Navajo nuclear family mother–infant interaction was characterized by shorter interactive bouts, the children spent less time on their mothers' laps, the mothers and infants alike both did less *approach, leave* to each other, and both tended to vocalize to each other less. They were also subject to a higher rate of behavior from others during their interaction.

At the opposite extreme were the Anglo nuclear families, with longer interactions, more time on lap, and higher rates of both *approach, leave* and vocalization by both mother and child and a very low rate of behavior from other people around them (who were very few in number anyway). Intermediate in all respects were the Navajo extended family mothers and infants—similar to the Navajo nuclear families, having many others around them during interaction, and similar to the Anglo nuclear families in that they had more opportunity for exclusive attention to each other. There were more adults and older children to free the mother from most of the demands the Navajo nuclear family mother had to handle alone. The Anglo mothers not only had many fewer other children to make such demands, they also had more time for exclusive attention to their children because of their economic and technological advantages.

The fact that the Anglo nuclear families and the Navajo nuclear families were on opposite ends of the distribution of all the variables suggests that abstract social structural variables might not always serve as adequate indirect measures of social opportunity, especially cross-culturally. For example, the spot observation data shows that Navajo nuclear family mothers held their infants less than did the Navajo extended family mothers. Precisely the same picture emerged from the continuous observation of mother–infant interaction: again the nuclear family mothers held their children less than did the extended family mothers. This nuclear-extended family difference replicates the finding reported by Munroe and Munroe (1971) that in large Logoli households in Kenya, infants were held more often than in small households. In the present study, however, the Anglo nuclear families were the smallest, yet the Anglo mothers held their infants the most. So it is not only the number and identity of others that affects holding and other aspects of mother–infant interaction, but the way that these factors may interact with others which also affect the opportunity for interaction (e.g., work loads).

THE EFFECT OF THE SOCIAL CONTEXT ON NAVAJO NUCLEAR AND EXTENDED FAMILY CHILDREN'S FEAR OF STRANGERS

In addition to observing mother–infant interaction, Navajo and Anglo childrens' fear of strangers was also assessed. The purpose was to determine whether or not individual differences in fear of strangers were related to cradleboard use. It turned out that they were not related in any way for either group. Instead, the within- and between-culture differences in residence groups that had such effect on mother–infant interaction had a similar strong effect on the expression of fear of strangers.

Employing a method adapted from Konner (1972), each child's fear of strangers was tested once every 2 months. An event-sampling technique was used consisting of 22 behaviors that had been assigned numerical weights that were a rough indication of the degree of the child's fearfulness or friendliness: Crying or clinging to mother scored +3; laughing or touching the stranger scored −3 (see Chisholm, 1978 for further details).

Briefly, the development of fear of strangers in Navajo and Anglo children was similar in the first year. They did not differ either in the quantity of fearful or friendly behaviors shown or in the types and combinations of behaviors used to express fearfulness or friendliness. Both groups showed a preponderance of fearful behavior at about nine months. In the second year, however, the Anglo children showed significantly more friendly behavior while the Navajo children continued to show a preponderance of fear. No Anglo children over 2 years were tested, but the Navajo children showed a preponderance of fearful behavior which continued well into the third year. For obvious reasons it is not clear how much validity these Navajo-Anglo similarities and differences may have, for because I am an Anglo, I was definitely more strange to the Navajo children than I was to the Anglo children. Thus, I will limit discussion here to the within-sample differences among the Navajo.

I obtained a total of 71 fear of strangers scores for Navajo nuclear family children and 89 for extended family children between the ages of 6 and 33 months. While there were no differences in the types or combinations of behaviors shown in the tests, the nuclear family children began to show a preponderance of fearful behaviors at about 8 months while the extended family children showed a preponderance of fearful behaviors two months later—at about 10 months. Further, the nuclear family children showed a peak in their fear of strangers about 3 months earlier than the extended family children; 10 months as compared to about 13 months. Figure 1.1 is a schematic presentation of these developmental differences.

The residence group differences in the development of fear of strangers suggest that early exposure to strangers may influence the child's later response to strangers. On average, children in the nuclear family camps will have less experience with strangers than children in the extended families where there are more people and a wider social network to which the child will be exposed. And, as mentioned earlier, with more people in camp there are more opportunities for trips to the trading post, where more strangers can be seen. Also, the spot

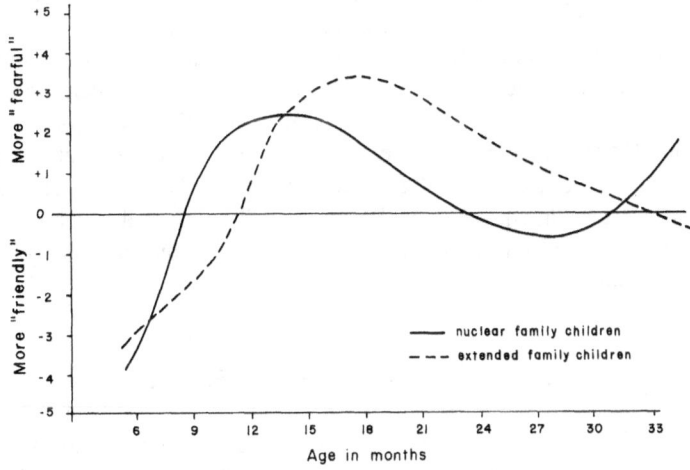

FIG. 1.1. Navajo nuclear and extended family camp children's fear of strangers.

observation data showed that extended family camp children were more likely to be away from home than nuclear family children.

Further support for this interpretation comes from two additional tests of association. First, there was a strong correlation between fear of strangers (controlling for age) and the number of people who the child was likely to see and/or interact with on a more-or-less daily basis. For this analysis I could not use simple camp population because a number of small nuclear family camps were located in the immediate vicinity of the trading post and the children in these camps were exposed not only to their next-door neighbors, but all the people who visited the trading post and local clinic daily. However, when I counted the number of potential interactors and estimated the number of probable passersby in each child's "neighborhood" and ignored the size of the camp per se, it turned out that this neighborhood figure was correlated with fear of strangers ($r = -.32$, $p < .001$).

Second, reasoning that those families (regardless of residence type) who lived farthest from the trading post would make fewer trips there, I related simple distance from the trading post to fear of strangers. Running separate regression analyses for *fearful* and *friendly* behavior, it turned out that fearful scores increased with distance from the trading post ($r = .27$, $p < .01$) while friendly scores decreased ($r = -.39$, $p < .001$).

These data on the effect of previous exposure to strangers are consistent with a number of cognitive developmental studies. The development of fear of strangers depends on maturational and experiential factors and interaction with unfamiliar persons is thought to be a major experiential variable. When maturation has proceeded sufficiently, the infant becomes capable of forming a schema of what is familiar, and a mismatch between the stimulus input and the schemata of familiarity is thought by some to be the cognitive basis for fear of strangers (Bronson, 1972; Kagan, 1974). The development of this novelty-induced fear cannot, however, proceed until the child has had enough experience with what is familiar to establish a sufficiently precise schemata against which the stimulus qualities of the stranger can be compared (Hoffman, 1974). Bronson (1972) and Rheingold (1961), among others, have shown effects of differential exposure to strangers on the development of fear that are similar to the nuclear-extended family differences shown here. As Konner (1972) says of the !Kung San, for more of the nuclear family children, "the class of strangers, as well as the individual stranger, is strange [p. 298]."

SUMMARY AND CONCLUSIONS

The primary finding of the research reported here is that the major determinant of within- and between-culture differences in Navajo and Anglo patterns of mother–infant interaction were differences in each child's opportunity for interaction with others besides mother. These differences in social opportunity were based on differences in the social context of the infants' residence groups, where there were significant group differences in the number and age/sex/kinship-familiarity identities of coresidents. These differences in infants' early social context were also related to their opportunities for experience with strangers and to parallel patterns of differences in their development of fear of strangers.

These conclusions constitute good support for the Whitings' (1975) argument that knowing the number and age/sex/kinship identities of potential interactors in the social settings that occupy most of the child's time will allow one to predict characteristic patterns of interpersonal behavior. The present study focused on mother–infant interpersonal behavior and infant–stranger interpersonal behavior, and not only were these children younger than most studied by the Whitings and their colleagues, the interactions themselves were described in ethological terms quite different than those used in the Whiting studies. The fact that the same conclusion was reached in spite of these differences in focus and method suggests that the central finding may be especially robust.

One of the most significant implications of this finding is the way it stresses the necessity of "unpacking" culture as an independent variable (cf. B. Whiting, 1976). As Leiderman and Leiderman (1977) argue in their own work on the differential developmental effects of mono- vs. polymatric households among the Kikuyu, "it is no longer possible to assume either a homogeneity of caretaking arrangements or a constancy of social forces within a relatively homogeneous society even over the short time span of the infant's first year [p. 430]." The material presented here shows that in many respects there was as much variability in mother–infant interaction and its determinants *within* Navajo culture as between Navajo and Anglo culture. Thus, using "culture" as an explicit or implicit independent variable may obscure as much as it reveals.

By focusing on the social settings in which a child spends most of its time, and on the number and age/sex/kinship identity and specific roles and functions of the individuals in these settings, one is in a much better position to relate both within- and between-group similarities and differences in behavior not only to common patterns and styles of interaction learned in these settings, but also to the larger historical, economic and ecological factors that so greatly determine the nature and composition of these early social settings through their effect on subsistence activities, work loads, the sexual division of labor, daily routines, and so forth. With such an approach, one is then able to test hypotheses about specific developmental/causal pathways whereby the infant responds to the larger environment he or she will face as an adult through the effects of this larger environment on the infant's early social environment.

Finally, just as group differences in behavior, which happen to parallel group differences in known genetic markers, cannot themselves be logically attributed to the genetic differences, group differences in behavior that happen to parallel group differences in obvious cultural markers (e.g., language, kinship, religion, etc.) cannot themselves be attributed to the vague gestalt of cultural differences. Instead, one must approach the problem in such a way that one can test the hypothesis that these group differences in behavior exist because of simple group differences in the distribution of larger economic and ecological factors that cause individual differences. Explaining group differences in behavior in terms of "culture" is too simple and tends to preclude the search for the developmental/causal pathways whereby behavior may be generated from the interaction between the infant and his environment.

ACKNOWLEDGMENTS

The research on which this paper is based was supported by a grant from the Harry Frank Guggenheim Foundation to Dr. N. G. Blurton Jones of the Institute of Child Health, University of London and by a grant from the National Science Foundation. I am indebted to these organizations for their support and to Nick Blurton Jones and R. H. Woodson for their helpful comments. I am also greatly indebted to the Navajo and Anglo mothers and infants who took part in the research and to the people of the Navajo Nation as a whole.

REFERENCES

Ainsworth, M. D. S. *Infancy in Uganda: Infant care and the growth of attachment*. Baltimore: Johns Hopkins University Press, 1967.

Basso, K. To give up on words: Silence in Western Apache culture. *Southwestern Journal of Anthropology*, 1970, *26*, 213–230.

Blurton Jones, N. G. (Ed.), *Ethological studies of child behaviour*. Cambridge, England: Cambridge University Press, 1972.

Blurton Jones, N. G., & Woodson, R. H. Describing behavior: The ethologists' perspective. In M. Lamb, S. Suomi & G. Stephenson (Eds.), *Social interaction analysis: Methodological issues*. Madison: University of Wisconsin Press, 1979.

Bronson, G. W. Infant's reaction to unfamiliar persons and novel objects. *Monographs of the society for research in child development*, 1972, *37* (3).

Chisholm, J. S. *Developmental Ethology of the Navajo*. Unpublished doctoral dissertation, Department of Anthropology, Rutgers University. (Ann Arbor: University Microfilms), 1978.

Chisholm, J. S. Development and adaptation in infancy. In C. Super & S. Harkness (Eds.), *Anthropological perspectives on child development*. San Francisco: Jossey-Bass, 1980.

Chisholm, J. S., & Richards, M. P. M. Swaddling, the cradleboard and the development of children. *Early Human Development*, 1978, *2*, 255–275.

Crosignani, P. G., & Robyn, C. (Eds.). *Prolactin and human reproduction*. London: Academic Press, 1977.

Ember, C. Female task assignment and the social behavior of boys. *Ethos*, 1973, *1*, 424–439.

Hoffman, H. S. Fear-mediated processes in the context of imprinting. In M. Lewis & L. Rosenblum (Eds.), *The origins of fear*. New York: Wiley, 1974.

Kagan, J. Discrepancy, temperament and infant distress. In M. Lewis & L. Rosenblum (Eds.), *The origins of fear*. New York: Wiley, 1974.

Konner, M. J. Aspects of the developmental ethology of a foraging people. In N. Blurton Jones (Ed.), *Ethological studies of child behaviour.* Cambridge, England: Cambridge University Press, 1972.

Konner, M. J., & Worthman, C. Nursing frequency, gonadal function and birth-spacing among !Kung hunter-gatherers. *Science,* 1980, *207,* 788-791.

Leiderman, P. H., & Leiderman, G. Economic change and infant care in an East African agricultural community. In P. Leiderman, S. Tulkin & A. Rosenfeld (Eds.), *Culture and infancy.* New York: Academic Press, 1977.

Minturn, L., & Lambert, W. W. *Mothers of six cultures: Antecedents of child rearing.* New York: Wiley, 1964.

Munroe, R. H., & Munroe, R. L. Household density and infant care in an East African society. *J. Social Psychology,* 1971, *83,* 3-13.

Raphael, D. *The tender gift: Breastfeeding.* New York: Prentice-Hall, 1974.

Rheingold, H. The effect of environmental stimulation upon social and exploratory behavior in the human infant. In B. Foss (Ed.), *Determinants of infant behavior.* Vol. 1, London: Methuen, 1961.

Sears, R. R., Maccoby, E. E., & Levin, H. *Patterns of child rearing.* Evanston, Illinois: Row & Peterson, 1957.

Weisner, T. S., & Gallimore, R. My brother's keeper: Child and sibling caretaking. *Current Anthropology,* 1977, *18,* 169-190.

Whiting, B. Culture and social behavior: A model for the development of social behavior. *Ethos,* 1980, *8,* 95-116.

Whiting, B. The problem of the packaged variable. In K. F. Reigel & J. A. Meacham (Eds.), *The developing individual in a changing world.* The Hague: Mouton, 1976.

Whiting, B. B., & Whiting, J. W. M. *Children of six cultures: A psycho-cultural analysis.* Cambridge, Mass.: Harvard University Press, 1975.

Whiting, J. W. M., & Child, I. *Child training and personality.* New Haven: Yale University Press, 1953.

2 Social Context in Caregiver-Infant Interaction: A Film Study of Fais and the United States

Anita Miller Sostek
Georgetown University School of Medicine

Peter Vietze
Martha Zaslow
National Institute of Child Health and Human Development

Laura Kreiss
National Institute of Neurological and Communicative Diseases and Stroke

Fransje van der Waals
National Institute of Child Health and Human Development

Donald Rubinstein
Stanford University

INTRODUCTION

Western theories of early development point to the importance of a consistent, stimulating, and warm relationship between infant and a single caregiver (Fraiberg, 1968). However, since much of the empirical support for these theories comes from western cultures, the universality of patterns of caregiver-infant interaction can be questioned (Leiderman, Tulkin & Rosenfeld, 1977). From ethnographic data it is clear that infants in some cultures have multiple caregivers; that provision of infant stimulation is not universally viewed as important; and that infants are not invariably seen as social partners for adults.

Ethnographic evidence suggests that not only dyadic but social contextual aspects of early interaction vary cross culturally as well. The extent to which social context can vary from the situation usually studied in mother–infant research is offered by Konner (1977) in his description of the Kalahari Desert San: "This relationship exists in a very dense social context; the mother–infant pair is typically in constant contact with other adults/relatives and friends. This overall social context is in marked contrast to the isolation of American mothers [p. 290]." Because cross-cultural comparisons that overlook differences in social context may be confounded, we hypothesized that the characteristic social context in which caregivers and infants were found might differ among cultures, and that differences in context might consequently influence interactive behaviors.

In addition to this basic study of cross-cultural and contextual influences on caregiver–infant interaction, we sought to establish the feasibility of analyzing existing film shot in other cultures. Apart from the obvious practical advantages of using available data, the rapid acculturation occurring in many parts of the world often makes existing footage an irreplaceable source of information on cultural practices.

Selection of a culture for this research was therefore largely determined by access to suitable cinema footage. The criteria for our choice included frequency and duration of interaction sequences in which both partners were visible, footage of several different dyads, and the availability of background information on ages and kinship relationships from the ethnographer. After inspection of footage at the Smithsonian Institution and the National Institutes of Health, we found only one data base that met all the criteria. This was the 16 mm color, silent footage shot by Donald Rubinstein in the Micronesian island of Fais following two years of field work and familiarization. Although caregiver–infant interaction was not a specific focus during filming, the ethnographer's interest in children was reflected in the footage. The following description of the island and the people of Fais is based entirely on Rubinstein's observations (1978a, 1978b, 1979).

PHYSICAL GEOGRAPHY OF FAIS ISLAND

Fais Island is a small, isolated raised coral island in the western corner of the Pacific Ocean, nearly bordering the Philippine Sea. Situated at 9° 46′ N., and 140° 31′ E., the island forms part of the western Caroline Islands, within the Micronesian culture area. Under the present political status, Fais belongs to the Yap District of the United States Trust Territory of the Pacific Islands.

A relatively level, central plateau 65 feet high accounts for most of the island's 1.083 square miles; sheer cliffs at the northeast and southwest ends of the island interrupt sandy beaches with moderate inland slopes. Fais enjoys a typical equatorial oceanic climate with a nearly constant temperature of about

82°F. during the day, and perhaps 10° cooler at night. Humidity averages 83% with 120 inches of rainfall.

Because of the phosphatic nature of the soil, and the elevated interior of the island, Fais supports more varied and luxuriant flora than most low coral islands. A number of species introduced from Yap thrive on Fais, and islanders continue to experiment with new useful plants including sweet potato (*Ipomoea batatas*), "true" taro (*Colocasia esculenta*), "dry" taro (*Alocasia macrorrhiza*) and about 10 varieties of breadfruit. A number of other fruit and root crops contribute to the Fais diet, such as bananas, mangoes, papayas, coconuts, cassava and yams (*Dioscorea alata* and *Dioscorea esculenta*), and tobacco grows well and has become an important item of interisland trade.

The variety of land animals is limited to chickens. a few pigs, stray dogs, and cats. Marine and shore birds are few in species. Rats, mice, and numerous varieties of lizards and insects are common. Marine fauna shows the richest variety and abundance.

DEMOGRAPHY

The resident population of Fais lives in a clustered settlement in the southwest corner of the island, which affords the best protection from the prevailing northeast trade winds, and also provides good beach and channel access to the ocean for canoes and small boats. The entire population of Fais islanders, at the time of data collection, was about 240; of these, about 200 were residing on the island at any given time. Most of the 40 or so emigrant islanders were living transiently on Ulithi or Yap, while six or seven were attending school in Palau, Truk, Guam, or the United States.

Physically the islanders are fairly heterogeneous, although on the whole they tend to be short and heavily built. Adult men range in weight from 95 to 216 lbs. (average 145 lbs.) and in height from 60" to 67" (average 63"). Adult women's weight varies between 80 and 207 lbs. (average 123 lbs.) and in height from 56" to 66" (average 61"). Hair color and texture are also variable, from medium brown with some reddishness or blondism, to black, and from straight to wavy to kinky. Skin color is varying shades of light brown. As with hair, skin and physique, facial features vary, from people with a strongly Melanesian appearance, to others with a more Malaysian or Polynesian aspect.

According to available reports, the population has been roughly stationary until recent decades when it declined about 25%. The American administration of Micronesia, as a Strategic Trust Territory since 1947, has brought in the past thirty years, accelerating changes to Fais in the areas of health, missionization, education, political structure, cash economy, and cultural values. With the arrival of a resident Jesuit priest on Ulithi in 1948 who made periodic circuits throughout the outer islands, Fais received direct evangelical pressure for the first time. By 1977 the entire population was nominally Catholic. The island women especially are conscientious churchgoers; many of the younger ones make a daily habit of stopping by the church in early morning, to recite a prayer. Christian forms and paraphernalia are increasingly substituted for traditional observances. The primary impact of missionization (aside from the encouragement of health care and education, and the facilitation of emigration to Yap), however, has probably been upon adolescent courtship and marriage practices.

With increased U.S. interest in Micronesia in the 1960s education programs expanded and a high school was built on Fais. As western vocational and academic knowledge increased during the past generation, traditional specialized skills declined. These include ritual and magical formulae, genealogical and historical accounts of land transactions, tattooing and weaving designs, skill in traditional massage and native medicine, calendrical knowledge, and ethnohistorical lore. More disturbing still was the gradual extinction of subsistence skills—the knowledge of offshore fishing sites, or the measurements and proportions for constructing wicker fish traps or carving outrigger canoes. The increasing reliance upon small motorboats and fuel is creating a new demand for cash on Fais, and thus a growing respect for education.

The appearance of the Fais community is that of a single, compact, internally undifferentiated settlement. Spatially and socially, however, the settlement is highly differentiated, divided into three distinct villages. Each village is parcelled into about twelve named house compounds (*bogot*), which may comprise a single house, or as many as five or six, with a common cookhouse. Boundaries between the three villages are not physically elaborated, but nevertheless are economically, socially, and politically explicit, being expressed in such multiple domains as the distribution of reef rights, communal lodges, and movable property; the daily flow and exchange of food, fish and goods; the distribution of specialist skills, ritual knowledge, and ceremonial dances; the linguistic hierarchy of commands and communication of information; origin myths and historical legends; and finally in particular behavioral expectations attached to different social contexts around the villages.

The typical *bogot* (house compound) includes two or more male agnates residing patrilocally with their families, in addition perhaps to an adoptive male or widowed female living on the land. Separate *bogot* are the primary landholding groups on Fais. Villages do not hold any interior garden land in communal ownership, nor do individual people (barring one or two exceptional cases) own land. People work and exchange the land associated with their *bogot*. As men remain on their *bogot*, positions of chieftainship and other male ritual and specialist occupations (tattooing, divining, agricultural, magic and fishing magic) also are associated with particular *bogot*.

Men's work, such as fishing, is largely communal while women's work, such as weaving is largely individual. Furthermore, specialist occupations and ritual knowledge such as magical specialists, diviners, dance instructors, canoe carpenters, and navigators are dominated by men. Both men and women may be ritually removed from the normal course of daily social contacts. Women are secluded during menstruation and after childbirth. Men are secluded when they undertake male specialist work, and this seclusion acts primarily to guarantee their removal from menstruating women. Both forms of seclusion entail a constellation of restrictions: with whom one talks or shares food, where one walks, what one eats and drinks. And, as opposed to normal, sexually-mixed daily life, both forms of seclusion are sexually separate spheres. Ritually "unmarked" men, however—those uninvolved with magical practices or chieftainship, and going about normal village life—may freely enter the menstrual yard and even sleep in the menstrual lodge, accompanying a menstrual or postpartum wife. However when a woman returns to her *bogot* after seclusion in the menstrual lodge, under most circumstances she resumes normal activities.

CHILDBIRTH, CHILDREARING AND ADOPTION

Women give birth in their own houses within the village area, but within minutes of severing the umbilical cord, the infant is carried down to the menstrual lodge, and the new mother, partially assisted perhaps by one or two other women, walks down to join her infant. There both mother and infant remain for the "three-month" postpartum seclusion that lasts until the second rising of the new moon. With continuous attendance by the mother, several of the mother's relatives or the infant's older sisters, or perhaps an adoptive mother, the infant is virtually never left alone during this period. The newborn has nearly unbroken attention of several adult women during the first month or two. A specially woven U-shaped baby basket, lined with soft pandanus mat, provdes a snug but not constrictive cradle. In recent years parents are constructing small flat-bottomed cribs with overarching frames of wood and screen to protect the infant from the ubiquitous swarming flies. There is also an increasing use of store-bought sheets, receiving blankets, baby oil, powder, and cloth diapers, which are often initial gifts adopting parents present to the infant's mother. The mother sits or lies beside the infant for much of the day, fanning flies from its face, picking it up to nurse at the least sign of hunger or discontent, and keeping the infant clean. On about the tenth day the infant is carried outside for the first time and carefully bathed in a shallow depression of warm seawater along the reef.

Around the time of birth, adoption by a family from another *bogot* is customarily arranged. The agreement involves an exchange of land between the natural and the adoptive parents, in order to legitimize the adoption. as well as theoretically to provide the child with lands on its adoptive *bogot*. The adopting parents give several plots of land to be distributed among the child's close relatives, and the child's natural parents reciprocate with several plots of land, for distribution among the adoptive relatives. The child generally has rights of use and residence at both places. This exchange of land points up the dual nature of kinship relations: Adoption entails not only an additional set of parents, but also an association with an additional *bogot*. Ideally, both associations endure throughout the lives of the children and their adoptive parents.

Typically, children live with their natal household on their father's *bogot* throughout childhood, although about a third of the children do reside elsewhere. The usual alternative to residence on the natal *bogot* is to live on the *bogot* of an adoptive father. The children who live with their adoptive families begin sleeping with them during their second or third year, at about the time of weaning, or when the natural mother is again pregnant. Owing to the residential mobility of both the young and the very old, there is a tendency for households to be multigenerational—children sharing the house of an aged relative, or a widowed parent living with grown children or grandchildren. Mean household density at the time of data collection for the sixty households on Fais was 3.9 (Rubinstein, 1979). What we can term a "complete nuclear family" i.e., husband plus wife living in one household with all of their natural children rarely occurs.

The early attention and interest that Fais people bestow upon their adoptive children varies widely from parent to parent. In a number of cases the adoptive parents assist during the early weeks and months of the child's infancy but then allow the relationship largely to lapse. No cases were observed in which an adoption, once validated by land exchange, was later denied or terminated by a return of the exchanged lands. There are frequent instances, however, of an adoptive set of parents showing little interest in the child after infancy, and as the child grows older, he or she fades into the social distance of peripheral "relatives." On the other hand, adoptive parents who desire a close and permanent relationship with the child, especially those who intend to negotiate a later change in the child's residence, to "sleep the child" with them. They take an early and continuing intense interest in the child, which they show by continual small gifts of food and daily visits to "hold the child," and to assist the child's parents in domestic routines of fishing and food preparation.

Coresidence, however, is not a necessary condition for a close relationship between adoptive parents and children, and people on Fais do not consider adoptive residence to be necessarily a mark of "fuller" or "truer" adoption. Children living with their adoptive parents at first seem to believe that these are their natural parents, or possibly, that the multiple adoptive and natural parents, as well as senior authority figures on the *bogot* are all equally "parents," even though the young children may recognize some special kinship with parents in whose *bogot* they reside.

Socialization on Fais does not involve much physical intimidation or punishment of children, and parental or paternal authority carries little threat of force or direct coercion. What begins as an extremely indulgent and gentle handling of infants continues as a fairly sensitive and responsive interaction with toddlers and children. Although after the age of about two, children no longer enjoy the special devotion and nearly exclusive attention of their parents, the relationship appears generally easy and affectionate. The style of confrontation avoidance that is apparent among adults on Fais also characterizes relationships between parents and children. Parents are reluctant to impose their will and authority over children. Rather they employ various and seemingly continuous forms of persuasion, pleading, cajoling, explaining, shaming, scolding, and indirect threats with children. Thus Fais parents understand clearly that socialization depends largely on "talk." The "well-mannered" child on Fais is the one who "listens to talk."

By 4 to 6 years of age children already are receiving the clear expectation, from parents as well as older children and adolescents, that they should assume a role of responsibility and nurturance towards still younger toddlers and infants. They are expected to assist in feeding, watching over, or carrying younger siblings. Five and 6-year-olds still make occasional appeals to adult authority, but slightly older children, the 7- or 8-year-olds, seem to feel fully confident in their own authority as caretakers.

AIMS AND METHODS

The aims of this research were threefold. We sought to investigate (1) cross-cultural differences in caregiver–infant interaction between the United States and Fais; (2) the influence of social context on caregiver–infant interaction within each culture; and (3) the feasibility of coding and analyzing existing ethnographic film for addressing these research questions. To accomplish these goals, sixteen segments of caregiver-infant interaction were selected from the Fais footage according to the following criteria: (1) age of infant (<30 months) (2) length of sequence (at least 300 cinema feet) and (3) physical proximity between the caregiver and the infant (within 3 yards of one another). The infants ranged in age from 10 days to 16 months with a mean age of 8.7 months; 11 were male and 5 female. The caregivers included natural and adoptive parents, various other natural relatives including siblings, and unrelated adults.

A coding system was developed to describe nonverbal social behavior of infants and caregivers from the film records. The categories were adapted from methodologies previously developed for use with digital recording devices (Anderson, Vietze, Faulstich & Ashe, 1978). The coded behaviors are described in Table 2.1. They include mutually exclusive subcategories of infant visual and manual activities, posture, facial expression, and the varieties of stimulation provided by the caregiver. In addition, a number of interactive behaviors such as mutual regard, head orientation and play were coded. The coding system was applied by four raters trained to reliability. Durations of each behavior were coded for each record during several runs through the data using the film foot counter on the editing table and were later transferred to the Datamyte 900. Coding disagreements were resolved consensually by discussion.

TABLE 2.1
Cross-Cultural Codes for Caregiver-Infant Interaction

Infant Codes	Adult Codes	Dyadic Codes
Hands	*Kinesthetic-Vestibular*	*Proximity*
reach toward caregiver	active manual	hold close
manipulate caregiver's body	touch/stimulate with object	hold far
reach for other person	moving	within arm's reach (medium)
manipulate other person's body	rocking	within 3 yds. (far)
auto-manipulation	carrying	beyond 3 yds. (very far)
reach toward object	vigorous tactile/kinesthetic	
manipulate object	other	*Head Orientation*
other manual activity		en face
	Caregiving	face other angle
Eyes	feeding	face out same or different
closed	grooming	direction, same 180° arc
directed to adult near	bathing	on shoulder
directed to adult far	changing/dressing	on back
directed to child near	other caregiving	other position
directed to child far		
directed to object		*Mutual Regard*
directed to self	*Facial Expression (third digit codes)*	caregiver−, infant−
other visual activity	(change in expression only)	caregiver−, infant+
	sad	caregiver+, infant−
Position/Locomotion	grimace	caregiver+, infant+
lying prone	neutral	
lying supine	interest/alert	*Play (third digit modifier)*
sitting	smile/laugh	change in dyadic play
crawling	play face	without object
standing	other expressions	with object
walking/running		stop play/nothing
carried - hard carrier		
carried - soft carrier		*Social Context (immediate)*
held upright		alone
other position		1–3 other people (small group)
		4+ other people (large group)
Facial Expression (third digit codes)		
(change in expression only)		*Distant Context (third digit)*
cry-face		alone
neutral		1–3 adults (small group)
interest/alert		4+ adults (large group)
smile/laugh		
other expressions		

For purposes of cross-cultural comparison, 13 sequences of American infants and caregivers were filmed with a specific attempt to include dyads alone and in the presence of others. The sample was middle class and Caucasian and located in the Washington, D.C. metropolitan area. The 8 male and 5 female infants ranged from 10 days to 28 months with a mean of 12 months. The caregivers included parents, siblings, and grandparents. The same coding system was applied to the footage of both cultures by four raters trained to reliability.

CROSS-CULTURAL COMPARISONS

Durations of behaviors were converted to proportions of the recording period because the segments coded were of unequal length. Because mean infant age differed for Fais and the United States, cross-cultural comparisons were made with infant age as a covariate. Analysis of covariance was applied to each variable as a proportion of its overall category. Examples of these variables are "manipulates object" as a proportion of all infant manual activity or "faces out" as a proportion of all head orientations. Mean proportions and F values in individual infant and adult behaviors are listed in Table 2.2. Because cross-cultural differences were very limited, only dyadic behaviors are presented.

For the dyadic behaviors, the infant and caregiver faced one another more frequently in the U.S. In Fais the most common head orientation was the infant facing outward (defined as baby in front of caregiver with back of baby's head facing adult's face and both looking within the same 180° arc) (see Figure 2.1). The prevalence of this posturing in the South Pacific is supported by Martini and Kirkpatrick's (this volume) observations in Ua Pou in the Marquesan Islands. As a corollary of these differences it was more frequent in Fais for neither the caregiver nor the infant to be looking at the other person (caregiver−, infant−). American caregivers looked at the infants significantly more often (caregiver+, infant−). However, no cross-cultural differences were noted for mutual social regard (caregiver+, infant+) (see Figures 2.2 and 2.3).

SOCIAL CONTEXT ANALYSES

It became clear in viewing the films that the predominant social context differed markedly between the cultures. Whereas mothers and infants are typically alone in the United States, they tend to be outdoors and in social groupings in Fais. In

TABLE 2.2
Cross-Cultural Differences Between Fais and the United States:
Mean Proportions Covaried for Infant Age

Dyadic Behavior	Fais	United States	$F(1,26)$	$p<$
Head orientation				
Facing one another	29.33	32.70	4.29	.05
Infant faces out	50.55	29.11	10.09	.005
Mutual regard				
No looking at each other	65.69	42.29	4.50	.05
Caregiver looks at infant	26.28	50.78	6.73	.02

FIG. 2.1. Characteristic positioning of infant facing out on caregiver's lap in Fais. (Photo by D. Rubinstein)

FIG. 2.2. Mother and infant in Fais demonstrating face-to-face (but not en face) positioning and mutual regard. (Photo by D. Rubinstein)

FIG. 2.3. Mutual regard and en face positioning of an American grandmother and 12 day old infant. (Photo by A. Sostek)

an attempt to address the question of how the presence of additional people influences caregiver-infant interaction within both cultures, the film segments were divided into three groups: those in which the dyad was alone; those in which between one and three other people were in proximity to the dyad (small group); and those in which more than three other people were present (large group). Although we attempted to code distant as well as immediate social context, these distinctions were necessarily based on the number of people who could be seen within the cinema frame (immediate context). Because the average age of the American infants was older than that of the Fais group and age was not matched across social contexts, age was again treated as a covariate. Social context analyses within Fais and the U.S. are reported in Table 2.3 (including F values and n's per cell).

Within Fais, interaction patterns were most similar when the dyad was alone and in the large grouping. In contrast to these contexts, with one to three people present, infants walked or ran and kept his or her eyes on self more often. In the small group, adult grimaces and playfaces increased and holding decreased. Compared to the two smaller groups, being with more than three other people reduced face-to-face positioning both for en face and other angles, and holding was particularly prevalent. When the dyad was alone both aspects of face-to-face interaction occurred more often.

TABLE 2.3.
Social Context and Caregiver-Infant Behaviors Within Each Culture:
Mean Proportions Covaried for Infant Age

Behaviors	Alone	1-3 People	>3 People	F	p<
Fais	(n=3)	(n=6)	(n=7)	F(3,12)	
Infant walk/run	1.53	8.79	0.20	3.57	.05
Infant eyes on self	-0.9	1.4	-0.1	4.72	.02
Adult grimace	-3.4	4.9	-0.5	4.72	.02
Adult playface	-2.2	4.9	-0.3	3.55	.05
Any holding	64.4	51.1	98.2	7.49	.01
Hold close	40.0	19.8	71.7	4.35	.05
Within arm's reach	27.4	30.9	1.5	4.87	.02
Arm's reach to 3 yards	3.1	17.7	0.4	.97	ns
Facing one another (any angle)	64.3	42.6	9.7	10.50	.005
Facing one another (not en face)	55.6	30.2	8.3	8.43	.01
United States	(n=6)	(n=7)	(omitted)	F(1,10)	p<
Infant walk/run	17.7	1.8		5.10	.05
Infant eyes on self	0.1	1.8		1.07	ns
Adult grimace	—	—		—	—
Adult playface	0.4	0.1		1.06	ns
Any holding	37.4	58.8		.58	ns
Hold close	27.1	30.7		.05	ns
Within arm's reach	45.5	42.7		.13	ns
Arm's reach to 3 yards	17.0	-1.4		7.98	.02
Facing one another (any angle)	42.8	17.4		5.98	.05
Facing one another (not en face)	39.3	12.8		6.58	.05

In America, infrequent large groups made it necessary to restrict the comparisons to the dyad alone versus the small group context (1-3 other people). When the dyad was alone, walking and/or running increased and the infants wandered further away. Furthermore, face-to-face positioning was again more frequent (again for both en face and face other angle).

These differences suggest that the small group context was characterized in both cultures by less intense interaction between caregiver and infant. Although adults in this context used more facial expressions such as playface and grimaces which can engage the infant's attention, close holding was infrequent and the infant's eyes were more likely to be on him or herself. When the dyad was alone, two patterns emerged. Either intense face-to-face interaction occurred (U.S. and Fais) or the infants were more likely to wander (U.S. only). It is probable that two characteristics of the dyad being alone serve to facilitate the infant's increased walk/running and distance from the caregiver. First, no one else is present who might inhibit the infant from separating from the caregiver, and second, no restrictions need be placed on exploration because the caregiver does not need to divide his or her attention between the infant and others.

In the largest group (which occurred only in Fais), infants were generally held, but without face-to-face interaction. It is likely that the infants choose to remain close to the "home base" of the caregiver and/or the caregiver may attempt to keep the infant within a manageable proximity. Whereas in the larger group context there may not be the direct demand for the caregiver to interact with others that there is in the small group context, the lack of face-to-face contact in the largest grouping suggests that one or both partners are attending to surrounding people or events.

DISCUSSION

It is interesting that cross-cultural comparisons between individual infant and adult behaviors yielded few differences. Our data on the dyadic behaviors involved in head orientation and mutual regard indicate a pattern that is essentially consistent with other cross-cultural studies of the South Pacific (Martini & Kirkpatrick, this volume). Infants in Fais were far more likely to be facing out and were less likely to be in face-to-face contact. This positioning also resembles the characteristic head orientation of the Kanela Indians of Brazil (Sorenson, Crocker, Balikci, Schecter & Maloney, 1978) and may be widespread in other cultures.

Analyzing the four possibilities for mutual regard (see Table 2.1), it was more likely in Fais for neither partner of the dyad to be looking at the other and it was more likely in the United States for the caregiver to be looking at the infant. Surprisingly, the two cultures did not differ in proportions of time that the infant looked at the caregiver and the caregiver and infant looked at one another. These "negative results" are particularly intriguing in view of the current interest in eye contact in caregiver–infant interaction.

Our attempt to address the second issue with which we were concerned—the influence of social context on caregiver–infant interaction—must be viewed as preliminary because the numbers of dyads within each context were small and the large group context was not observed in America. With this restriction in mind, the extent of differences among the social contexts is quite remarkable. In Fais, group size related to infant locomotion, visual activity, adult facial expression, holding, proximity and head orientation. In the United States, infant locomotion and caregiver–infant proximity and head orientation were influenced by the presence of others.

The effects of number of people present are bolstered by a growing body of literature on the importance of social context (Bronfenbrenner, 1979; Chisholm, this volume; Konner, 1977). The studies tend to fall into two categories: (1) comparisons between parent–infant interaction in solitude versus in the presence of the spouse (Clark-Stewart, 1978; Lamb, 1977, 1978; Parke, 1978; Pedersen, Anderson & Cain, 1979), and (2) studies of household or colony density in humans or primates (Chisolm, this volume; Hinde & Spencer-Booth, 1967; Kaplan, 1972; Monroe & Monroe, 1971; Wolfheim, Jensen & Bobbitt, 1970). The former approach examines the second-order effects on parent–infant interaction produced by the presence of the spouse. Typically, focused attention on the infant decreases with both parents present and parental smiles and physical stimulation declines (Parke, 1978; Pedersen et al., 1979). When the infant is old enough to initiate social interactions, affiliative behaviors originating from him or her are reduced in the triad as compared to a dyad with either the mother or the father alone (Lamb, 1977, 1978). Parke (1978) cautions against generalizing from dyadic observations of parent–infant interaction without considering the characteristic social context of the family.

In another approach to the general issue of social context, comparisons of low and high density households among the Logoli of Western Kenya indicate more indulgence (reflected by shorter latency to intervene when the infant cries and more infant holding) in high density households in spite of the fact that mothers were somewhat less available (Monroe & Monroe, 1971). Primate studies also associated group living with greater acceptance of dependency demands in infancy with paradoxically less proximity seeking and dependency in later youth (Hinde & Spencer-Booth, 1967; Kaplan, 1972; Wolfheim et al., 1970).

For those behaviors that varied by social context, the greatest similarities lay in comparisons between the small group in Fais and the dyad alone in the United States. Such patterning of behaviors seems to reflect the distribution of social contexts within the two cultures. The function served by different characteristic behaviors in different contexts is most likely preparation for continued socialization into small groups in Fais and dyads in the United States. In Fais caregiving is shared not only among cross-generational members of the natural family but also with the adoptive relatives in another *bogot*. For this reason, parents may avoid imposing unique authority and discipline tends to consist of verbal persuasion coming from many different persons including children and adults (Rubinstein, 1979).

Research demonstrating clear effects of social context has important consequences for cross-cultural comparisons. Unlike the United States or other Western societies in which the predominant context for a caregiver and infant is dyadic, in many other cultures it is rare for a caregiver and infant to be alone together (Goldberg, 1977; Konner, 1977; Martini & Kirkpatrick, this volume). Imposition of Western-based dyadic laboratory paradigms or their facsimiles in another culture might yield data on caregiver–infant interaction confounded by reactions to isolation from the customary others in both the adult and the child.

The findings that, for a given culture, interaction behaviors differ according to the number of people present underline the importance of maintaining sensitivity to social context but leave open the question of how to handle this issue optimally. Controlling for social context sacrifices ecological validity because it would place the caregiver and infant in at least one of the cultures under study out of their characteristic environment. On the other hand, total dedication to ecological validity raises the possibility that cross-cultural differences may be confounded by social context. The present study represents a compromise between the two research strategies. At a minimum, awareness of this complex issue can be reflected in interpretation of cross-cultural data even if the research design does not address the problem.

USE OF EXISTING ETHNOGRAPHIC FILM

The final aim of this research was to evaluate the feasibility of coding and analyzing existing anthropological film for social interactive behaviors. A disadvantage of the Fais footage was the lack of sound that obviously eliminated a record of vocalization. This limitation probably made our task more difficult, which may in turn bolster our positive conclusions.

When compared to the caregiver–infant interaction literature on Asian cultures, the cross-cultural data presented here have face validity. Since the other data were based on direct observations (Brazelton, 1977; Caudill & Weinstein, 1969; Martini & Kirkpatrick, this volume; Sorenson et al., 1978), similarities among the results suggest that analysis of existing ethnographic film can yield worthwhile information. It is important to realize, however, that confidence in the data derived from existing film is directly dependent on the quality of the footage selected and the availability of the necessary documentation.

At the outset, we proposed several criteria for selecting footage, including adequacy of the data base in terms of frequency and duration of appropriate sequences and sufficient variety of subjects to allow for generalizability. Finally, we found it essential to have extensive background information particularly concerning ages and relationships of the interactants. Although it is preferable, but not always possible, that the ethnographer be accessible, permanent detailed records should make this unnecessary. As Margaret Mead (1975) asserts:

> Surely any ethnologist with the intelligence to pass examinations based on a critical knowledge of the current sacred texts and worthy of being supported in the field can learn to make such records which can be analyzed by our steadily developing methods of microanalysis of dance, song, language and transactional relations between persons [p. 18].

Given a choice it would be preferable to have strategic filming of a particular research problem in order to use the most appropriate cinema technique and subject selection criteria. Practical considerations of course make field research opportunities, even without filming, very rare. More importantly, rapid development in many areas of the world may have changed indigenous behavior patterns, social roles and interpersonal relationships. Existing anthropological film therefore provides a unique data base which, with attention to quality and documentation, can be analyzed behaviorally.

ACKNOWLEDGMENTS

We thank Carleton Gajdusek and Andrew Sostek for their support and inspiration and the caregivers and infants in both cultures for their cooperation.

REFERENCES

Anderson, B. J., Vietze, P. M., Faulstich, G., & Ashe, M. L. Observational manual for assessment of behavioral sequences between infant and mother: Newborn to 24 months. *Journal Supplement Abstract Service Catalog of Selected Documents in Psychology,* 1978, *8,* 31.

Brazelton, T. B. Implications of infant development among the Mayan Indians of Mexico. In P. H. Leiderman, S. R. Tulkin & A. Rosenfeld (Eds.), *Culture and infancy: Variations in the human experience.* New York: Academic Press, 1977.

Bronfenbrenner, U. *The ecology of human development: Experiments by nature and design.* Cambridge, Massachusetts: Harvard University Press, 1979.

Caudill, W., & Weinstein, H. Maternal care and infant behavior in Japan and America. *Psychiatry,* 1969, *32,* 12–43.

Clarke-Stewart, K. A. And daddy makes three: The father's impact on mother and young child. *Child Development,* 1978, *49,* 466–478.

Fraiberg, S. *The magic years.* New York: Scribner, 1968.

Goldberg, S. Infant development and mother–infant interaction in urban Zambia. In P. H. Leiderman, S. R. Tulkin & A. Rosenfeld (Eds.), *Culture and infancy: Variations in the human experience.* New York: Academic Press, 1977.

Hinde, R. & Spencer-Booth, Y. The effect of social companions on mother–infant relations in rhesus monkeys. In D. Morris (Ed.), *Primate ethology,* Chicago: Aldine, 1967.

Kaplan, J. Differences in the mother–infant relations of squirrel monkeys housed in social and restricted environments. *Developmental Psychology,* 1972, *5,* 43–52.

Konner, M. Infancy among the Kalahari Desert San. In P. H. Leiderman, S. R. Tulkin & A. Rosenfeld (Eds.), *Culture and infancy: Variations in the human experience.* New York: Academic Press, 1977.

Lamb, M. E. The development of mother–infant and father–infant attachments in the second year of life. *Developmental Psychology,* 1977, *13,* 637–648.

Lamb, M. E. Infant social cognition and "second-order" effects. *Infant Behavior and Development,* 1978, *1,* 1–10.

Leiderman, P. H., Tulkin, S. R., & Rosenfeld, A. (Eds.), *Culture and infancy: Variations in the human experience.* New York: Academic Press, 1977.

Mead, M. Visual anthropology in a discipline of words. In P. Hockings (Ed.), *Principles of visual anthropology*. The Hague: Mouton, 1975.

Monroe, R. H., & Monroe, R. L. Household density and infant care in an East African society. *The Journal of Social Psychology,* 1971, *83,* 3-13.

Parke, R. Parent-infant interaction: Progress, paradigms and problems. In G. P. Sackett (Ed.), *Observing behavior, Vol. 1: Theory and applications in mental retardation.* Baltimore: University Park Press, 1978.

Pedersen, F. A., Anderson, B. J., & Cain, R. L. *Parent-infant interaction observed in a family setting at age 5-months.* Paper presented at the biennial meetings of the Society for Research in Child Development, San Francisco, 1979.

Rubinstein, D. H. *Adoption on Fais Island: An ethnography of childhood.* Paper presented at the 77th annual meeting of the American Anthropological Association, 1978.

Rubinstein, D. H. Native place names and geographic systems of Fais, Caroline Islands. *Micronesica,* 1978, *14,* 69-82.(b)

Rubinstein, D. H. *An ethnography of Micronesian childhood: Contexts of socialization on Fais Island.* Doctoral dissertation, Department of Anthropology, Stanford University, 1979.

Sorenson, E. R., Crocker, W. H., Balikci, A., Schecter, S., & Maloney, M. M. *Keystones of culture: The discovery of culturally specific behavior patterns through research film analysis.* Paper presented at the annual meetings of the American Association for the Advancement of Science, Washington, D.C., 1978.

Wolfheim, J. H., Jensen, G. D., & Bobbitt, R. A. Effects of group environment on the mother-infant relationship in pigtailed monkeys (Macaca nemestrina). *Primates,* 1970, *11,* 119-124.

II
CULTURAL AND SOCIOECONOMIC STATUS

3   Mother-Infant Interactions Among Lower SES Black, Cuban, Puerto Rican and South American Immigrants

Tiffany M. Field
Susan M. Widmayer
Mailman Center for Child Development
University of Miami Medical School

INTRODUCTION

Mother–infant interaction studies conducted in the United States are cross-cultural by nature. Curiously, however, while socioeconomic status is noted typically for the groups studied, the cultural or ethnic make-up, despite its variability in lower SES groups, is rarely mentioned. The early interaction studies of Beckwith and her colleagues with lower SES groups in California, for example, undoubtedly included Mexican–American, Puerto Rican, Oriental, Black and Caucasian American groups (Beckwith & Cohen, 1980; Beckwith, Sigman, Cohen & Parmelee, 1977). Studies by Brazelton, Koslowski, and Main (1974) in Boston, and Stern (1974) in New York City, likely included a heterogenous lower SES group of Puerto Rican, Italian, Black and Caucasian American mothers. Researchers in medical schools, which are often located in inner cities frequently recruit culturally heterogeneous groups of lower SES people.

Although the literature suggests that early interactions are extremely different, for example, in Oriental cultures such as Japan (Caudill, 1962) and Hispanic cultures such as Mexico (Brazelton, 1977) and Guatemala (Klein, Lasky, Yarbrough, Habicht & Sellers, 1977), it is not clear whether those differences persist following immigration to survive the process of acculturation. Although there are some dramatic differences between cultures that are geographically remote: Japanese living in Japan versus Americans living in the U.S. (Caudill, 1962), these differences may disappear as the Japanese move to Hawaii or to California. There may be a gradient, as there is for coronary heart disease, with the Japanese becoming increasingly like Americans in their interaction styles as they move from Japan to Hawaii to California. Then, depending on whether they isolate themselves somewhat in a separate area or acculturate themselves in an inner city or suburban neighborhood, they may share varying degrees of similarity to the local interaction patterns. In the event of "real" acculturation their cultural group identity may be subsumed by or become secondary to their lifestyle or living conditions as represented by SES. Socioeconomic status may then become a more critical independent variable than one's cultural group membership. An example of this phenomenon is a comparison between the Florida Seminole and Miccosukee Indians who at one time belonged to the same tribe. The Miccosukee wishes to remain separatist (from the American culture) while the Seminoles wanted to become more assimilated. The distinguishing identity or characteristic of the Miccosukees today is that they are still a separate Indian tribe affected only peripherally by Anglo-American mores. Although the Seminoles also constitute a tribe, they are commonly identified as part of a lower SES group living in Southern Florida (Lefley, 1979).

If differences among groups tend to dissipate following immigration, ethnic groups could be lumped together with native Americans as a lower SES group, but if differences remain, researchers may be mixing apples and oranges in their studies of lower SES groups, which may explain some of the inconsistencies in the literature. For example, although Tulkin (1977) did not note the cultural makeup of his lower and middle SES groups, or even mention that his study was conducted in Boston, he did note that the middle class was non-Catholic and the lower class Catholic, suggesting that he included a large number of Irish mothers in his lower SES sample (because the lower class Catholic mothers in Boston are Irish). We know from the work of Peter Wolff (1969) that Irish mothers living in Boston have different patterns of feeding infants, e.g., bottle propping, which would appear to be a nonoptimal feeding interaction. Thus, cultural differences may have been contributing to those differences labeled "social class" differences by Tulkin.

Another example comes from our own SES comparisons of early interactions that by necessity of numbers were a comparison between black lower SES and white middle SES (because our geographic location at the time featured too small a black middle SES and too small a white lower SES sample) (See Field, 1979). The most dramatic difference noted in this comparison was the small amount of mother talk in the lower SES group. A subsequent comparison of white middle and lower SES groups in the U.S. and England (Field & Pawlby, 1980) suggested that although the lower SES British mothers talked less than the middle SES mothers, they talked a great deal. Thus, our earlier observation of minimal maternal vocalization appears to have been an ethnic more than an SES group characteristic.

A comparison of SES group differences in lifestyle may be of such magnitude as to dwarf cultural differences, and thus may be considered a more potent independent variable for early interaction studies. In fact, a number of cross-

3. MOTHER-INFANT INTERACTIONS AMONG LOWER SES GROUPS

cultural studies on early interactions have reported SES differences of greater magnitude than cross-cultural differences even when the cultures have been geographically remote. Some examples are Yugoslavian-American comparisons (Lewis & Ban, 1977), Italian-American comparisons (Pearlin & Kohn, 1967) and British-American differences (Field & Pawlby, 1980). Of course, comparisons suggesting larger SES than cross-cultural differences may also be plagued by the problem of a heterogenous, lower SES group. Lower SES groups in other countries are equally as likely to be comprised of a cultural mix. A lower SES sample in London, for example, may include South African, Pakistani, Welsh, Scottish, Irish, and British mothers. Such a mix may produce interaction patterns that are more similar when the groups are living together in the same neighborhood than would be observed in their native regions.

The present study investigates the question of whether groups immigrating to the U.S. might develop some of the same early interaction patterns as groups endogenous to the area or retain their individual cultural patterns. Whereas a full investigation of that question would require field trips to the exotic places of origin, this study is confined to that American neighborhood to which the groups immigrated. As such, we could not address questions of behavioral change before and after immigration but we could examine cross-cultural differences as well as SES versus cultural influences.

The neighborhood is a lower SES, inner city area surrounding the University of Miami Medical School complex and the Miami Civic Center. The cultural groups living there include American Blacks, Cubans, Puerto Ricans, and South Americans immigrating from a number of countries including Honduras, Columbia, Chile, etc. Before describing the study of these groups, some historical background and major cultural values of these groups might provide some perspective.

HISTORICAL BACKGROUND AND CULTURAL VALUES

Cuban-Americans

The influx of Cuban political refugees began in early 1959 when approximately 3000 *Bastistianos,* members of the elite power structure of President Fulgenica Batista escaped to Miami. These people left Cuba with many of their assets and were able to establish themselves quite comfortably in Miami, an area used to large numbers of Cuban tourists and businessmen (Rogg, 1974).

The second phase of refugees arrived in Miami in late 1959 and throughout 1960 when businesses, ranches, and plantations were systematically confiscated by the Castro regime. These refugees were almost exclusively upper SES and were able to liquidate some of their assets prior to their exodus, arriving in the U.S. with money and, in many cases, having numerous American friends. In late

1960 and the first half of 1961 the upper-middle class, including professionals, managers, directors, stockholders and executives of U.S. businesses in Cuba arrived in Miami. Most of these refugees had tourist visas, paid the airfare themselves, and had enough money to support themselves well in this country for at least a few months. This group represents about 50% of the refugee population. It did not occur to most of these refugees that it would not be possible to return to Cuba within the year. The heads of most families had come to Miami to protect their wives and children, to regroup themselves as a military operation, to solicit military aid from the U.S., and to launch a counter-revolution to overthrow Castro as soon as possible (Rogg, 1974; Senior, 1965).

Following the futile Bay of Pigs operation, however, new waves of refugees arrived, recognizing that Castro's regime was more stable than previously thought and that it was being kept afloat through the assistance of the USSR. These refugees, initially, were allowed only $5.00 in American money, one suit of clothing, and a few changes of underwear. Subsequently they were allowed nothing but the clothes they were wearing (Rogg, 1974).

The composition of the emigré group began to change at this juncture with increasing numbers of lower-middle SES people arriving and fewer formerly wealthy people. The "Freedom Flights" were bringing an average of 1700 Cubans to Miami each week until the Cuban missile crisis of October 1962 when Castro stopped the flights. Most of the people arriving subsequently escaped in row boats and were primarily women and children because males of military age (15 to 26 years) were conscripted into the army and had little opportunity to escape (Rogg, 1974).

The New York Times (Dec. 9, 1962) reported that there were 400,000 Cubans living in Miami–Dade county, Florida. Until very recently many Cubans arriving in Miami were less political refugees than migrants with relatives in the United States. Large numbers of these people entered the U.S. through Spain or Mexico under the sponsorship of their American relatives, almost all searching for work, and for better housing and living conditions than currently exist in Cuba. These are essentially the "disaffected" and were primarily lower-middle SES people in their own country (Weidman, 1978).

The upper SES and upper-middle SES refugee had the least trouble with acculturation in the United States. Most spoke fair to good English and many had received at least part of their education in the United States. Many of these people established their own businesses in Miami or moved to other urban areas of the East coast to find work or to return to various universities to qualify for licensure in numerous fields. This was comparatively easy in the case of physicians, dentists, architects, engineers, etc., but particularly difficult in other fields such as law (Senior, 1965).

The profile of the Cuban family of the Miami area is as diversified as the pluralistic American family of the United States. There are some, particularly among more recent arrivals, who are lower SES and live in substandard housing with insufficient food. For the most part, however, the Cuban is able to find employment, usually skilled labor, at least. There is much emphasis placed on education and both parents will work long hours to provide a college education for a son or daughter (Weidman, 1978). In general, the children are indulged and very much protected by American standards. The wealthier, more acculturated Cuban-Americans, appear to have fewer problems with their childrens' adaptations to the American way of life and many of these children leave home for college and subsequently live independently, unlike their own mothers who lived at home until marriage and whose mother, aunts and in-laws usually live nearby to provide assistance when necessary. The upper-middle SES Cuban-American infrequently encounters prejudice from the native-born American as they tend to associate with Americans who value their business acumen and bilingualism. The lower-middle and lower SES Cuban-Americans, however, tend to isolate themselves in urban areas and are frequently subject to prejudicial remarks and attitudes. These people are consequently less enamored of the American way of life, tend to insist that their children speak Spanish exclusively, and feel great conflicts in dealings with their adolescents, particularly those who ridicule the ideas and traditions of their parents (Rogg, 1974).

Cuban-American children of the lower-middle SES behave toward their parents with much *respeto* within the family, but in the neighborhood and at school the traditional ways are looked down upon, and many adolescents feel trapped between the two cultures, neither of which totally accepts them nor is completely acceptable to them. Representatives of the Miami Mental Health Clinics report ever increasing numbers of school-age children with serious emotional conflicts within the Cuban community. Most of these children live in exclusively Cuban areas, are from the lower-middle class, and have parents who speak little or no English (Gurri, 1979). An example of the seriousness of this problem is the extremely high incidence of elective abortion among Cuban-American teenagers. Pregnancy prior to marriage is considered to be an unconscionable disgrace among Cubans of all income groups, but particularly the lower-middle SES. Girls of this SES group will have abortions rather than admit to being pregnant, even though abortion is contrary to their religious beliefs (Scott, 1979).

The Cuban child of the middle and lower SES groups is the center of the household on whom everyone dotes, including parents, grandparents, aunts, uncles, etc. Male children are particularly esteemed. However, both boys and girls are expected to receive comparable educations, although married women seldom worked before coming to the United States. The children are protected from contact with persons outside the family and children, particularly from the lower middle groups, are often very shy and have difficulty adjusting to school. Many of these children speak very little English and retain an accent for many years, though they speak Spanish early and develop language quickly. Cuban infants and children are encouraged to eat very well, particularly by their grandmothers, and many are obese as they begin with solids by one month. They are not precocious motorically and appear to enjoy being carried everywhere and rocked a great deal. The children are scolded infrequently and seldom physically punished. Many seem demanding and somewhat immature.

As SES increases, there appears to be less isolation of the children from people outside the family, more emphasis on the proper learning of English, and on the value of independence and self-sufficiency (Gurri, 1979).

Puerto Ricans

The 55,000 Puerto Ricans of the Miami area are much like the peoples from other South and Central American countries. They are divided into two groups: a wealthy upper-middle SES and a lower SES group, with comparatively few representatives of the intervening socioeconomic groups. The wealthier Puerto Ricans live in Miami for financial reasons as Miami is fast becoming the United States' door to Latin America. The better educated, bilingual Puerto Rican business person uses Miami as a base of economic operations (Senior, 1965).

Lower SES Puerto Ricans come to the United States mainland to find work. With the high rate of unemployment in New York and the crisis of public assistance programs there, the Puerto Rican migrant is moving to other industralized areas with increasing frequency. Miami is growing in its appeal to the poor Puerto Rican because of its bilingualism, its growing number of industries, and because there is less competition for jobs in unskilled markets than in areas such as New York, New Jersey, and Chicago. Nevertheless, large numbers of Puerto Ricans in Miami are forced to avail themselves of public assistance, especially women with dependent children (Senior, 1965).

The attitude of the lower SES Puerto Rican is less positive than is that of the Cuban toward the Federal Government. The political undercurrents on the island are demanding either full statehood or independence and the lower SES peoples believe that their economic problems, particularly unemployment, stem from what they perceive as a colonial role in relation to the United States mainland.

The Puerto Rican child is highly valued by his or her parents, but may be the victim of much prejudice in the neighborhood, particularly if she or he is of mixed parentage and is made to feel somewhat of an outcast in these communities. There is, in general, much antagonism between blacks and the Spanish-speaking populations of Miami (Weidman, 1978). This is the result of the competition between the two groups for jobs and the fact that Hispanic Americans, particularly Cubans and Puerto Ricans, have become politically, socially, and economically more powerful in 20 years than have the blacks in almost a century. Moreover, though Puerto Rican parents esteem education, it is often difficult for parents to provide their older children the leisure needed to complete high school and very few children of the lower income groups go on to college (Senior, 1965).

South Americans

There are approximately 32,000 South and Central Americans living in Miami-Dade County, Florida. Large numbers of these people are here with temporary visas so that they may attend universities and colleges in the area; many others are here working as representatives of large Latin American banks and businesses. Most of these individuals are from the upper classes of their respective countries, which include Colombia and Venezuela, particularly, as well as Chile, Peru, Brazil and some Central American nations (Census data–Dade County, 1979). These people have been attracted to the Miami area because of its bilingualism, its Latin atmosphere, tropical climate, and its potential as a place of residence in the event of political unrest at home. They also seem to find it easier to deal with Cuban-Americans than with non-Latin groups within the United States.

South and Central America are also represented by members of the lower socioeconomic groups of their countries. For example, for many years "maid flights" from Guatemala to the United States have been a common occurrence. Young women, often married with small children at home, will come to the United States as live-in maids, cooks and nurses, particularly to work in Cuban homes. Here they receive room and board and enough salary to send money home to support their parents and/or children. This separation represents an extraordinary hardship for most of these women and many return home after a year or two. Single women also come to this country on temporary work permits, hoping to marry Americans and/or to have American-born babies so that they may stay here permanently. Also, of course, there are numbers of South and Central Americans living in Miami without status (Truss & Benson, 1979).

The lower socioeconomic families from these Latin American areas often live in very crowded conditions on the fringes of other groups. They are not accepted by the blacks in the neighborhood who view them as economic rivals and aliens, by the white non-Latin lower SES who cannot communicate with them, or by other Spanish-speaking groups who consider them to be of inferior social status. These people tend not to be demanding or aggressive in their dealings with others, are often on public assistance, and are often the last people served in the public health clinics and government offices. As a result of their isolation relatively few learn English and all appear very diffident to others, particularly white Americans who are authority figures for them (Truss & Benson, 1979).

The lower SES South and Central Americans appear to be very much involved with their infants and enjoy talking about them—emphasizing their intelligence, etc. When an infant must be hospitalized for any reason, the entire family, particularly the mother of the infant, is disconsolate. Because they are poor some mothers cannot dress their children and many appear to be unkempt much of the time. What money is available is used for food and the children in this group are surprisingly healthy (Weidman, 1978).

Southern Black

Approximately 17% of the population of Miami is black. This includes groups of Haitian refugees, Bahamians, as well as southern blacks (Census data–Dade County, 1979). The regional origins of the southern black population of Miami are complex. Many have reported that their parents or grandparents moved here from Georgia or the Carolinas. One mentioned that her parents sent herself and her sisters to Miami from the "country" so that they could get more education. A minority have intermarried with the Bahamians who have lived in Miami since the mid-1700s. It appears that the majority of blacks in Miami have lived here for several generations.

As is typical of urban areas of the deep South, the economic and social position of the black person in Miami has always been an inferior one (DuBois, 1969). Although there is a growing group of black professionals in Miami, this group is proportionately small compared to similar groups in cities of the Border South such as Washington, D.C. and of the North such as Chicago and New York. The black person is at a particular disadvantage in Miami as his or her upward mobility is blocked by large numbers of lower SES Hispanic groups who are more frequently employed by their middle SES "countrymen" who prefer Spanish-speaking employees dealing with Latin-American customers. Middle SES blacks, frequently educated in the North, maintain a precarious status in Miami as there are few areas where they can live and not be identified with the lower socioeconomic status blacks. The middle SES black's overriding concern is with maintaining respectability and he expends much effort in making the proper associations and belonging to upwardly mobile social groups. Most middle SES blacks in Miami are educators, (considered upper-middle SES in this ethnic group), small business owners, health professionals, and government employees (Pinkney, 1969).

Until the major Supreme Court decisions prohibiting overt discrimination, segregated schools, restaurants, etc., the lower socioeconomic status black in Miami–Dade county could find only the most minimal work as domestic servants and day laborers. Although there was hope that this situation would change with legal reforms demanding equal opportunity, the great influx of Latin American immigrants to the area also in need of work, has resulted in comparatively little economic improvement among the southern blacks in Miami. Even today, groups of black men may be seen very early in the morning on different street corners, waiting to be picked up by large buses to take them to construction jobs or other day-labor occupations. Though many black women find jobs as maids, white non-Latin and Latin employers often tend to hire live-in help from South and Central American countries.

Most black men, except older ones, do not marry or live with their girlfriends to avoid welfare problems. The black woman has the highest unemployment rate in this country and she and her children are generally on public assistance. The presence of a male on the premises who is capable of work will exempt the women from benefits.

The children, particularly when they are infants, are much appreciated and, for the very young mother, are much like play things. The mother will go without food or clothes herself in order to provide these for the baby. The babies are often overdressed, even in intense heat, and frequently have colds and runny noses. If the infant is the last of several, less attention is given to him and most of his care may be entrusted to a sibling, often only 4 or 5 years old herself. The black mother believes that a child is easily spoiled by too much attention, by being held and carried, and by being praised. She refrains from doing these things and typically leaves the baby unattended, often on a bed, for long periods of time. The child soon learns that if he is to move he must move himself.

Housing for the majority of blacks in Miami is substandard, and roaches and rodents are almost domestics in some households. The more fortunate often live in public housing, which is very cheap, but which quickly becomes run down. Often a woman lives in a one or two bedroom apartment with several teenagers and some younger children. Children of her teenagers may live with her too, and often are raised as her own (Harrington, 1962).

Teenage pregnancy is not disapproved of but promiscuity is frowned upon. The teenage mother, often 14 or 15 years old, changes and feeds the baby during the day but reports that she does not feed the baby at night because he or she "never cries." Grandmothers often mention that the babies do cry but that their daughters sleep through it. Apparently the grandmother does not tend to the baby either. The teenage mother is extremely involved with the baby during the first few days and weeks, but then appears to become disinterested, leaving much of the baby's care to her mother. The grandmothers are more expressive in their interactions with the babies but as the children grow older, discipline at home becomes very rigid; shaking and spanking, often with belts and switches, becomes the rule. The children grow up familiar with physical aggression but are unable to express their feelings at home where complaining and self-pity are not permitted. Children and adolescents soon learn to keep silent, to acquiesce, but to do more or less as they please. In dealings with the establishment, the black adolescent continues to agree to all the rules and regulations, but then refuses to conform (Harrington, 1962).

The rate of illness, particularly hypertension and chronic heart disease, among blacks is very high, and the median age for death in Dade County is 51.9 years as compared to 70.2 years for whites (Miami Herald, May 15, 1979).

Commonalities Among These Cultures

The majority of the southern black and Latin groups represented in this study were unskilled employees. Most of the participants live within a twenty block radius of the Hospital/Civic Center Complex, although each group is somewhat segregated from the others by living area. Within these areas approximately 21% of the Cubans own their own homes, as do 17% of the Puerto Ricans, whereas all of the southern black population rent their homes (Weidman, 1978). The housing of the poorest of the southern black is markedly substandard with poor plumbing, rodents and roaches, little ventilation, and almost no privacy. The crowding index of the southern black home is 1.4 as compared with 1.0 for the Puerto Ricans and .9 for the Cubans. In many instances grandparents with their children and their children's children are found living together in a small two or three bedroom house in both the black and the South and Central American areas. The Cubans were found to live very near, often next-door to, parents, aunts, uncles, brothers, sisters, etc., but they invite only widowed or single mothers, fathers, uncles, or aunts to live with them.

Common to the four groups studied in this project, aside from poverty and much interest in their children, is a highly religious attitude. Although most of the Latin groups report themselves to be Roman Catholic and the black to be southern baptist, an extraordinary number of these people are only nominal participants in these more traditional faiths, and are actually affiliated with Santeri, Espiritismo, or Vodun, syncretic religions derived from an amalgamation of European Catholicism, Indian, and West African and Nigerian belief systems. Witchcraft and sorcery play a very significant role in these groups with a belief in spirits as the most predominant feature of these secret traditions. Most participants deny any affiliation with these cults but will seek out Rootworkers in cases of serious illness, particularly, as they often believe these to be the result of "curses" or "spells." Living in an unpredictable, unintelligible world, these lower SES groups who are plagued with poverty and continual sickness share tremendous feelings of helplessness, which manifests itself as a type of floating anxiety that appears to be alleviated by spiritualism and banishing of evil spirits. When, due to inability to pay the rootworker or conflicts in seeking help, the individual attempts to cope with this anxiety himself, a phenomenon known as *falling out* among the southern black and a related behavior called *ataques* among the Latins is common among these lower SES groups. This transient paralytic seizure may take place at any time, anywhere and may seriously interfere with many types of employment, etc. (Weidman, 1978).

Certain similarities in world view, commonalities in education and income levels, little or no acceptance of the mores of these low SES ethnic groups by the predominant culture, language barriers even among the southern black populace who speak dialect, and religious customs and beliefs, suggest that socioeconomic status may be a more potent factor in separating these groups from the mainstream of American culture in Miami than is ethnicity. In their relationships with their children, however, subtle differences among these cocultures continue to manifest themselves.

METHOD OF STUDY

Subjects

Thirty-two mother–infant dyads of Cuban, Puerto Rican, South American and black American backgrounds comprised the sample of this study. All of the mothers were lower SES based on maternal education and paternal occupation. Maternal education ranged from 7- to 12-years (M = 10), and paternal occupations included mainly skilled labor jobs such as truck driver, factory worker, and cab driver. None of the Hispanic mothers spoke English to us. Age of mothers ranged from 18 to 40 years (M = 25). There was a considerable group variability on number of years residence on the mainland U.S. (Cubans = 11 years; Puerto Ricans = 16 years; and South Americans = 5 years). This demographic information appears in Table 3.1.

Procedure

The mothers and infants visited our interaction lab when the infants were 3- to 4-months of age (M = 14 weeks). They were first videotaped in a feeding interaction, followed by a face-to-face interaction. Subsequently the infants were given a pediatric examination, a developmental assessment, and the mothers were interviewed on demographic, attitudinal, and infant nutrition information by a bilingual research assistant.

The mother-infant feeding interaction was videotaped with one camera on the infant's face and torso and one camera on the mother's face and torso. The cameras were located approximately 6 feet away from the mother in order to be unobtrusive. A split screen generator in the adjacent room made possible simultaneous viewing of mother and infant images on each side of the video screen. A digital clock entered time in seconds across the lower portion of the video field to facilitate coding.

Following a 3 minute videotaped feeding segment, the mother and infant were videotaped in a face-to-face interaction for 3 minutes. The mothers were simply

TABLE 3.1
Demographic Data

	Group Means			
Measures	Cuban	Puerto Rican	South American	Black
Years in U.S.	11	16	5	25
Maternal Age	28	24	27	25
Maternal Education	10	10	10	10

asked to pretend they were home playing with their infant during this interaction segment. The infant was placed in an upright infant seat on a table approximately 18 inches from the mother. Again, one camera filmed the torso and face of the mother and the other the torso and face of the infant.

Coding and Data Analyses

The videotapes of the interactions were coded for mother vocalization and infant gaze activity as these two measures have discriminated mother–infant dyads in previous studies. In addition, both infants and mothers were rated on a number of feeding and face-fo-face interaction dimensions using an interaction rating scale (IRS) (Field, 1980a). The face-to-face interaction dimensions included infant state, head orientation, facial expressions, fussiness and vocalizations, mother's facial expressions, infantized behaviors, contingent responsivity, and game playing. In addition, the videotapes were transcribed for the mother's language record, again by a bilingual researcher. The transcripts were then coded for the following measures: total number of words, total number utterances, mean length of utterance, number of statements, imperatives and questions.

These interaction measures, together with the infant growth data (weight, length and head circumference) and the Denver developmental assessment scores, were then entered into a multivariate analysis of variance (Rao, 1973), using a *sex* (2) × *cultural group* (4) design. Since the F value for this analysis was significant ($p < .01$), univariate analyses of variance were conducted for each of the measures followed by post hoc comparisons made by Bonferonni t tests (Myers, 1972).

Results

Growth and development measures. There were no differences on growth measures, although the nutritionist reported a greater incidence of obesity among the Cuban infants. The only developmental difference as measured by the Denver scale was the superior performance of the Puerto Rican infants on the Denver adaptability subtest (tracking, reaching and grasping items).

Face-to-face interactions. The face-to-face play behaviors that most reliably differentiated the groups were amount of maternal vocalization and infant gaze (or proportion of total interaction time the mother talked and the infant looked at the mother). Cuban mothers talked to their infants almost continuously whereas black mothers talked very little. The rank order of mean percentage of time talking was: Cuban (82%) > South American (75%) > Puerto Rican (56%) > black (14%), each of the group differences being significant at least at the $p < .05$. Mothers' mean length of utterance followed the same rank order (Fig. 3.2): Cubans (5.10) > South American (4.51) > Puerto Rican (3.60) > black

(1.62). Interestingly, a reverse order appeared for infant gaze: Puerto Rican (67%) > black (57%) > South American (50%) > Cuban (32%), with Cuban infants gazing at mother the least or gaze averting the most. These results are depicted in Figs. 3.1 and 3.2.

These data are consistent with previously reported inverse relationships between amount of mother talking and infant gaze (Field, 1977a; 1980a, 1980b). However, the data do not support the frequently reported low levels or amounts of verbal activity for lower SES mothers except in the case of black mothers (Bee, Van Egeren, Streissguth, Nyman & Lockie, 1969; Field, 1980a; Kilbride, Johnson & Streissguth, 1977; Tulkin & Kagan, 1972). Generalizing from black mothers to all low SES groups therefore distorts the picture of interactions in the lower SES groups. Although the most dramatic differences occurred between the Hispanic and black dyads, the aforementioned differences between Hispanic dyads were also reliable indicating further heterogeneity in the low SES populations.

On the interaction rating scale (IRS) (Field, 1980a) significant differences emerged for the following maternal dimensions (all $p < .05$): (1) infantized behavior — Puerto Rican > Cuban > South American > black; (2) contingent responsivity — Puerto Rican > Cuban > South American > black; and (3)

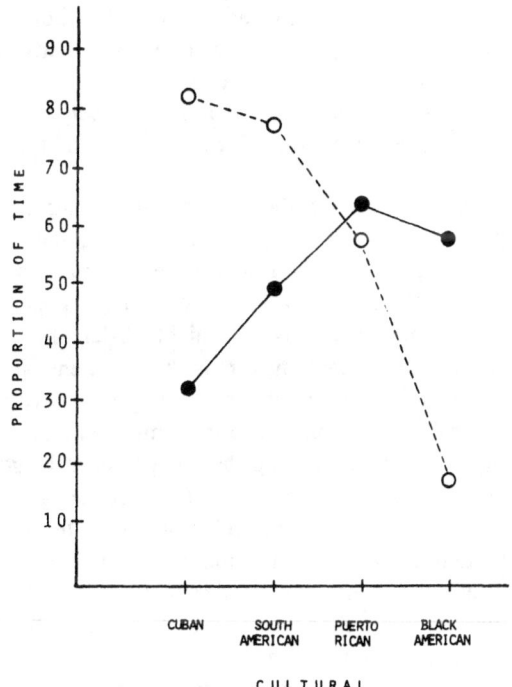

FIG. 3.1. Proportion of interaction time that mothers talked (---) to their infants and infants gazed (—) at their mothers.

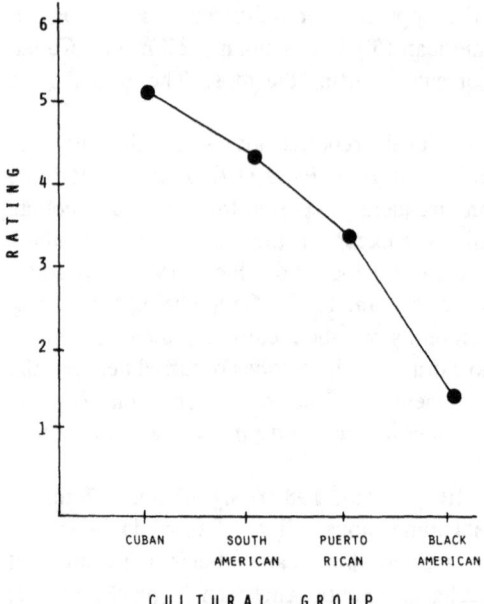

FIG. 3.2. Mean length of utterances by mothers talking to their infants.

gameplaying — Puerto Rican > Cuban ~ South American > black. On the same interaction rating scale, the following significant differences on infant dimensions emerged: (1) facial expressions — Cuban > South American > Puerto Rican ~ black; and (2) fussiness — Cuban > Puerto Rican > South American ~ black. The mean ratings for the mother and infant interaction dimensions appear in Table 3.2.

Again, although the most significant differences occurred between the Hispanic and black dyads, there also were reliable differences among the Hispanic dyads. In addition, at least for the maternal dimensions, there was a consistently similar ranking of groups. Thus, there appear to be some salient face-to-face interaction dimensions that reliably differentiated all four cultural groups, and the consistency in ranking across these dimensions suggests relationships between the infantized behavior, contingent responsivity, and gameplaying dimensions.

Profiles that emerged, for example, characterized the Cuban mothers as talking the most and having the longest mean length of utterance and their infants, being the most expressive facially, but engaging in the most gaze averting and fussing. Relative to the Cuban mothers, the Puerto Ricans talked less, showed more infantized behavior, more contingent responsivity, and played more games. The South Americans ranked between the Puerto Ricans and blacks with the black mothers showing the least talking, infantized behavior, contingent responsivity, and gameplaying.

Differences between the groups on the types of gameplaying during the face-to-face interactions were also intriguing. The Cuban mothers engaged in more teaching or instructional-cognitive games, whereas the Puerto Rican mothers

3. MOTHER-INFANT INTERACTIONS AMONG LOWER SES GROUPS

engaged in more social games. The South American mothers showed a mixture of these while the black mothers did little of either. These gameplaying differences appeared to be consistent with the mother's objectives for the face-to-face interactions, for example, the Cuban mother's primary objective of "educating her children" and the Black mother's expressed concern that she not "spoil her child by giving him too much attention." Thus, the mothers' "hidden agendas" appeared to differ across these cultures which may have contributed to their differential behaviors.

Feeding interactions. All of the mothers bottlefed their infants, and all showed the "universal" pattern of holding the infant on their left side (Richards & Finger, 1975; Salk, 1962; Weiland, 1964). There were differences in the amount of mother talking during the feeding with Cuban mothers talking 43% of the time, South American mothers 31% and Puerto Rican and black mothers talking very little.

Differences emerged on the feeding interaction rating scale (IRS: Field, 1980a). The maternal dimensions on which the group differed significantly were as follows:

1. mother's state (i.e., depressed/anxious or alert/attentive)—with Puerto Rican mothers being more alert/attentive than Cuban mothers > South American > black mothers;

TABLE 3.2
Interaction Ratings

Rating*	Groups			
	Cuban	Puerto Rican	South American	Black
Face-to-face interaction				
mother-infantized behavior	2.6	2.8	2.4	1.9
-contingent responsivity	2.6	2.8	2.4	1.8
-gameplaying	2.4	2.8	2.3	1.8
infant-facial expression	3.0	2.6	2.8	2.5
-fussiness	2.2	2.6	2.9	3.0
Feeding Interaction				
mother-state	2.6	3.0	2.3	2.0
-physical activity	2.6	2.8	2.5	1.6
-head orientation	2.8	3.0	2.1	1.5
-initiation bottle				
removal	2.2	3.0	1.9	3.0
-summary	2.4	2.6	2.4	2.3
infant-physical activity	2.8	3.0	2.3	1.9
-summary	2.6	2.8	2.3	2.2

*higher ratings are optimal

2. physical activity (overly active/inactive or minimal activity) with Puerto Rican mothers being less active than South American and Cuban mothers, and black mothers being inactive;
3. head orientation (frequent or infrequent head aversion) with Puerto Rican mothers' heads oriented toward their infants more frequently than Cuban mothers > South American > black mothers;
4. initiation of bottle removal (infants' or mothers' initiation) with Puerto Ricans and black mothers initiating bottle removal less often than Cuban and South American mothers (Puerto Rican ~ black > Cuban ~ South American); and
5. the overall summary feeding rating for mothers (a summary of nine ratings) showed a ranking of Puerto Rican mothers being more optimally rated than Cuban mothers who were equivalent to South American and black mothers.

In light of these findings it is interesting that their infants received the same rank order ratings for: (1) physical activity (frequent squirming or relaxed body/molding to mother)–Puerto Rican infants showing less squirming and more relaxed body than Cuban > South American > black; and (2) summary feeding rating—Puerto Rican > Cuban > South American ~ black. Thus, the profile that emerged was that Puerto Rican mothers more frequently oriented their heads toward their infants, were more attentive to their infants, engaged in the least amount of physical activity (such as rocking and repositioning of the infant) and were least likely to initiate bottle removal or more likely to let their infants initiate the termination of the feeding.

It is interesting that the rank order for a number of the feeding ratings followed that of the face-to-face interaction ratings with Puerto Rican mothers and infants receiving more optimal ratings on this particular rating scale than Cuban mother–infant dyads, in turn, more optimal than South American or black dyads. Although the relative ranking for mother–infant feeding ratings approximated that of the face-to-face interaction ratings, the feeding interactions in general were less optimal than the face-to-face interaction ratings. For example, during feeding interactions, Cubans engaged in considerable verbal and physical stimulation. In light of this finding, it is interesting that infant obesity was a pediatric problem, primarily for the Cuban infants of this study.

DISCUSSION

The number and magnitude of differences in early interaction patterns among the mothers of these cultures were somewhat surprising to us given the following:

1. All mothers were of similar age, education and parity. A number of studies have suggested that early interaction behaviors vary as a function of the mother's

age (Field, 1980a), education (Cohen & Beckwith, 1976) and parity (Jacobs & Moss, 1976; Kilbride et al., 1977);

2. All mothers were lower SES with similar lifestyle and living conditions. The literature on interaction patterns of lower SES mothers is fairly consistent (Bee et al., 1969; Field, 1980a; Kilbride et al., 1977; Tulkin & Kagan, 1972);

3. All four groups of mothers have lived in the same neighborhood for a number of years, although there was some variability between groups on number of years in the U.S.;

4. The Hispanic groups, at least, share a common language (Spanish) and a common nonlanguage (failure to use English); and

5. Members of all four groups have been noted to hold similar belief systems and engage in similar religious rituals (Weidman, 1978), and may have similar ways of coping with stress (e.g., "falling out"; Weidman, 1978), and similar attitudes toward institutions such as medical facilities (Weidman. 1978), etc. Despite these seeming similarities, there were dramatic differences between the groups on a number of early interaction dimensions.

Some group differences that may have contributed to these interaction pattern differences were years in this country, relative prestige ranking of groups within the community, larger cultural values such as respect and value for higher education or other "hidden agendas" of the mothers from a very early stage in their relationship with their infants. Also, possible constitutional differences in the infants may have contributed to differences in the behaviors of the mothers.

Among the Hispanic groups, years in this country followed the same rank order as interaction ratings. That is, the Puerto Ricans who had resided in the U.S. for the longest period (an average of 16 years) received the most "optimal" interaction ratings, whereas the South Americans who resided here the shortest time (M = 5 years) received the least optimal ratings. And the Cubans fell in between these groups both on length of residence and interaction ratings. It is conceivable that a longer period of time in the U.S. may have influenced interaction patterns directly or may have contributed to their feeling comfortable around non-Latin, middle SES researchers. The length of time in the U.S., however, did not appear to relate to degree of acculturation in other ways, for example, language. Despite 16 years in this country, these mothers still elected not to speak English.

The relative prestige ranking of each of these groups within the community or that assigned to each other by each other is not clear. All four groups appear to compete for a similar job market. The Cubans may have greater stature among this particular community because there are many more upwardly mobile Cubans than other Hispanics in the area. The Puerto Ricans may feel more confident of their rank because of their citizenship, and their being on the U.S. mainland as a cultural group for a longer period of time. And the South Americans may feel some diffidence in their small numbers but confidence in their status related to their compatriots recently bringing in wealth and buying up the real estate market in the Miami area. It is not clear how these factors may affect the behaviors of these people.

An interesting aside, which points to the complexity of cultural values, is provided by the recently arrived Haitian lower SES immigrants living in Miami. In Haiti, lower SES Haitians breast-feed their infants whereas the upper SES Haitians bottle-feed their infants (there is no middle class). When the lower SES Haitians move to this country they no longer breast-feed but bottle-feed: they say "because it is the modern thing to do." But it also may be related to their attitude about "coming to the promised land," which might make them "more like their upper SES countrymen back home"; or it may be because their role models in the hospital lying-in period are lower SES Hispanics and American blacks who do not typically breast-feed, and there are no nurses who can speak Creole to encourage or assist them in establishing breast-feeding during the lying-in period. In addition to these possible explanations there are countless other possibilities that would be difficult to confirm.

"Hidden agendas" for early interactions may differ dramatically as manifested by mother behaviors. Although mothers' attitudes or expressed objectives for early interactions are rarely tapped by researchers, differences in behaviors suggest the mothers may have different objectives for early interactions. A study comparing British and American mothers suggested, for example, that British mothers played more instructional/cognitive games with their infants whereas American mothers played more social games (Field & Pawlby, 1980). The kinds of games referred to here are "infant" games such as peek-a-boo, pat-a-cake, I'm gonna get you, etc. British mothers more frequently attempted to elicit tracking, searching, reaching. and grasping behaviors in their infants, whereas American mothers attempted more often to elicit eye contact, smiling, and cooing. British mothers sang more nursery rhymes (as if instructing) whereas American mothers attempted to engage their infants in "conversation." In the present study, these same kinds of contrasts were noted for the Cuban/Puerto Rican dyads with the Cuban mothers being more "instructional" i.e., counting, going through the A, B, Cs, asking "what's this?" questions in polysyllabic words and long utterances, whereas the Puerto Rican mothers were more frequently talking "baby talk" in very exaggerated intonations and brief phrases with very little instructional content. The South American mothers showed a mixture of infant games, whereas the black mothers played infant games very infrequently. These game-playing differences may have been consistent with the mothers' objectives for the face-to-face interactions—for example. the Cuban mother's primary objective of "educating children" and the black mother's expressed concern that she not "spoil her child by giving him too much attention." Thus, the mothers' "hidden agendas" may have differed and differentially contributed to the behaviors observed.

Another analogy between the British/American and the present data is that the mean length of utterance for the British mother is to that of the American mothers as the mean length of utterance of the Cuban mother is to that of the American black mother. Even with general conversation among adults, British and Cuban women may be more "chatty" than American white or black women. What is certainly not true is that, on the whole, lower SES mothers are nontalkative or inactive. Although American black mothers may be less talkative than the middle SES white mothers, the lower SES Cuban mothers of this study and the lower SES British mothers of the Field and Pawlby (1980) study were certainly highly verbal.

The infants themselves differed during their interactions, with the Cuban infants being the most active and the most expressive, but also engaging in the least eye contact and most fussing. That was, perhaps, not surprising given that the high levels of stimulation provided by their mothers might be strongly arousing and evoke greater positive, as well as negative reactions in their infants.

The generally inverse relationship or "inverted U" relationship of mother vocalization and infant gaze aversion noted in this study (see Fig. 3.1) is very similar to that noted in our American samples of normal and high-risk infants and their mothers (Field, 1977a; 1980a, 1980b). There appears to be more infant gaze aversion and fussiness with high levels of maternal activity.

On the other hand, the infants may have differed in these ways at birth, and it is not clear whether the stimulating mother or the labile infant came first. A number of cross-cultural studies have reported significant differences between neonates of various cultures (Brazelton, 1977; Freedman & Freedman, 1969) on orienting and early behaviors. Unfortunately, we did not recruit this sample immediately after birth and cannot address this issue. Although causality may remain unclear, the development of the infants appeared to relate to feeding and play interactions. Among the Cuban infants who experienced a less optimal feeding interaction, there was a developmental problem of obesity. In the Puerto Ricans, who experienced a more optimal face-to-face interaction, there was more accelerated development of skills tapped by Denver adaptability items (e.g., tracking, searching, reaching, grasping).

The specific behaviors that differentiated the groups are certainly not independent of each other. Game-playing involves contingent responsivity and infantized behavior and vice versa, just as infant facial expressions, gaze behaviors, and fussiness are related. These types of behaviors are very often measured in early interaction studies and cross-cultural studies as if they are universal mother-infant interaction behaviors. Although they may occur universally, their variability in these cultures was considerable. Similarly, the feeding interaction ratings that discriminated the groups were those that are frequently cited as markers of "sensitivity to infant signals" or sensitive feedings, i.e., head orientation, amount of stimulation during sucking, initiation of bottle removal (Field, 1977b; Kaye & Brazelton, 1971).

It is interesting that although the rank order of groups on face-to-face and feeding interactions were similar, there were a number of individual dyads, e.g.,

Honduran dyads, who received optimal ratings on one of these interactions and nonoptimal on the other. In general, the feeding interaction ratings were less optimal than the face-to-face interaction ratings, which may derive from the mothers feeling uncomfortable bottle-feeding (native Cubans and Puerto Ricans, for example, typically breast-feed in their own country).

Comparisons between these lower SES Hispanic groups and our middle SES American groups demonstrate less baby talk, more frequent and longer speech utterances, less game-playing, more singing, more acceleration of activity level (instead of deceleration) during infant fussiness, and more activity (both verbal and nonverbal) during feeding interactions in the lower SES Hispanic groups. Interestingly, however, there appear to be as many differences in interaction patterns between the lower SES, Hispanic groups living in the same neighborhood as there are between these socioeconomically and ethnically diverse lower SES Hispanic groups and middle SES non-Latin groups. Thus, a culturally heterogenous group may be as much a "mixed-bag" as socioeconomic mixtures of people, and must be considered in our attempts to understand the dynamics of early interactions.

ACKNOWLEDGMENTS

We would like to thank all mothers and infants who participated in this study. In addition, we are grateful to Jayne Brennan, Lorraine Gawley, Jenny Julien and Sheah Roeback for their assistance with data collection. This research was supported by a grant OHD 90CW605(1) from the Administration of Children, Youth and Families.

REFERENCES

Beckwith, L., & Cohen, E. S. Interactions of preterm infants with their caregivers and test performance at age two. In T. Field, S. Goldberg, D. Stern & A. Sostek (Eds.), *High-risk infants and children: Adult and peer interactions.* New York: Academic Press, 1980.

Beckwith, L., Sigman, M., Cohen, S. E. & Parmelee, A. H. Vocal output in preterm infants. *Developmental Psychobiology,* 1977, *10,* 543–554.

Bee, H. L., Van Egeren, L. F., Streissguth, A. P., Nyman, B. A., & Lockie, M. S. Social class differences in maternal teaching styles and speech patterns. *Developmental Psychology,* 1969, *1,* 726–734.

Brazelton, T. B. Implications of infant development among the Mayan Indians of Mexico. In P. H. Leiderman, S. R. Tulkin, & A. Rosenfeld (Eds.), *Culture and infancy.* N.Y.: Academic Press, 1977.

Brazelton, T. B., Koslowski, B. & Main, M. The origins of reciprocity: The early mother–infant interaction. In M. Lewis & L. Rosenblum (Eds.), *The effect of the infant on its caregiver.* New York: Wiley, 1974.

Caudill, W. Patterns of emotion in modern Japan. In R. J. Smith & R. K. Beardsley (Eds.), *Japanese culture: Its development and characteristics.* Chicago: Aldine, 1962.

Census data, Miami-Dade County Library System, 1979.

3. MOTHER-INFANT INTERACTIONS AMONG LOWER SES GROUPS 61

Cohen, E. S., & Beckwith, L. Maternal language in infancy. *Developmental Psychology*, 1976, *12*, 371-372.

DuBois, W. E. B. (Ed.) *The Negro American family*. Westport, Conn.: Negro Universities Press, 1969.

Field, T. Effects of early separation, interactive deficits and experimental manipulations on infant-mother face-to-face interaction. *Child Development*, 1977, *48*, 763-771. (a)

Field, T. Maternal stimulation during infant feeding. *Developmental Psychology*, 1977, *13*, 539-540. (b)

Field, T. Interaction patterns of preterm and term infants. In T. Field, A. Sostek, S. Goldberg, & H. H. Shuman (Eds.), *Infants born at risk*. New York: Spectrum, 1979.

Field, T. Interactions of preterm infants born to lower class teenage mothers. In T. Field, S. Goldberg, D. Stern, & A. Sostek (Eds.), *High-risk infants and children: Adult and peer interactions*. New York: Academic Press, 1980. (a)

Field, T. Interactions of high-risk infants: Quantitative and qualitative differences. In D. B. Sawin, R. C. Hawkins, L. O. Walker, & J. H. Penticuff (Eds.), *Current perspectives on psycho-social risks during pregnancy and early infancy*. New York: Brunner/Mazel, 1980. (b)

Field, T. & Pawlby, S. Early face-to-face interactions of British and American working and middle class mother-infant dyads. *Child Development*, 1980, *51*, 250-253.

Freedman, D. G., & Freedman, N. Behavioral differences between Chinese-American and American newborns. *Nature*, 1969, *224*, 227.

Gurri, I. Personal communication, 1979.

Harrington, M. *The other America: Poverty in the United States*. N.Y.: Penguin Books, 1962.

Jacobs, B. A., & Moss, H. A. Birth order and sex of sibling as determinants of mother-infant interaction. *Child Development*, 1976, *47*, 315-327.

Kaye, K., & Brazelton, T. B. *Mother-infant interaction in the organization of sucking*. Paper presented at the meeting of the Society for Research in Child Development, Minneapolis, April 1971.

Kilbride, M. W., Johnson, D. C., & Streissguth, A. P. Social class, birth order and newborn experience. *Child Development*, 1977, *48*, 1686-1688.

Klein, R. E., Lasky, R. E., Yarbrough, C., Habicht, J. P., & Sellers, M. J. Relationship of infant/caretaker interaction, social class and nutritional status to developmental test performance among Guatemalan infants. In P. H. Leiderman, S. R. Tulkin, & A. Rosenfeld (Eds.), *Culture and Infancy*. N.Y.: Academic, 1977.

Lefley, H. Personal communication, 1979.

Lewis, M. & Ban, P. Variance and invariance in the mother-infant interaction: A cross-cultural study. In P. H. Leiderman, S. R. Tulkin, & A. Rosenfeld (Eds.), *Culture and infancy*. New York: Academic Press, 1977.

Myers, J. L. *Fundamentals of experimental design*. Boston: Allyn & Bacon, 1972.

Pearlin, L. I., & Kohn, M. C. Social class, occupation and parental values: A cross-national study. *American Sociological Review*, 1965, 466-479.

Pinkney, A. *Black Americans*. Englewood Cliffs, N.J.: Prentice-Hall, Inc., 1969.

Rao, C. R. *Linear statistical inference and its applications*. N.Y.: Wiley, 1973.

Richards, J. L., & Finger, S. Mother-child holding patterns. A cross-cultural photographic study. *Child Development*, 1975, *46*, 1001-1004.

Rogg, E. M. *The assimilation of Cuban exiles*. N.Y.: Aberdeen Press, 1974.

Salk, L. Mothers' heartbeat as an imprinting stimulus. *Transactions of the New York Academy of Science*. Ser. 2., 1962, *24*, 753-763.

Scott, K. Personal communication, 1979.

Senior, C. *Our citizens from the Caribbean*. St. Louis: McGraw-Hill, 1965.

Stern, D. Mother and infant at play. In M. Lewis & L. Rosenblum (Eds.), *The effect of the infant on its caregiver*. N.Y.: Wiley & Sons, 1974.

Truss, C., & Benson, J. *Parent training*. In Preprimary Behavioral Competence Project Report, 1979.

Tulkin, S. R. Social class differences in maternal and infant behavior. In P. H. Leiderman, S. R. Tulkin, & A. Rosenfeld (Eds.), *Culture and infancy*. N.Y.: Academic Press, 1977.

Tulkin, S., & Kagan, J. Mother-child interaction in the first few years of life. *Child Development*, 1972, *43*, 31-41.

Weidman, H. H. *Miami Health Ecology Project Report*. Volume I. University of Miami, 1978.

Weiland, I. H. Heartbeat rhythm and maternal behavior. *American Academy of Child Psychiatry*, 1964, *3*, 161-164.

Wolff, P. H. The natural history of crying and other vocalizations in early infancy. In B. M. Foss (Ed.), *Determinants of infant behaviour, IV*. London: Methuen, 1969.

4 Middle Class Differences in the Mother-Child Interaction and the Child's Cognitive Development

Candice Feiring
Michael Lewis
Educational Testing Service
Princeton, New Jersey

In any discussion of socioeconomic status, it is important to remember that this designation is not in itself a psychological variable. Socioeconomic status (SES) is a variable that others, historians or economists, for example, have used to identify differences among people. However, SES is inadequate as a psychological explanation for differences. The relationship between psychological process and behavioral outcome as a function of SES must be observed in order to understand how group differences are generated. The presence or absence of individual differences between different economic and/or social groups should not be the main focus of scientific investigation. Rather, it is the study of those processes that produce outcomes that provide us with more precise and useful information for explaining differences. The present analysis, which explores social class differences, attempts to understand underlying processes rather than to demonstrate class differences.

In general terms, the variable of social-economic status (SES) refers to the amount of income and the way in which it is acquired. Acquisition of income or occupation assumes an attribution of status often concommitent with the amount of formal education. Although SES is a continuous variable that may be viewed as varying from extreme wealth and formal education to extreme poverty and lack of formal education, the majority of research on SES differences has tended to compare groups that were fairly far apart on the income-education dimensions. Frequently, middle income groups have been compared with impoverished groups resulting in a confounding of SES and race (cf. Deutsch, 1973). Another unfortunate consequence of choosing SES extremes for comparison is that theoretical explanations for differences too easily acquire good-bad evaluations that are ethnocentric in nature. The ethnocentrism in the SES literature has tended to be based on the investigators' standards; a problem with research in general (Edel, 1976), but particularly a problem in the SES literature given the "status attribution" inherent in the variable itself.

Still a third difficulty is that the middle SES studied most often is the highly educated middle SES, a group readily available as subjects, rather than the total middle SES group. Differences between lower- and -middle SES often reflect differences between the poor and a highly educated middle SES group. It may be the case that this highly educated group although labeled middle SES does not reflect the entire middle income group. Consequently the middle-lower SES distinction may be misleading because the educational level of what researchers label middle SES is much higher than the education level within the general middle income group. If this were the case, one would expect to find differences between this highly educated middle SES group and others of the middle income who have somewhat less education but who would not be classified as lower SES group. Research by Shipman and her colleagues (1972) supports this view. It was found that similar magnitudes of cognitive differences existed between children of college educated parents and children of high school educated parents and between children of college educated parents and children of parents with a 10th grade education or less. Thus it may be the case that in many studies of SES differences a biased sampling of the highly educated middle income group and the tendency to call this group "middle class" without specifying its unique educational characteristics has contributed to our misinterpretation of SES differences.

Actually, the implicit assumption that the SES designation of "middle class" describes some homogeneous group is part of the more fundamental problem of failure to examine process as compared to status variables (cf. Dave, 1963; Hess Shipman, Brophy, & Bear, 1969; Schaefer, 1972). Status variables, such as education or occupation reflect standard demographic descriptions of families. Unlike process variables, they offer little information concerning patterns of parent-child interaction or child rearing attitudes that may influence a child's development. As indicated previously, status variables are gross proxies for assessing the child's environment. Status variables used to define SES inappropriately assume constancies of meaning *within* as well as across SES groups (cf. Light & Smith, 1971) and indicate little about the type of stimulation the child receives from parents, siblings, teachers, friends, etc. Consequently, within a given SES level, the range of home environment, or parent-child interaction can be so varied as to render extremely tenuous any generalizations about SES level and development (Pavenstedt, 1965; Shipman, 1972; Tulkin, 1968; & Zigler, 1968). In the study reported here our interest in socioeconomic status is motivated by our desire to find the psychological processes that underline group differences within middle income groups. We are particularly interested in comparing a highly educated group, which we shall label upper-middle SES, to a moderately educated group, which we shall label middle SES, in regard to the mother-child interaction in the opening years of life and its effect on the child's emerging verbal-symbolic competence.

As in other areas of inquiry, research efforts aimed at explaining differences in socioeconomic status in infancy have yielded mixed results. Many studies have been unable to find SES differences in children in the first two years of life. Bayley (1965) reported no SES differences in infants 1 to 15 months of age on her scales of motor and mental development. Levine, Fishman, Kagan (1967) reported no SES differences in the behavior of 4-month-old infants observed at home. On the other hand, Wachs, Uzgiris, and Hunt (1967, 1971) have noted SES differences in tasks involving motor imitation and verbal facility as well as differences on subjects of Piagetian infant psychological development scales. At 7 months of age, middle SES infants were more skilled than lower SES infants in the ability to obtain a distant object. At 15 months, lower SES infants were more proficient at stacking rings on a pole than middle SES infants whereas middle SES infants scored better than low SES infants on verbal measures of the number of appropriate words used spontaneously for objects and the number of words that were elicited through imitation. Messer and Lewis (1972), in a study of attachment and play behavior in 12-month-old infants of different SES level, in general failed to find any differences. However, they did note that middle SES infants vocalized seven times more frequently in the presence of their mothers than did lower SES infants. Counter to expectation Lewis and Wilson (1972) found that at 3 months of age lower SES infants vocalized, smiled more, and cried less than upper-middle SES infants. The maternal behaviors of touch, smile, look, play, and TV watching were more frequently observed in low as compared to middle SES parents. However, and most important for language development, middle SES mothers were twice as likely to respond with vocalization to infant vocalization than were low SES mothers (cf. also Lewis & Freedle, 1977).

Lewis and Freedle (1973) examined patterns of vocal interaction between mothers and their 3-month-old infants as measured by naturalistic observation in the home. Although no SES differences were noted in how much the mothers spoke to their children, how much the infant vocalized was related to socioeconomic status. Lower SES infants vocalized more frequently than middle SES infants. However, the patterns of infant-mother vocal responses appeared to be less conversational; lower SES infants were more likely to vocalize when their mothers were speaking whereas middle SES infants were more likely to stop vocalizing and to listen. Finally, the poorest children in terms of general behavior were placed in a more physically restricted environment than middle class children.

Tulkin and Kagan (1972) and Tulkin (1972) found SES differences in the behavior of 10-month-old females from middle and working class families. As in the Lewis and Freedle (1973) findings, middle SES infants spent less time in a playpen and more time crawling and playing with objects than working class infants. The children were also exposed to an experimental treatment involving tape recorded passages of a fairy tale read by the mother. The middle SES infants quieted more when they heard their mothers voice, vocalized more when their mother stopped speaking, and tended to look more at the mother after hearing her voice than did working class infants.

Golden and Birns (1968) found no SES differences in black male and female infants 1 to 2 years of age on the Cattell Infant Intelligence Scale or on the Piaget Object Scale. However, these same investigators (Golden & Birns, 1976) found SES differences in the cognitive skills of white males at 2 years of age. Children with mothers in the higher education group scored significantly better on the Bayley as well as on both the production and comprehension tests of a verbal inventory. White (1975) found no SES difference at 12 months of age on measures of children's social and intellectual competence. At 3 years of age, there was still no relationship between SES and social competence. However, the Stanford-Binet measure of intellectual competence varied significantly as a positively linear function of SES.

In summary, SES differences in infant cognitive skills are not prevalent during the first 18 months of life. Although differences in maternal and child social behavior may vary by SES, especially when patterns of verbal interaction are examined at early ages, differences in sensorimotor behavior in general have not been demonstrated. Although vocalization differences exist as a function of SES, this is not reflected in measures of early sensorimotor intelligence. Because vocalization patterns are related to later measures of verbal performance and intelligence (Moore, 1968), it would seem reasonable to expect that SES differences in language-based measures of intelligence should begin to emerge between 18 to 24 months (cf. Golden & Birns, 1976). As verbal skills become more important for exploring and conceptualizing the environment, those infants who have been getting more verbal input may have an advantage in the development of cognitive skills. At around 24 months, language skills seem to take precedence over sensorimotor skills and it is at this point that SES differences in "intelligence" as well as parent-child vocalization patterns are noted. By 3 years of age, SES differences in children's intelligence is a fairly reliable finding (cf. Coleman, Campell, Hobson, McPartland, Mood, Weinfeld & York, 1966; Hess & Shipman, 1968; Palmer, 1972). The increase in SES differences over time may be a function of the shift in the cognitive task from sensorimotor to verbal-symbolic operations. These differences can be caused by several factors; some have considered them genetic (Wilson, 1975) and others cultural (Lewis & McGurk, 1972). Given that the most marked SES differences in mother-infant interactions appear to be around verbal-communication competence, it may be the case that these early differences, although having no effect on infant cognitive ability in the first 18 months, make their effects felt when the verbal-symbolic operations emerge.

4. MIDDLE CLASS DIFFERENCES IN COGNITIVE DEVELOPMENT

As noted earlier, SES is not viewed here as a unitary variable but rather as a conglomerate of several factors. The specific purpose of the analysis reported here is the determination of SES related factors that comprise differences in the social behaviors of mothers and children and the cognitive development of children at 3, 12, and 24 months of age. Thus, we are interested in SES differences in specific mother-child behaviors and interactions and their influence on cognitive development. SES constitutes an implied description of environmental stimuli that influence the child's development. Although it is easy to suggest that life style, value systems, child rearing patterns, etc., vary with SES, it is more difficult to specify the nature and content of these variations. In this study it was assumed that the mother is particularly influential in transmitting to the young child behaviors and adaptations related to the environment. For this reason greater priority was given in our analysis to the mother's input to the child, although we recognize the importance of the child's influence on its environment (cf. Bell, 1971; Lewis & Rosenblum, 1974). Information about the status variables of education and occupation of parents was used to identify subpopulations of the middle socioeconomic status group, which should be analyzed separately in light of possible process and environment differences.

Another focus of this study was how possible SES differences in mother-child interaction were related to the child's cognitive skills as these skills shifted from a preverbal to a verbal mode. Although we expected to find SES differences in the mothers' and children's vocal patterns at the earlier ages (cf. Lewis & Freedle, 1977), we did not expect to find differences in the cognitive measures until the children were 24 months of age (cf. Golden & Birns, 1976).

METHOD

Subjects

Social class of the families was determined by using a modification of the Hollingshead's scales of socioeconomic status. An average of the father's and mother's score was computed and this average score was used to assign the family to either an upper or middle SES group. The families were divided into two instead of the five Hollingshead's categories with the division of 27.5, the lower numbers being assigned to the upper SES group. At 3 months there were 193 families (92 families were classified as upper-middle SES and 101 families were classified as middle SES), at 12 months 174 families (87 upper-middle and 87 middle), and at 24 months 156 (74 upper-middle and 87 middle families were examined).

Having stressed the importance of specifying the defining characteristics of SES that may relate to differences in the processes of mother-child interaction, a more complete description of the families studied here follows. Considering education, upper-middle SES parents had an average of 17.53 and 15.76 years of education for father and mother respectively, whereas middle SES parents had on the average 13.82 and 12.84 years of education for father and mother respectively. Table 4.1 gives a breakdown by SES of the educational degrees earned by the mothers and fathers in the sample. As Table 4.1 indicates, the major difference in upper-middle and middle SES mothers is that the majority of the former have completed college whereas the majority of the latter have finished high school. Both groups are similar in the number of junior college degrees whereas the upper-middle class mothers have earned more master's degrees. Examining the fathers' education, we note that the majority of upper-middle SES fathers have earned college degrees, with a large percentage having completed graduate work. For the middle SES fathers, the majority have finished high school with a substantial percentage having finished 2 to 4 years of college. In summary, middle SES families tend to have mothers with high school degrees and fathers with high school or college degrees. Upper-middle SES families tend to have mothers with college degrees and fathers with college or graduate degrees.

Table 4.2 presents the occupations that characterized the parents in the upper-middle and middle SES groups. The majority of upper-middle SES mothers were teachers, with a number of nurses and business-related jobs also represented. The data indicate that the majority of middle SES mothers were secretaries followed by a large number of clerical positions. The majority of upper-middle SES fathers held management-level business jobs. Engineers and college professors were also well represented in the upper-middle SES father

TABLE 4.1
Educational Degrees of Mothers and Fathers by SES

Degree	Upper-Middle Fathers	Middle Fathers	Upper-Middle Mothers	Middle Mothers	Total
Less than high school	0	2	0	1	3
High school	2	44	7	74	127
Two years college	3	21	14	15	53
Four years college	36	27	52	10	125
Master's Degree	30	5	19	1	55
PHD	21	1	0	0	22
Did not respond	0	1	0	0	1
Total	92	101	92	101	386

TABLE 4.2
Occupations of Mothers and Fathers by SES

Occupation	Upper Middle Fathers	Middle Fathers	Upper Middle Mothers	Middle Mothers	Total
Accountant	6	6			12
Architect	1				1
Artist		1		1	2
Baker		1			1
Business Related	27	32	10	7	76
Butcher		1			1
Clerk	1	2	1	22	26
Computer Related	6	7	1		14
Construction		7			7
Doctor	3				3
Draftsperson				1	1
Economist			1		1
Engineer	16	2	1		19
Factory Worker	1	4		3	8
Fashion Stylist			1		1
Film Maker	1				1
Foreman					1
Hairdresser				6	6
Hospital Aide				3	3
Housewife			1	5	6
Journalist			2		2
Lawyer	6				6
Machinist		15			16
Mechanic		3			3
Military		1			1
Musician		1			1
Nursing			11	4	15
Physical Therapist			2		2
Professor	12	1			13
Public Servant	1	3		1	5
Science Related	4		5		9
Secretary			6	34	40
Social Worker	1		1		2
Student	1	1	7	3	12
Teacher	5	3	34	5	47
Technician		6	5	2	13
Travel Agent			3	1	4
Truck Driver		3			3
Waitress/Waiter				2	2
Total	92	101	92	101	386

occupations. Other high status occupations such as medical doctor, attorney, accountant, and computer programmer were also represented in the upper-middle SES sample. The majority of middle SES fathers were employed in middle level business management positions. The next most frequent occupation for middle SES fathers was machinists. Skilled tradesmen such as electricians, mechanics, carpenters, and computer technicians were represented in the middle as contrasted with upper-middle SES fathers. Although much less frequent than in the upper-middle SES sample, some middle SES fathers were also engineers, accountants, and teachers.

Observation and Recording of Mother–Infant Interaction at Age Three Months: Home Observation

Each mother–infant pair was observed in the home for a 2-hour period while the infant was awake. Preparatory to observation, the observer briefly explained the purpose of the observation, showed the mother the materials being used, tried to put the mother at ease, and instructed the mother to continue with her normal routine and to ignore the observer.

All behaviors (13 for the mother and 13 for the infant) were coded every 10 seconds on machine-scorable checklists; primary activities (such as crib or lap) were noted for each 1-minute interval. In order to ensure accurate timing for coding behavior, the observer used a small timing device which only she could hear.

In addition to recording the amount of behavior exhibited, the observation checklist was designed to capture any one of three types of behaviors during a given 10-second period: (1) occurrence, (2) initiation, and (3) response. Any of the 13 infant and 13 mother behaviors could be recorded as occurrences (non-interactive behavior) or as part of an interaction as initiations or responses. Infant behaviors at 3 months were:

1. eyes closed,
2. vocalization,
3. extra movement,
4. fret/cry,
5. feed—bottle,
6. feed—spoon,
7. play—object,
8. play—person,
9. play—self,
10. smile/laugh,
11. burp, sneeze, cough,
12. looking at mother, and,
13. sucking—non-feed.

4. MIDDLE CLASS DIFFERENCES IN COGNITIVE DEVELOPMENT

Mother behaviors at 3 months were:

1. touch,
2. hold,
3. vocalization,
4. vocalization to other,
5. look,
6. smile/laugh,
7. play w/child,
8. change diaper/bathe,
9. feed,
10. rocks child,
11. read/TV,
12. kiss, and,
13. give toy/pacifier.

Measurement of Cognitive Performance at 3 Months

Cognitive performance at 3 months was measured by (1) the Bayley Mental Scale of Infant Development; and (2) the Corman-Escalona Object Permanence Scale. In the case of the Bayley Mental Scale, items 26 through 73 were administered during the home visit. These items represent an average age placement ranging from 2.1 to 5.8 months according to Bayley. The first five items of the Corman-Escalona Scale, tapping early behaviors that are likely precursors to the concept of object permanence, were administered at the Infant Laboratory. All perceptual-cognitive tasks were administered within 2 weeks of the infant's 3 month birthday.

Observation and Recording of Mother-Infant Interactions at Ages 12 and 24 Months: Playroom Observation

At ages 12 and 24 months, mother-infant dyads were observed in a playroom at the laboratory. The dyad was left alone in the 10 x 12 foot playroom, marked with carpet squares and containing 13 toys, a chair, table, and magazine. Both mother and infant were observed through a one-way mirror and videotaped. The observation consisted of a 15 minute free play period in an unstructured situation in which mother and infant had the opportunity to interact with toys.

In order to tap the interactive quality of the mother-infant relationship, the coding sheets were designed for recording behaviors during a given 15-sec period as occurrences, initiations, or responses, as was the case at 3 months. The recording of interactive behaviors was reciprocal. That is, if one or more behaviors were checked for the mother as an initiation, then one or more behaviors had to be recorded for the infant as a response for any given 15-sec period.

Infant behaviors at 12 and 24 months were (1) vocalization, (2) looking, (3) smile, (4) touch, (5) fret/cry, (6) seek approval, (7) seek help, (8) gesture, (9) seek proximity, (10) toy/non-toy, (11) move/door, (12) lap, and (13) hold/hug. Maternal behaviors at 12 and 24 months were (1) vocalization, (2) looking, (3) smile, (4) touch, (5) kiss, (6) hold, (7) give directions, (8) read, (9) seek proximity, (10) toy/non-toy, (11) show toy, (12) manipulate toy, and (13) demonstrate toy.

Measurement of Cognitive Performance at 12 Months

Cognitive performance at 12 months was measured in the laboratory by (1) the Bayley Mental Scale of Infant Development, and (2) the Uzgiris-Hunt Scales of Infant Development. In the case of the Bayley Mental Scale, items 99 through 125 were administered. These items represent an average age placement ranging from 11.3 to 17.8 months according to Bayley. Two subscales of the Uzgiris-Hunt Scale were administered and included Scale I—the Development of Visual Pursuit and the Permanence of Objects, and Scale II—the Development of Means for Obtaining Desired Environmental Events. All cognitive measures were administered within 4 weeks of the infant's first birthday.

Measurement of Cognitive Performance at 24 Months

The cognitive measures at 24 months consisted of the infant's performance on (1) the Bayley Mental Scale of Infant Development, (2) the Infant Laboratory Language Test, a test of prepositions and adjectives, and (3) the Peabody Picture Vocabulary Test. Each of the measures was administered in the Infant Laboratory within 4 weeks of the child's second birthday. The Bayley Scale items 124 through 163, which represent an age placement range from 17.8 months to 30+ months were administered to the 24-month-old children.

The Peabody Picture Vocabulary Test (PPVT), a measure of verbal intelligence, generated three performance scores for each subject: (1) comprehension; (2) production; and (3) mental age. In the case of comprehension, the child was presented with a series of cards divided into four sections with a picture in each section. Children were asked to "point to" the picture the experimenter named. When the child failed six of eight consecutive items, testing was terminated. The number of correct responses determined the comprehension score. The mental age score is an age equivalent derived from the comprehension score. In the case of production, the child was again shown the picture cards, but this time the experimenter pointed to a picture and asked the child to name it. The production score was determined by the number of correct responses made by the infant until six of eight consecutive items were failed. Because the production and comprehension tasks employed the same picture cards, the two tasks were given at least 1 week apart.

The Infant Laboratory Language Test (ILLT) provided an estimate of the child's knowledge of prepositions and adjective contrasts. In the prepositions part of the test, children were asked to manipulate objects—such that they placed a block *into* a cup or put a plate *on top* of the block. In the adjective contrast part of the test, children were asked to show the experimenter, for example, the *big* versus the *small* ball.

Measurement of Maternal Language Skill at 24 Months

The vocabulary test of the Wechsler Adult Intelligence Scale (WAIS) which provides an estimate of verbal intelligence was administered to the mother of each 24-month-old child. The mothers were given a list of words and asked to give their meanings while an experimenter recorded their responses. Items were scored on a 3-point scale; 0 for an incorrect answer, 1 for a partially correct answer, and 2 for a correct answer. After five consecutive items were failed or after all the items had been defined, testing was terminated. The total number of points equaled the raw score.

Coding of Mother-Infant Interaction Data

The mother-infant interaction data for all ages were coded in several ways. It will be recalled that a distinction was made in recording behaviors between those that occurred in interaction (as an initiation or a response) and those that simply occurred. This scheme allowed for the analysis of the interactive nature of mother-infant behavior both in terms of frequency of interaction and nature of interaction in terms of chains of behavior. Of specific interest was the amount of maternal initiations and responses toward her child.

Behavior Frequency and Groups. The first type of coding analysis involved the frequency of behavior occurrences. At 3 months behaviors were coded in 10-sec intervals. Because a given behavior could be recorded only once (as an occurrence, initiation, or response) within one 10-sec period, a particular frequency reflects the number of 10-sec intervals in which the behavior occurred. At 12 and 24 months, the amount of behavior was reported in terms of the actual frequency or number of times each behavior occurred over the observation period. At 3, 12 and 24 months, mother behaviors were also grouped as proximal (e.g., touch, kiss, hold, proximity) and distal (e.g., vocalize, look, smile, give directions). Infant behaviors were also grouped as proximal (same square, touch, seek proximity, lap, hold/hug) and distal (vocalize, look, smile, fret/cry, gesture).

Interactive Analyses. In addition to the generation of behavior frequencies and groups, more complex levels of coding were employed as an attempt to characterize the nature of mother–infant interaction. One type of interactive analysis involved interactions between mother and infant in terms of initiation and response frequencies. In the *complex interactive* analysis, total interactions as well as maternal initiating and responding behavior were examined. As a result of the complex interactive coding, a selection of interactions that occurred with relatively high frequency were also subjected to analysis. These selected interactions were directed interactions; that is, they were either mother-initiated (e.g., mother vocalize—infant look) or infant-initiated (e.g., infant fret/cry—mother look) and could be characterized by two-link chains. These *selected-directed interactions* were, like the complex interactions, examined in terms of frequency.

RESULTS
AGE LEVEL ANALYSES

Three Month Data

Maternal Behavior. The frequency of each maternal behavior at 3 months shows some effect of SES. Although the differences are not large, upper middle SES mothers in general engage in more activities, specifically in more proximal activity and vocalization. For the proximal behaviors of kiss, rock, hug, hold and touch the mean number of 10-sec periods is 109.8 for the upper middle and 97.1 for the middle SES mothers out of a total of 720 10-second periods. The mean of the distal behaviors of smile, look, and vocalize are 183.1 and 185.6 for the upper-middle and middle SES mothers respectively. Considering the number of 10-second periods in which a behavior occurred, upper SES mothers vocalize (upper-middle) = 210.3, middle = 185.9; $F(1, 187) = 2.62$ $p \leq .10$), kiss (upper-middle = 13.2, middle = 10.0; $F(1, 187) = 3.02$ $p \leq .08$), feed (upper-middle = 120.4, middle = 105.0; $F(1, 187) = 2.76, p \leq .10$), and hold (upper-middle = 268.8, middle = 230.8; $F(1, 187) = 6.01, p \leq .02$) their infants more than middle SES mothers. On the other hand, middle-SES mothers show a greater frequency of smiling (upper middle = 66.1, middle = 82.5; $F(1, 187) = 5.31, p \leq .02$) and read/watch TV (upper middle = 15.9, middle = 25.0; $F(1, 187) = 6.47. p \leq .01$) as compared to upper middle-SES mothers.

Infant Behavior. The only difference worth noting was that upper-middle class infants tended to vocalize more frequently than middle SES infants (upper-middle = 153.3, middle = 132.7; $F(1, 187) = 3.28, p \leq .07$).

Mother-Infant Interaction. The interactive data indicated that middle SES dyads tended to engage in a greater frequency of interactions than upper-middle

SES dyads (middle = 116, upper-middle = 99; F (1, 187) = 3.69, $p \leq .06$) with middle SES mothers showing more initiative behavior than upper-middle SES mothers (upper-middle = 37.0, middle = 50.0; F (1, 187) = 5.66, $p \leq .02$). In addition, maternal initiation as a proportion of total maternal behavior was higher for middle SES mothers (upper-middle = 5.0, middle = 8.0; F (1, 187) = 5.63, $p \leq .02$). The only exception to this pattern was in maternal initiation of vocalization. Although the data indicated that both upper-middle and middle SES mothers initiated more vocalization than other behaviors, the percentage of time infants were responsive was greater for the upper-middle SES infants than middle SES infants (percentage of interaction time = 7.1 vs. 5.1 respectively).

Infant Cognitive Skills. At 3 months, there was no difference in infant performance on the MDI of the Bayley or the Object Permanence Scale as a function of SES.

In summary, at 3 months, there were few SES differences in maternal or infant behavior and no differences in the child's cognitive performance. Upper-middle SES mothers more frequently hold and vocalize to their infants whereas middle SES mothers smile and read/watch TV to a greater degree. Upper-middle SES infants show a tendency to vocalize more than middle SES infants although the two groups do not differ in cognitive performance.

Twelve Month Data

Maternal Behavior. There were few differences in maternal behavior at 12 months, although middle SES mothers tended to engage in proximal types of behavior somewhat more frequently than upper-middle SES mothers (upper-middle = 2.8, middle = 4.0; F (1, 161) = 3.65, $p \leq .06$), especially in regard to touch (upper-middle = 2.2, middle = 3.4; F (1, 161) = 5.26, $p \leq .02$). Although there were no overall differences in distal behavior (upper-middle = 123.4, middle = 121.6), middle SES mothers tended to look at their infants more frequently than upper-middle SES mothers (upper-middle = 46.2, middle = 49.0, F (1, 161) = 3.14, $p \leq .08$), whereas upper-middle SES mothers smiled more than middle SES mothers (upper-middle = 26.8, middle = 21.1; F (1, 161) = 9.33, $p \leq .003$).

Infant Behavior. Although there were no SES differences in overall distal behavior, upper-middle SES infants vocalized and looked somewhat more frequently than middle SES infants. Middle SES infants cried more frequently than upper-middle SES infants (upper-middle = .3, middle = 1.4; F (1, 161) = 5.49, $p \leq .02$). Consistent with this finding, middle SES infants engaged in more proximal behavior (upper-middle = 12.1, middle = 16.1; F (1, 161) = 4.68, $p \leq .03$), and shared the same square with the mothers more often than upper-middle SES infants (upper-middle = 9.9, middle = 13.5; $F (1, 161) = 5.57$, $p \leq .02$). In addition, middle SES infants were on their mothers' laps about four times more frequently than upper-middle SES infants.

Mother–Infant Interactions. At 12 months upper-middle SES mothers initiated more interactions than middle SES mothers through their looking and smiling behavior. In particular, maternal smile—infant smile interaction was greater for upper-middle than middle SES mothers (upper-middle = 9.0, middle = 5.0; $F (1, 161) = 4.95$, $p \leq .03$). The data also reveal that upper-middle mothers were more responsive to infant vocalization than middle SES mothers. In particular, upper-middle mothers vocalized, looked, smiled, and toy played more in response to infant vocalization than did middle SES mothers. These differences were significant for both smiling in response to infant vocalization (upper-middle = 4.5, middle = 4.0; $F (1, 161) = 12.58$, $p \leq .001$) and toy play in response to infant vocalization (upper-middle = .1, middle = 0; $F (1, 161) = 3.52$, $p \leq .05$).

Infant Cognitive Skills. There were no differences as a function of SES on the Bayley MDI (upper-middle = 115.8, middle = 116.2), or Uzgiris-Hunt Scales of Object Permanence of Means and Ends.

In summary, there are still only few SES differences in either maternal or infant behavior at 12 months. The differences that do appear indicate somewhat more maternal distal behavior for the upper-middle and somewhat more proximal behaviors for the middle SES mothers. Infants of upper-middle mothers smile and vocalize more and cry less than middle SES infants. In particular, maternal infant interaction centering around positive affect and vocalization are more prevalent in the upper-middle whereas more infant upset maternal comforting behavior is found in the middle SES dyads. There are still little SES differences in cognitive competence although vocalization differences begin to appear.

Twenty-Four Month Data

Maternal Behavior. Clear SES differences in distal behavior emerge here. Upper-middle mothers engage in significantly more distal behavior than the middle SES mothers (upper-middle = 159.9, middle = 147.6; $F (1, 150) = 8.15$, $p \leq .005$). The specific distal behaviors of vocalization (upper-middle = 84.3, middle = 78.2; $F (1, 150) = 4.69$, $p \leq .03$), look (upper-middle = 45.5, middle = 42.9; $F (1,150) = 3.21$, $p \leq .08$), and smile (upper-middle = 22.0, middle = 18.6; $F (1, 150) = 4.77$, $p \leq .03$) are more frequent in upper-middle as compared to middle SES mothers. Although there was no overall difference in toy play the style of play between the mothers was quite different. Middle mothers gave directions (upper-middle = 4.3, middle = 5.7; $F (1, 150) = 4.33$, $p \leq .04$) and demonstrated toys more frequently than upper-middle SES mothers (upper-middle = 8.3, middle = 11.2; $F\ (1,\ 150) = 6.10$, $p \leq .01$). Upper-middle mothers manipulated toys (upper-middle = 6.4, middle = 3.6; $F\ (1,\ 150) = 11.24$, $p \leq .001$) and showed approval (upper-middle = 3.8, middle = 2.2; $F\ (1,\ 150) = 14.6$, $p \leq .001$) more frequently than middle SES mothers.

Child Behavior. During the free play episode there were few child differences as a function of SES. Surprisingly, middle children engaged in more toy play (upper-middle = 69.0, middle = 72.2; $F\ (1,\ 150) = 2.99$, $p \leq .09$), and in particular, explored the toys more than the upper-middle SES children (upper-middle = 54.9, middle = 60.1; $F\ (1,\ 150) = 5.89$, $p \leq .02$). The upper-middle SES children tended to engage in more distal behavior, especially vocalization and smiling, than did the middle SES children, although these differences were not significant.

Mother-Child Interaction. Overall levels of maternal interaction and responsivity did not vary significantly with SES. However, upper-middle mothers did show more responsivity especially around vocalization and smiling behavior. In particular, upper-middle mothers responded more frequently than middle SES mothers with vocalization to their childrens' toy play (upper-middle = 13.7, middle = 11.3; $F\ (1,\ 150) = 5.63$, $p \leq .02$). It was also the case that upper-middle = .1, middle = 0.0; $F\ (1,\ 150) = 3.98$, $p \leq .05$) and toy play (upper-middle = 2.7, middle = 1.7; $F\ (1,\ 150) = 9.3$, $p \leq .003$).

Child's Cognitive Skills. By 24 months social class differences in childrens' cognitive ability emerge. Upper-middle children were found to perform significantly better than middle SES children on the Bayley MDI ($F(1,\ 133) = 5.68$, $p \leq .02$). The mean Bayley MDI score for the upper-middle child was 107.2 while the middle SES child mean was 101.2.

The Infant Laboratory Language Test (ILLT) is a test of prepositional and adjective knowledge. These competencies also show the effects of SES. Upper-middle children performed significantly better than middle SES children on ILLT total score (upper-middle = 1.36, middle = 1.09; $F\ (1,\ 133) = 9.28$, $p \leq .01$), as well as for both prepositional (upper-middle = 1.18, middle = 1.04; $F\ (1,\ 128) = 2.98$, $p \leq .09$) and adjective knowledge (upper-middle = 1.56, middle = 1.10; $F\ (1,\ 117) = 12.24$, $p \leq .01$).

An analysis of the production task of the Peabody Picture Vocabulary Test (PPVT) revealed that upper-middle children performed significantly better than middle SES children ($F\ (1,\ 98) = 5.03$, $p \leq .03$). Upper-middle children correctly named an average of 6.39 pictures whereas middle SES children correctly identified 5.20 pictures. The effect of SES on comprehension performance revealed a trend ($F\ (1,\ 103) = 2.55$, $p \leq .12$). Once again it was the upper-middle children (upper-middle = 13.39) who pointed more often to the correct picture than middle SES children (middle = 11.88). However, the mental age equivalent based on the comprehension scores was very similar for both groups of children (upper-middle = 2.21, middle = 2.17).

It is also interesting, but not surprising, to note that the mother's language skills as measured by the vocabulary subscale WAIS was found to vary with SES (upper-middle = 62.42, middle = 51.21; $F(1, 145) = 46.55, p \leq .001$), with upper-middle SES mothers performing better. SES level, therefore, was found to have a significant relationship not only to the child's language performance but to the performance of the mother as well.

DEVELOPMENTAL CHANGES

Mother-Infant Behavior. The data gathered at 3 months and at 12 and 24 months were collected using different time bases, in the former case a 10-sec base while in the latter a 15-sec base. In order to look at the data in a comparable fashion over age, the data were converted into a percentage of observation time measure. This measure is presented in Fig. 4.1 for maternal toy play (including behaviors such as demonstrates or give toy), read or watch TV, distal and proximal behaviors (see Fig. 4.1a), and infant vocalization and smile (see Fig. 4.1b).

Percent of maternal toy play increases with age with few significant SES differences that are apparent. By 24 months the style of toy play differentiated with mothers rather than with amount. If anything, middle SES mothers were engaged in more dyadic teaching styles whereas upper-middle mothers were engaged in more ongoing play and positive affect.

The amount of maternal reading or TV watching also increased with age between 3 and 12 months leveling off between 12 and 24 months. The increase in nonchild directed activity is facilitated by the child's ability to care for itself. The lack of strong SES differences may reflect several issues, not the least of which is the fact that under the conditions of being observed mothers may realize that it would be inappropriate to engage in this activity and thus we would observe few individual or group differences. Even so, middle rather than upper-middle SES mothers engage in more of this activity at 24 months.

The distal and proximal modes of interaction show important age changes; proximal contact decreases over age while distal contact increases. These differences have been observed before and appear to reflect a general socializing effect of moving the child physically away from the mother (Lewis, 1972). Although there are few differences in proximal behavior as a function of SES over the entire 2 years the upper-middle mothers show significantly more proximal behavior at 3 months than do the middle. Most impressive is the increase in distal behavior for both groups but especially for the upper-middle SES mothers. By 24 months these differences are quite significant.

The two distal behaviors in particular, maternal vocalization and maternal smile, both show an increase with age (maternal smile appears to level off

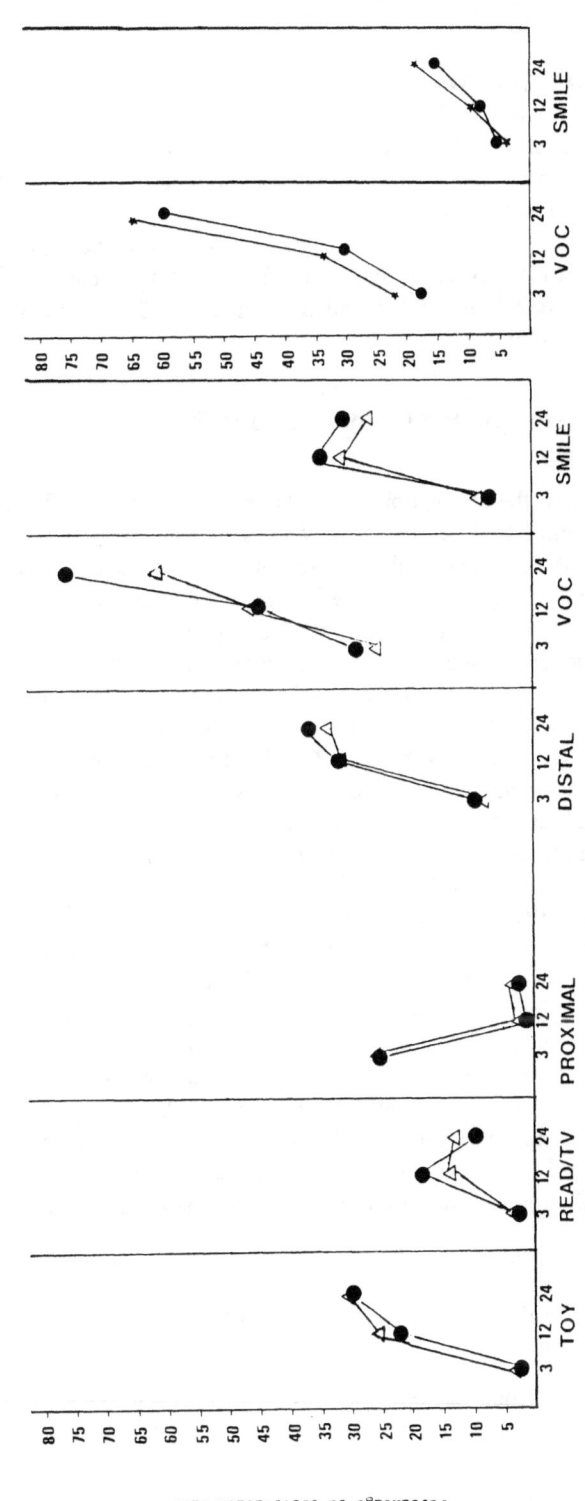

FIG. 4.1a. The percentage of observation time mothers toy play, read/watch TV, vocalize, smile, and distal and proximal contact with the child at 3, 12, and 24 months as a function of SES.

FIG. 4.1b. The percentage of observation time children vocalize and smile at 3, 12, and 24 months as a function of SES.

between 12 to 24 months). Socioeconomic status differences in these maternal behaviors are paralleled in the infant behaviors that also show both an age and status effect change.

These data as well as the more complex interaction data support the suggestion that SES differences in maternal-infant interaction make their appearance within the first 2 years of life and have an effect on the infant's subsequent cognitive development.

Maternal Behavior and Children's Cognitive Development

Until this point, the description of SES has resulted in several findings that favor the upper-middle SES family. However, as indicated earlier it is not SES differences but the psychological processes underlying these differences that should be of maximal concern. To a large degree, developmental theory has assumed that environmental factors, at the very least, play some small role in cognitive development, and at the very most, are largely responsible for differences observed. In order to explore the role of the environment in cognitive growth, data on maternal behavior and infant cognitive performance is next considered. Although most theories support a causal model, that is, the environment affects the child's development, we recognize that it is equally likely that the child's development can affect the environment (Bell, 1971; Lewis & Rosenblum, 1974). In the correlations presented here, this causal model, namely the effect of the environment on the child's cognitive growth is assumed, however, it is recognized that other models are possible.

Present results indicate maternal and infant differences in interaction from the earliest months onward as a function of SES. Infant cognitive differences, however, do not appear to emerge until after the first year. Important from a process point of view is are these cognitive differences independent of the earlier social interactions or do these early social interactions lead to cognitive differences? To better understand the relationship between maternal behavior and infant cognitive development, maternal behavior was correlated with infant cognitive performance, first for the whole sample in order to study general processes, and second for each SES group in order to observe whether there are SES differences in this process.

Maternal Vocalization and Infant Cognitive Development[1]

Maternal vocalization has been held to be an important factor in the language development of the child. An enriched vocal environment should facilitate not

---

[1] In the correlations reported here the symbols * and + indicate correlations different from zero at the $p \leq .05$ and $p \leq .10$ levels respectively.

4. MIDDLE CLASS DIFFERENCES IN COGNITIVE DEVELOPMENT 81

only language development but general cognitive growth as well. Figure 4.2 presents correlations between the mother's vocalization at 3 months and the child's cognitive performance at 3(MDI), 12(MDI) and 24(MDI, PPVT-PROD) months; the mother's vocalization at 12 months and the child cognitive measures at 12 and 24 months and the mother's vocalization at 24 months and the cognitive measures at 24 months for both SES groups and the total sample. Thus Fig. 4.2 shows the relationship within and across time between maternal vocalization and the child's cognitive skills.

Although there is relatively little relationship between maternal vocalization at 3 months and infant cognitive development at 3 months and 12 months (for both the MDI as seen in Fig. 4.2 as well as object permanence and Uzgiris-Hunt Scales), there does appear to be a significant relationship between maternal vocalization at 3 months and infants' performance on the PPVT at 24 months. In particular, for the total sample there is a significant correlation between 3 months maternal vocalization and 24 months infant PPVT performance (Upper-middle = .30*, Middle = .22*, Total = .28*). Maternal vocalization at 12 months tends to show a relationship to infant cognitive performance at 12 and 24 months. Maternal vocalization at 12 months is significantly related to the child's 12 month MDI scores only for the middle SES dyads (Upper-middle = −.03, middle = .20+, Total = .10). However, there are many more significant relationships between maternal vocalization at 12 months and infant cognitive and language performance at 24 months (for mother's vocalization at 12 months

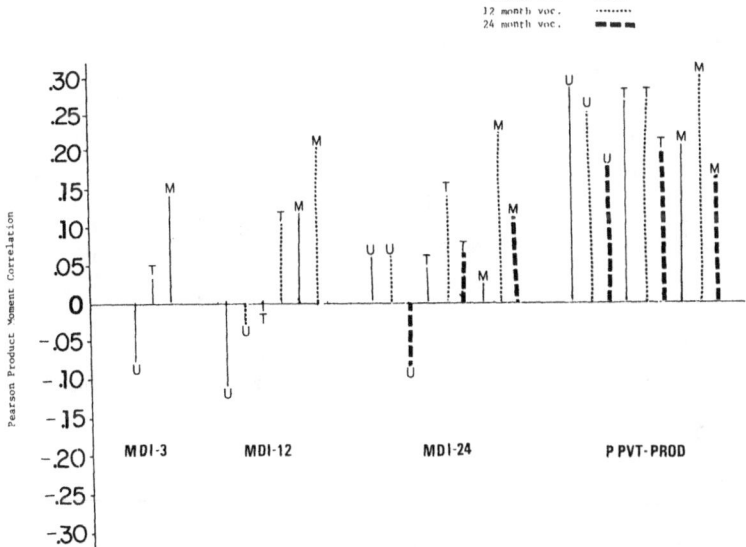

FIG. 4.2. Correlations between maternal vocalization at 3, 12, and 24 months and the child's cognitive performance at 3, 12, and 24 months for upper middle (U), middle (M), and the total (T) sample.

and MDI at 24 months: Upper-middle = .07, Middle = .22*, Total = .13; for mother's vocalization at 12 months and PPVT prod: Upper-middle = .27*, Middle = .31*, Total = .28*). Finally, maternal vocalization at 24 months is related to the child's language (PPVT prod: Upper-middle = .19*, Middle = .18*, Total = .21+) but not the child's cognitive performance (MDI: Upper-middle = .07, Middle = .12, Total = .06). These data support the view that early maternal differences in behavior toward their infants, while having little concurrent effect on the infants' cognitive performance, may show significant effects in later cognitive growth.

Maternal Smile and Infant Cognitive Growth

Other maternal behaviors such as socioemotional behavior reflect other domains of development and provide data on the effects of these domains on the child's cognitive growth. In particular, maternal smiling behavior was related to the child's cognitive performance. Figure 4.3 presents the correlations between the mother's smiling behavior at 3 months and the child's cognitive skills at 3 (MDI), 12 (MDI), and 24 (MDI and PPVT PROD) months; the mother's

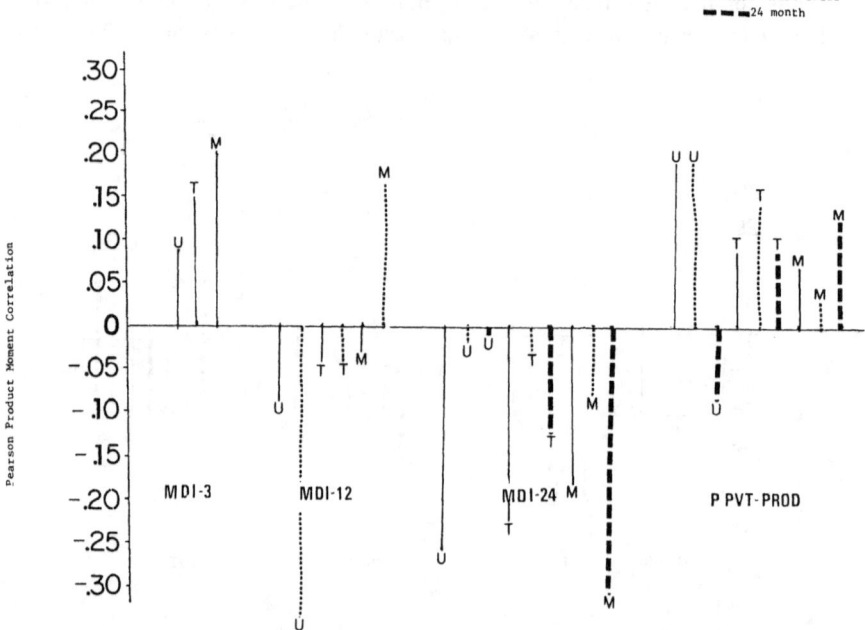

FIG. 4.3. Correlations between maternal smile at 3, 12, and 24 months and the child's cognitive performance at 3, 12, and 24 months for upper middle (U), middle (M), and the total (T) sample.

4. MIDDLE CLASS DIFFERENCES IN COGNITIVE DEVELOPMENT 83

smiling behavior at 12 months and the child's cognitive measures at 12 and 24 months; and the mother's smiling behavior at 24 months and the child's cognitive performance at 24 months, for both SES groups and the total sample. In general, the data indicate that early maternal smile although positively related to early cognitive development is not significantly related to later cognition or language skills. Specifically, maternal smile at 3 months is positively related to the 3-month MDI (Upper-middle = .08, Middle = $.20^+$, Total = .15) and the 12 months Uzgiris Hunt Scales (Upper-middle = $.21^+$, Middle = $.21^+$, Total = $.21^*$). However, maternal smile at 3 months is negatively related to the 24 month MDI (Upper-middle = $-.26^*$, Middle = $-.17$, Total = $-.23^*$). Maternal smile at 12 months shows significant SES differences in relationship to the child's cognitive performance at 12 months. In particular, maternal smile is positively related to the MDI_{12} for the middle group (R = .17) but is negatively related to the MDI_{12} for the upper-middle SES group (R = $-.26^*$). Maternal smile at 12 months is not related to the MDI at 24 months although it shows a tendency to be positively related to language skills (Upper-middle = $.19^+$, Middle = .02, Total = .15). Maternal smile at 24 months is not related to language skill for either SES group but is significantly negatively related to the 24 month MDI only for the middle SES group (Upper-middle = .01, Middle = $-.32^*$, Total = $-.13$). Considering the child's cognitive development as it relates to the maternal behavior of vocalization and smile, it appears as if, in general, early maternal smiling is related to early cognitive and language development while early vocalization, although not related to early cognitive skill, is related to later cognitive and language growth.

Maternal Proximal and Distal Behavior and the Child's Cognitive Development

Patterns of early mother–child interaction as they relate to proximal and distal modes of behavior are noted to have an influence on cognitive and language development. In particular, proximal modes of contact have been suggested as facilitative of earlier but not later cognitive skill (cf. Lewis & Ban, 1971; Yarrow, Rubensten, & Pedersen, 1975) whereas the distal mode of contact has been related to cognitive and language skills as of the second year of life but not earlier. Figure 4.4 presents the correlations for the maternal distal behaviors at 3 months and the child's cognitive measures at 3 (MDI), 12 (MDI) and 24 (MDI and PPVT PROD) months; the mother's distal behavior at 12 months and the child's cognitive measures at 12 and 24 months; and the mother's distal behavior at 24 months and the child's cognitive measures at 24 months for both SES groups and the total sample. Figure 4.5 presents the correlations for maternal proximal behavior at 3 months and the child's cognitive performance at 3- 12- and 24-months; the maternal proximal behavior at 12 months and the child's cognitive performance at 12 and 24 months and the maternal proximal behavior

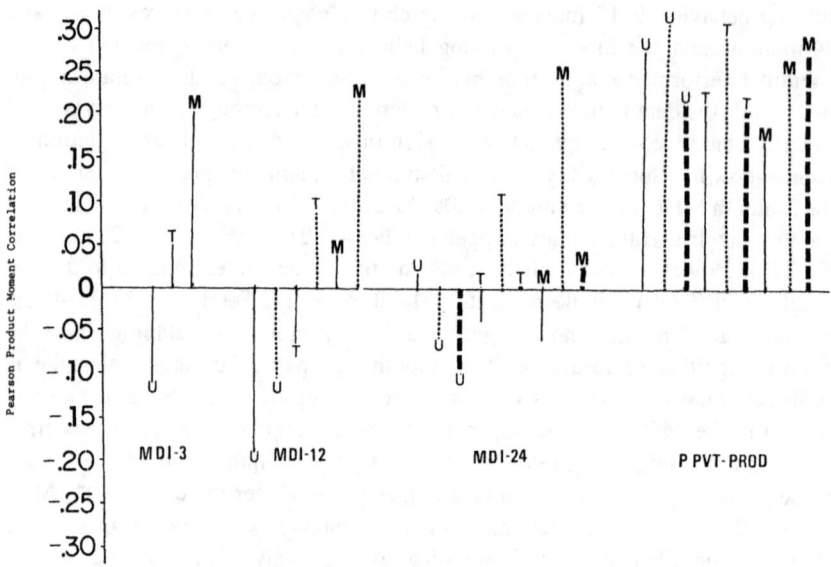

FIG. 4.4. Correlations between maternal distal behavior at 3, 12, and 24 months and the child's cognitive performance at 3, 12, and 24 months for upper middle (U), middle (M), and the total (T) sample.

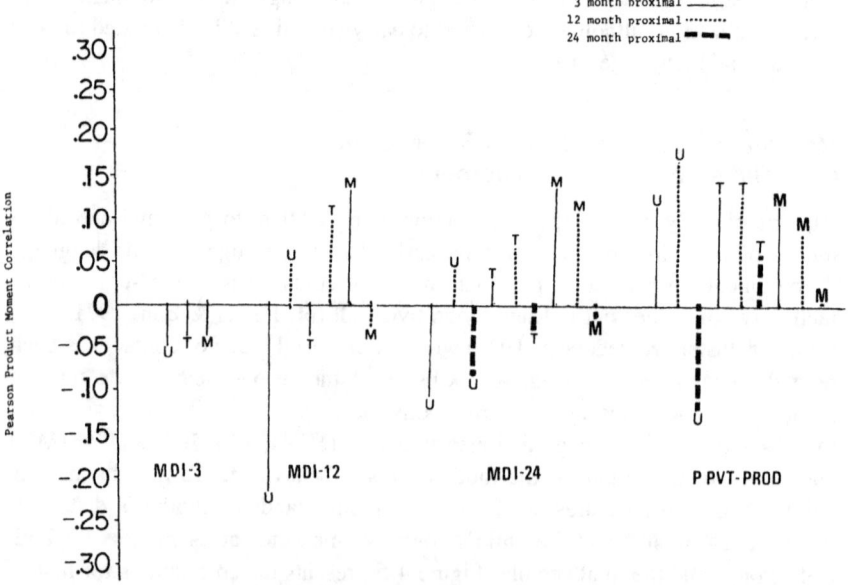

FIG. 4.5. Correlations between maternal proximal behavior at 3, 12, and 24 months and the child's cognitive performance at 3, 12, and 24 months for upper middle (U), middle (M), and the total (T) sample.

at 24 months and the child's cognitive skills at 24 months by SES group and for the total sample.

Examining the distal data first (see Fig. 4.4) we note that it is similar to the findings for maternal vocalization and child cognitive skills. That is, early maternal distal behavior is not significantly related to early cognitive skill although it is significantly positively related to language development at 24 months (for mother distal 3 months and PPVT PROD: Upper-middle = .27*, Middle = .17+, Total = .21+; for mother distal 12 months and PPVT: Upper-middle = .31*, Middle = .25*, Total = .29*). Maternal vocalization at 24 months is positively related to language skill only for the middle class and total sample but not for the upper middle class group (upper-middle = −.01, Middle = .27*, Total = .20*).

Maternal proximal behavior at 3 months is not related to early cognitive skills and shows a stronger but still insignificant relationship to later cognitive and language development (see Fig. 4.5). The data indicate that maternal proximal behavior at 3 months and child cognitive skill at 3 months are unrelated. Maternal proximal behavior at 3 months as it relates to the child's cognitive performance at 12 months shows an SES difference such that, for upper-middle SES maternal proximal behavior at 3 months is negatively related to the 12 month MDI ($r = -.22*$) while for the middle SES, maternal proximal behavior at 3 months is positively related to the MDI ($r = .14$) at 12 months. By 24 months, however, maternal proximal behavior at 3 months is positively related to language and cognitive measures for both groups, although this relationship is not significant. Proximal maternal behavior at 12 and 24 months is not significantly related to either cognitive or language measurement at 12 to 24 months.

Comparing the data for maternal proximal and distal behavior and their relationship to the child's cognitive skills and development we note that whereas early maternal distal behaviors are related to later cognitive development this is not the case for maternal proximal behavior. Although work of other investigators (Yarrow et al., 1975) would suggest that early proximal behaviors are related to early but not later cognitive development, the maternal proximal data examined here does not show this trend. However, the expected relationship between early maternal distal behavior and later language and cognitive development is observed for this sample.

DISCUSSION

Group differences as a function of SES have occupied considerable attention of social scientists and have usually generated more heat than clarity. Of major concern for any enterprise that seeks to understand SES effects is the definitional issue. Most studies when referring to socioeconomic status often fail to supply sufficient information necessary to appreciate what SES differences are being observed (for example, Deutsch, 1973). Often the middle SES samples that are examined and compared to lower SES groups are unspecified on status variables such as education or occupation of parents. However, even given the limited amount of information, especially about educational level, we can assume that many samples of middle SES groups contain an inordinate amount of families whose parents are college and professionally educated and as such probably represent a rather biased sample of the entire middle class. This may be due to the relative ease in locating and eliciting the help of these types of families because most of the reported studies take place in settings more available to the well educated middle SES groups who are willing to participate in such studies. More important than this potentially biased sampling of middle SES groups is the implication of the results showing that the middle SES performs better than the lower SES in many cognitive tasks starting with infants as young as 18 to 24 months. If this sample is biased toward the well educated, we would expect such differences between the poor and this group. However, and even more important for theory building, we might expect cognitive performance differences *within* the middle SES group, for example, between a well educated and a less well educated group of middle SES families. The view that SES differences in cognitive performance found between middle and lower SES children may exist within middle SES groups was demonstrated by our data. By two years of age upper-middle SES children of at least college educated parents performed better on measures of cognitive and language skills than children of at least high school educated parents. Yet, if we chose not to consider differences within the middle SES, we would have failed to notice such a difference. Thus, it is certainly possible that past investigations of SES differences between lower and middle SES groups were more specifically investigations of differences between what we have called here upper (highly educated) middle SES and a lower (e.g., skilled, semiskilled, impoverished, etc.) SES group. These data indicate further, that differences within as well as across SES are observable in regard to cognitive development (cf. Shipman, 1972).

The present findings show that within the middle SES group, the well educated subgroup shows superior cognitive performance, beginning at about the same time developmentally as the reported differences between poor and middle SES groups. Such findings have been reported by others (cf. Deutsch & Brown, 1964; Hess et al., 1969) and together with the present results indicate that the more educated the family, the better cognitive performance is shown by the child. The implication from such findings focuses our attention less on the differences between poor and middle SES groups and more on the process of development and the possible causes of these differences.

Although both middle SES groups are performing well on the cognitive measures for their age group, the most striking findings from the present analysis are the differences in the cognitive skills of the middle and upper-middle SES children at 24 months. It is striking but not surprising, given the work of other investigators, to note the absence of cognitive differences at 3 and 12 months (cf. Bayley, 1965; Golden & Birns, 1968) and their emergence by 24 months as a function of SES (cf. Golden & Birns, 1976). Given the fact that language skills become the predominant component of cognitive measures at 24 months, it is reasonable to find that children with more highly educated and verbally proficient mothers do better on tasks that contain a strong language component or on language tasks themselves. Also, considering the status variable of occupation it is instructive perhaps to recall that upper-middle children were more likely to have teachers for mothers while middle SES children were more likely to have secretaries for mothers. One might expect children of teachers to perform better on standard cognitive or language tasks.

The demonstration of cognitive differences of children from middle and upper-middle class families gives rise to the concern for process variables which might relate maternal–child interaction and the child's cognitive development over the first two years of life. Two important factors can be used to infer process; (1) cognitive differences in the MDI and PPVT emerge by 24 months and are affected by the educational-occupational level of the family; and (2) early maternal–child interactions appear to be related both to SES and to later cognitive development. Several aspects of maternal behavior have been considered, in particular, proximal contact and distal interactions as well as the maternal behaviors of smile and vocalization. Early and concurrent maternal behavior was shown to effect later infant cognitive development.

Contrary to expectation (Yarrow et al., 1975), the proximal mode of maternal contact was not significantly related to the 3 month or 12 month child's cognitive performance. In fact early maternal proximal contact showed only a tendency to be related to later cognitive performance. Distal contact, however, showed a different pattern; 3- and 12-month distal contact was related to 24 month cognitive performance, specifically PPVT. Mothers who showed more distal behavior earlier had infants who performed better on 24 month language tasks, although language or general cognitive performance was not affected before that time. Because vocalization data account for most of the distal contact and because maternal language usage might particularly effect children's language development, maternal vocalization was examined in detail. Like distal contact these data indicate that while vocalization at 3 and 12 months was not related to cognitive development at these age points, early maternal vocalization was related to cognitive growth and language development at 24 months. Regardless of SES, the frequency of maternal vocalization at 3 and 12 months is positively related to the child's language ability at 24 months.

The results of this analysis suggest that the child's development of cognitive and language skills at 24 months is related to the mother's language use at earlier age points. Mothers characterized here as upper-middle SES, i.e., college educated or more, tended to employ a greater amount of verbal interaction as compared to middle SES mothers and had children who performed better on language measures at 24 months. The amount of verbal interaction a child receives at an early age is important and is probably related to the mother's education level. Recall that there is a tendency at 3 months for upper-middle SES mothers to vocalize more to their infants. At 12 months, although both SES groups vocalize a similar amount, upper-middle class mothers were more responsive to their children's vocalization.

Vocalization may be one, albeit most important, aspect of the distal mode of interaction. In this regard, the developmental shift from a proximal to distal mode of interaction also may be important for subsequent cognitive development. It may be the ratio of distal to proximal maternal interaction that is an influencing factor in the child's language and cognitive skills at 2 years of age. In fact, Lewis and Coates (1978) looked at the ratio scores for all 5 groups of the Hollingshead SES classification. The results showed a significant increase in distal to proximal contact with increasing SES level, that is, higher SES mother used more distal to proximal than did lower SES mothers. In fact the lowest SES group showed more proximal to distal contact. The shift from the use of the proximal mode at 3 months to the use of the distal mode at 24 months has been noted by other researchers as possibly related to cognitive development. It has been argued that early developmental tasks require the kinesthetic stimulation of proximal contact (cf. Yarrow et al., 1975) whereas later developmental tasks require the exercise of distal modes of communication (cf. Golden & Birns, 1976; Lewis & Ban, 1971; Lewis & Coates, 1980). The result of this analysis suggests that all mothers evidence this shift and that this may be facilitative of their child's cognitive and language skills at 24 months.

The differential use of proximal and distal behavior and their subsequent effect on infant development needs more study. Coates and Lewis (1977) found that proximal contact at 3 months was predictive of infant MDI scores at 3 months but not of PPVT at 24 months, whereas maternal vocalization was not correlated at 3 months with infant MDI but was significantly correlated with the infant PPVT at 24 months. These results parallel, in part, what has been found with this sample. Developmental tasks are complex and environmental conditions that facilitate some may have no effect on others. Proximal contact early in the child's life may be a necessity in terms of the child's social and emotional development but may have little function for later emerging cognitive skills. Likewise, maternal verbal behavior may have no impact on the child's earlier development, but may be quite significant for later language growth. The process that has been outlined is still tentative, although there is some support for the role of proximal and distal (verbal) stimulation in the child's cognitive development. Although a few of the specific correlations between maternal and infant behavior vary as a function of SES level, all told the process appears applicable for both upper-middle and middle SES groups. For both groups it appears reasonable to suggest that early maternal distal interaction affects later infant cognitive performance. Differences in early and concurrent distal interaction, as a function of educational level of the family, produce differences in infant cognitive ability at a later time. Thus, differences cannot be perceived until such time as they emerge in the child's repertoire. One question remains, however, namely, how is it that relatively small differences in early maternal language make themselves felt in terms of consistently significant infant differences in cognitive capacity later? Although no clear explanation is currently available, it should be kept in mind that even small differences as measured at any one point in time may have a more profound effect when they occur over months or even years.

In conclusion, the classification of our middle class sample by the status variables and parent occupation and education yielded differences in the child's cognitive performance at 24 months, and examination of the process variables revealed the same process at work for the two middle SES groups. Regardless of parent education and occupation early maternal proximal contact was not related to the infant's cognitive performance whereas early maternal distal behavior, especially vocalization, was related to the child's later cognitive and language performance. Given the finding that status variables yielded differences in performance scores at 24 months, how might we understand the relationship between status and process? The relationship between status and process variables might be best interpreted as reflecting differences in the opportunities provided for the engagement of process variables (cf. Shipman, 1972). Thus, for example, a higher parental education or the maternal occupation of teacher might be associated with a greater likelihood that the mother would engage her child in verbal interaction, which appears to have a facilitative impact on the child's cognitive and language growth. Within this middle SES sample the status variables of education and occupation provide predictive power concerning the likelihood of how frequently the mother will engage in these processes facilitative of children's cognitive growth.

ACKNOWLEDGMENTS

This research was supported by an NICHD contract #N01-HD-82849 to Michael Lewis. Special thanks are to be given to Kenneth Provencher and John Jaskir for computer analysis of the data, to V. C. Shipman for helpful discussion on the meaning of SES, and to Linda Olivacz for typing the manuscript.

REFERENCES

Bayley, N. Comparisons of mental and motor test scores for ages 1–15 months by sex, birth order, race, geographic locale and education of parents. *Child Development.* 1965, *36*, 379–411.
Bell, R. Q. Stimulus control of parent or caretaker behavior by offspring. *Developmental Psychology,* 1971, *4*, 63–72.

Coates, D. L., & Lewis, M. *Social class ethnicity differences in early mother–infant interaction.* Paper presented at the annual meeting of the American Educational Research Association, New York, April 1977.

Coleman, J. S., Campell, E. R., Hobson, C. J., McPartland, J., Mood, A. M., Weinfeld, F. D. & York, R. L. Equality of educational opportunity, U. S. Department of Health, Education and Welfare, Office of Education, Washington, D.C., 1966.

Dave. R. H. *The identification and measurement of environmental process variables that are related to educational achievement.* Unpublished doctoral dissertation, University of Chicago, 1963.

Deutsch, C. P. Social class and social development. In B. M. Caldwell & H. N. Ricciuti (Eds.), *Child development research (Vol. 3.): Child development and social policy.* Chicago: University of Chicago Press, 1973.

Deutsch, M., & Brown, R. Social influences in Negro-white intelligence differences. *Journal of Social Issues,* 1964, *20,* 205-214.

Edel, A. The scientist and his findings: Some problems in scientific responsibility. In E. Tobach & H. M. Prochansky (Eds.), *Genetic destiny: Scientific controversy and social conflict.* New York: AMS Press, 1976.

Golden, M., & Birns, B. Social class and cognitive development in infancy. *Merrill Palmer Quarterly,* 1968, *14,* 139-149.

Golden, M., & Birns, B. Social class and infant intelligence. In M. Lewis (Ed.), *Origins of intelligence: Infancy and early childhood.* New York: Plenum Press, 1976.

Hess, R. D., & Shipman, V. C. Maternal influence upon early learning: The cognitive environments of infant and preschool children. In R. D. Hess & R. M. Bear (Eds.), *Early education.* Chicago: Aldine, 1968.

Hess, R. D., Shipman, V. C., Brophy, J. E., & Bear, R. M. *The cognitive environments of urban preschool children: Follow up phase.* Chicago: University of Chicago Press, 1969.

Levine, J., Fishman, C., & Kagan, J. *Sex of child and social class as determinants of maternal behavior.* Paper presented at the meeting of the American Orthopsychiatric Association, Washington, D.C., 1967.

Lewis, M. Mothers and fathers, boys and girls: Attachment behavior in the one-year-old. In F. J. Monks, W. W. Hartup, & J. DeWit (Eds.), *Determinants of behavioral development.* New York: Academic Press, 1972.

Lewis, M., & Ban, P. *Stability of attachment behavior: A transformational analysis.* Paper presented at a symposium on Attachment: Studies in Stability and Change, at the Society for Research in Child Development meetings, Minneapolis, April 1971.

Lewis, M., & Coates, D. Mother-infant interaction performance. In D. J. Chivers & J. Herbert (Eds.), *Advances in Primatology: Behavior* (Vol. 1). New York: Academic Press, 1978.

Lewis, M., & Coates, D. Mother–infant interactions and cognitive development in twelve-week-old infants. *Infant Behavior and Development,* 1980, *3,* 95-105.

Lewis, M., & Freedle, R. Mother–infant dyad: The cradle of meaning. In P. Pliner, L. Krames, & T. Alloway (Eds.), *Communication and affect: Language and thought.* New York: Academic Press, 1973.

Lewis, M., & Freedle, R. The mother and infant communication system: The effects of poverty. In H. McGurk (Ed.), *Ecological factors in human development.* Amsterdam, the Netherlands: North-Holland Publishing Co., 1977.

Lewis, M., & McGurk, H. Evaluation of infant intelligence: Infant intelligence scores—true or false? *Science,* 1972, *178,* 1174-1177.

Lewis, M., & Rosenblum, L. (Eds.), *The effect of the infant on its caregiver: The origins of behavior* (Vol. 1). New York: Wiley, 1974.

Lewis, M., & Wilson, C. D. Infant development in lower class American families. *Human Development,* 1972, *15,* 112-127.

Light, R. J., & Smith, P. V. Statistical issues in social allocation models of intelligence: A review and a response. *Review of Educational Research,* 1971, *41,* 351-367.

Messer, S. G., & Lewis, M. Social class and sex differences in the attachment and play behavior of the year old infant. *Merrill–Palmer Quarterly,* 1972, *18,* 295-306.

Moore, T. Language and intelligence: A longitudinal study of the first eight years, Part II: Environmental correlates of mental growth. *Human Development,* 1968, *11,* 88-106.

Palmer, F. H. Minimal intervention at age two and three and subsequent intellective changes. In R. K. Parker (Ed.), *The Preschool in Action.* Boston: Allyn and Bacon, 1972.

Pavenstedt, E. A comparison of the child-rearing environment of upper-lower and very low-lower class families. *American Journal of Orthopsychiatry,* 1965, *35,* 89-98.

Schaefer, E. S. Parents as educators: Evidence from cross-sectional, longitudinal and intervention research. *Young Children,* 1972, *27,* 227-239.

Shipman, V. C. *Disadvantaged children and their first school experiences: Demographic indexes of socioeconomic status and maternal behaviors and attitudes.* (PR 72-13). Prepared under Grant H-8256, Dept. of Health, Education & Welfare. Princeton, N.J.: Educational Testing Service, 1972.

Shipman, V. C. *Disadvantaged children and their first school experiences: Notable early characteristics of high and low achieving black low-SES children.* (PR 76-21). Prepared under Grant H-8256, Dept. of Health, Education & Welfare. Princeton, N.J.: Educational Testing Service, 1976.

Tulkin, S. R. Race, class, family, and social achievement. *Journal of Personality and Social Psychology.* 1968, *9,* 31-37.

Tulkin, S. R. An analysis of the concept of cultural deprivation. *Developmental Psychology,* 1972, *6,* 326-339.

Tulkin, S. R., & Kagan, J. Mother-child interaction in the first year of life. *Child Development,* 1972, *43,* 31-41.

Wachs, T. D., Uzgiris, I. C., & Hunt, J. McV. *Cognitive development in infants of different age levels and from different environmental backgrounds.* Paper presented at the Meetings of the Society for Research in Child Development, New York, 1967.

Wachs, T. D., Uzgiris, I. C., & Hunt, J. McV. Cognitive development in infants of different age levels and from different environmental backgrounds: An exploratory investigation. *Merrill–Palmer Quarterly,* 1971, *17,* 283-317.

White, B. *The first three years of life.* Englewood Cliffs, N.J.: Prentice-Hall, 1975.

Wilson, E. O. *Sociobiology.* Cambridge: Harvard University Press (Belknap Press), 1975.

Yarrow, L. J., Rubensten, J. L., & Pedersen, F. A. *Infant and environment: Early cognitive and motivational development.* New York: Wiley, 1975.

Zigler, E. I. Learning, development and social class in the socialization process. In M. H. Marx (Ed.), *Learning: Interactions.* New York: Macmillan, 1968.

III CULTURAL VALUES

5 Father-Mother-Infant Interaction in the Newborn Period: A German-American Comparison

Ross D. Parke
University of Illinois
Karin Grossmann
University of Regensburg, West Germany
Barbara R. Tinsley
University of Illinois

The extent to which social relationships reflect the more general political and economic societal structures in which they are embedded has been a subject of interest for researchers in various social sciences (LeVine, 1970, 1977; McGranahan, 1946). Anthropologists and sociologists, as well as psychologists, have conducted cross-cultural comparisons of both individual and group behavior in an effort to establish not only the cultural universality and generalizability of research findings, but also to delineate the ways in which a country's institutional structure interacts with the uniqueness of human behavior. This issue is a variation of the still unresolved nature-nurture question concerning the origin and maintenance of human characteristics. By conducting cross-cultural research, we are asking to what extent human behavior patterns form and exist independently of their cultural environment.

Child Rearing: German American Comparisons

Rohner (1977) suggests that one rationale for engaging in cross-cultural research is "to be able to systematically vary factors that cannot be varied within a single population or cultural system." An opportunity to examine the effect of one such factor, the effect of a country's transition to industrialization on parent-infant interaction patterns, was made available when the senior author spent six months in West Germany. West Germany has experienced profound societal change since the end of World War II. In achieving its present status as a major political and economic force in Western Europe, its political and economic characterization has radically changed from a militaristic and autocratic society to a democratic, industrialized country. Not only is it interesting to trace this transition by examining its effect on individual social behavior and attitudes, but we can also compare German parent-infant interaction with that of another western industrialized nation, the U.S., to provide evidence in determining the extent to which industrialization, a societal characteristic, affects individual social relationships (Rainwater, 1962).

Historically, a nation's shift to industrialization has been accompanied by two other related sociological phenomenon: large shifts of families from rural to urban areas and the reduction of socioeconomic class distinctions. Both of these trends have been documented in the studies of parent-child relationships in Germany over the past 25 years (Devereux, Bronfenbrenner, & Suci, 1962). Much of our knowledge concerning German parent-child interaction during the immediate post-war period comes from an analysis of German child care guidance literature available in the 1940s–1950s (Metraux, 1955). The main tenet of these advice books for German parents was one that emphasized the early provision of discipline and training as the way in which German parents could best provide their children with the "armor to face the battle of life." Families were organized to guide the children to the development of good character, defined as discipline of mind and body. The authoritarian structure of the German society was reflected in the patriarchial structure of the German family (Schaffner, 1948). However, the father seemed to maintain a contradictory position in his family. Although he was officially pictured as the distant, authority figure in the German family, child care experts in the 1940s and 1950s entrusted the actual fulfillment of the child's potential almost entirely to the German mother. As Metraux (1955) states:

> Father, as an immediately influential expert figure, has been eliminated from the picture... The family, as it appears in the pages of these (child-care guidance) books is truncated. Although the experts formally emphasize the importance of parental unity and of a full family life, the father appears only rather distantly and indistinctly as a co-educator or, in examples of parental misguidance and juvenile difficulty, either as the worried, angry, outraged companion of the mother or as a minor villain who disturbs the peace of the home, who excites, spoils, or spanks the darling or the naughty child, who interferes with proper education [p. 211].

Empirical documentation of German parent-child interaction has been conducted only recently. Assuming that the behavior of German parents in the 1940s and 1950s was, in part, reflected by German child care expert advice, German parent-child relationships and behavior have apparently undergone a significant change in recent decades.

Three independently conducted studies of West German parent-child behavior conducted in the 1960s suggest that family interaction patterns in West German families may be reflecting the transition of the German culture from an authoritarian-based system to a more democratic sociopolitical organization. Modern German parents seem to be maintaining a less authoritarian approach to child rearing and engaging in more egalitarian behavior and attitudes in their parental roles than in the past. This pattern closely approximates early parental behavior in the United States, and as our review indicates, in some cases, German parents even demonstrate more intense affectional patterns than U.S. parents.

In an interview study of 87 German men concerning their family-oriented daily routines and family relationships, Rainwater (1962) found that German fathers are very emotionally involved with their families and value intense family relationships. Although the results were modified to some extent by the social class of the respondents, these German fathers were very concerned with their relationships with their children. However, Rainwater suggests that although these German fathers consider family unity important, they were still concerned with being respected by their children. This attitude can be contrasted with the German father of the 1940s and 1950s who demanded obedience, rather than respect from his children.

Rapp (1961) compared the childrearing attitudes of U.S. and German mothers of 3- 5-year-old children. A questionnaire that measured the extent to which the mothers valued authority-oriented child guidance tactics was administered. Ths U.S. mothers were found to be significantly lower than the German mothers in demonstrating controlling attitudes. This study is best understood in the context of a U.S.-German comparative examination of sixth grade children's perceptions of their parents' behavior (Devereux, Bronfenbrenner & Suci, 1962). The children were asked to complete questionnaires concerned with their parents' nurturance, companionship, discipline strategies, and desire for the children's achievement. The German children reported higher levels of affection, companionship, punitiveness and control than the American children who suggested their parents were more likely to subject them to more indirect pressures such as criticism.

German fathers were reported to be very involved with their children and were compared to American mothers in the intensity of this involvement (Devereux et al., 1962). These investigators concluded that mothers and fathers play different roles in the two cultures, with German fathers very active in expressing direct discipline and affection and American mothers demonstrating high levels of disapproval and pressure to excel. Fathers were found to interact more with their sons than their daughters and mothers were at least as active, if not more so, with their daughters than their sons. This finding is consistent with the preponderance of parent-child as well as parent-infant interaction data both in the U.S. and cross-culturally, although this pattern was stronger for the American families.

A complex picture of U.S.-German parent-child relationship differences and the historical changes in German parent-child interaction pattern emerges. German parents (especially fathers) are characterized as highly emotionally involved and controlling with their children. Yet these German parents are also providing greater amounts of affection for their children than are American parents. American parents (especially mothers) are portrayed as dispensing higher levels of criticism, disapproval, and pressure to achieve than German parents, but are also characterized as less controlling than German parents. These data suggest that American and German parents are becoming more similar in their child care practices, but that some striking differences in the affectional and control domains remain.

One way of evaluating whether or not the hypothesized shifts in family organization and role allocation discussed earlier have, in fact, occurred is to examine both German and American families in similar contexts and at similar time periods. To date there has been only a single observational study comparing the patterns of parent-child interaction in the United States and West Germany. This study (Grossmann & Grossmann, 1980) compared German children's behavior towards their mother at 12 months and their father at 18 months. By using the Ainsworth strange situation, these investigators were able to compare their findings with American findings based on this same test situation (Ainsworth, Blehar, Waters, & Wall, 1978). These investigators found marked differences in the distribution of secure and insecure attachment between their sample and comparable American samples with insecure attachment being observed with greater frequency in the German than American samples.

This study suggests that further examination of parent-infant interaction patterns across the two cultures would be worthwhile. One purpose of the present investigation was to provide a preliminary observational examination of American and German parent-infant interaction patterns during the early days of life.

Father-Infant and Mother-Infant Interaction

Our investigation is based on the assumption that socialization patterns are evident in the earliest interactions between parents and their infants. Historically, however, only limited attention has been systematically paid to the nature of the interactions among family members during this early infancy period. In recent years, investigators have more often addressed the socialization roles of *both* mother and father in this period and have viewed mother and father and infant as partners in a family system. However, only rarely have both fathers and mothers been included in recent cross-cultural investigations.

To provide an appropriate backdrop for our cross-cultural investigation, the main findings that have emerged in these earlier studies will be briefly reviewed. In order to evaluate the general proposition that German child-rearing practices have, in fact, become more similar to the U.S. pattern, we have chosen parent-infant interaction patterns as a specific example of this overall trend. A second purpose is to evaluate the generality of earlier American findings to another western culture, West Germany.

Bronfenbrenner (1958, 1961) summarizes U.S. trends in child-rearing behavior from 1935 through 1960 as characterized by greater permissiveness and expression of affection, increased reliance on indirect forms of discipline (e.g., "reasoning" with the child) rather than more direct methods of discipline (e.g., punishment), and a narrowing of the dichotomy between mother and father behavior patterns (i.e., fathers have become more affectionate and less authoritarian in their interaction with their children and mothers are more involved in discipline, especially with boys).

Most relevant to the current research are earlier empirical studies of father and mother involvement with newborn infants by Greenberg and Morris, and Parke and his associates. In the Greenberg and Morris (1974) study, two groups of fathers were questioned: (1) those whose first contact with their newborns occurred at the birth (in the delivery room); and (2) those whose first contact with the newborn occurred after the birth when the newborn was shown to them by nursing personnel. Both groups of fathers showed evidence of strong paternal feelings and of involvement with their newborn, with 97% of the fathers rating their paternal feelings as average to very high. The majority were generally "very glad" immediately after the delivery and pleased about the sex of their infant (97%), While both groups of fathers judged themselves able to distinguish their own newborn from other babies by the way the infant looked (90%), fathers who had been present at birth thought they could do this all the time while the fathers who were not present thought they could do this only some of the time. Finally, there was some indication that fathers who were present at the delivery felt more comfortable in holding their baby. Combined with clinical interview data, Greenberg and Morris (1974) suggested that:

> ... fathers begin developing a bond to their newborn by the first three days after birth and often earlier. Furthermore, there are certain characteristics of this bond which we call 'engrossment,'... a feeling of preoccupation, absorption, and interest in their newborn [p. 526].

Although suggestive, these verbal reports need to be supplemented by direct behavioral observations to determine whether these self-reports of feelings and interest are reflected in behavior.

A series of observational studies by Parke and associates were conducted in order to describe—in behavioral terms—the nature of father's interaction with his newborn infant. In the first study, Parke, O'Leary and West (1972) observed the behavior of fathers in the family triad of mother, father, and infant. The results indicated that fathers were just as involved as mothers and that mothers and fathers did not differ on the majority of observational measures. In fact, fathers tended to hold the infant more than mothers and rock the infant in their arms more than mothers. In short, fathers, in a context where participation was voluntary, were just as involved as the mother in interaction with their infants.

Although there were few differences in the nurturance and stimulatory activities of the parents, fathers did play a less active role in caretaking activities than mothers. In the Parke and O'Leary (1976) study in which all infants were bottle-fed, fathers fed significantly less than mothers when they were alone with the baby. Additional support for this mother-father difference comes from another study (Parke & Sawin, 1975) of father-newborn interaction that involved a detailed examination of early parent-infant interaction in a feeding context. Comparisons of the frequencies and durations of specific caretaking activities of mothers and fathers while alone with their infants in a feeding context indicate that mothers spend more time engaged in feeding the infant and in related caretaking activities, such as wiping the baby's face, than do fathers. These findings suggest that parental role allocation begins in the earliest days of life.

Sex of Infant as a Determinant of Parent-Infant Interaction

One of the most consistent determinants of parent-infant interaction patterns is the sex of the infant. There are marked and relatively consistent differences in paternal and maternal reactions to male and female infants. Evidence of differential parental reactions to males and females is evident even before the infant is born. Parents prefer male offspring across a wide variety of cultures (Arnold, Bulatao, Buripakdi, Chung, Fawcett, Iritani, Lee, & Wu, 1975; Poffenberger & Poffenberger, 1973) including India and Asia as well as the United States. In a 1975 survey of 1500 women and approximately one-fourth of their husbands in the United States, Hoffman (1977) found that there was a 2:1 preference for boys over girls. Coombs, Coombs, and McClelland (1975) reported a similar result. The respondents were given a series of choices about the sexes they would prefer if they had three children; a consistent pattern of choosing more male infants than female babies emerged. Of particular relevance is Hoffman's (1977) finding that the pattern of boy preference was more pronounced for men: "Between three and four times as many men preferred boys than girls [p. 11]." Reproduction patterns are revealing as well. According to Hoffman, "Couples are more likely to continue to have children if they only have girls. They will have more children than they originally planned to try for a boy [p. 11]."

After the birth of the infant, parents have clear stereotypes concerning the particular type of behavior that they expect to be associated with infants of different sexes. One set of investigators (Rubin, Provenzano, & Luria, 1974) found that parents, especially fathers, expected boys to be firmer, stronger, and hardier than girls, who were expected to be smaller and cuter.

Although these father-mother differences in attitude toward male and female infants remain only suggestive, there are threads of evidence from both American and cross-cultural studies that support these general trends. According to recent American studies by Parke and O'Leary (1976), differential treatment of male and female children starts as early as the newborn period. In their hospital-based observational study, they found that fathers touched first-born newborn boys more than either later-born boys or girls of either ordinal position. Fathers vocalized more to first-born boys than to first-born girls, whereas they vocalized equally to later-born infants irrespective of their sex. Parke and Sawin (1980) in an observational study of feeding both in the hospital and again in the home at 3 weeks and 3 months found that both visually and tactually fathers stimulated their sons more than their daughters. Consistent with these findings are Kotelchuck's (1976) data that fathers report that they play about one-half hour per day longer with their first-born sons than with their first-born daughters. Although other investigators using American samples (Osofsky & Danzger, 1974) find no differences in maternal behavior toward male and female infants, in those studies where differences are evident, mothers tend to stimulate girls more than boys. For example, Parke and Sawin (1980) found that mothers provided more stimulation for their daughters than their sons and Thoman, Leiderman, and Olson (1972) found that mothers are more likely to vocalize to their newborn girls during feeding than to their boys.

Nor are these patterns limited to American samples. In a study of visiting patterns in Israeli Kibbutzim, Gewirtz and Gewirtz (1968) found that fathers stayed for longer periods in the children's house with their infant sons than their infant daughters. West and Konner's (1976) observations of male parental behavior among the !Kung San (Bushmen) of Botswana, a warm-climate hunting and gathering group, reveal sex of infant differences. Although fathers interact more with male than female infants at both age levels studied (0–26 weeks, 27–99 weeks), the effect was significant only for the older infants. Finally, Mackey and Day (1979) conducted a cross-cultural comparison of adult male-child interaction patterns in five countries including the United States, Ireland, Spain, Japan, and Mexico. Adult males, especially when adult females are not present, associate to a higher degree with boys than girls not only in the United States, but also in Japan and Mexico. The pattern was not significant for the two remaining cultures of Ireland and Spain. As in the case of the American samples, however, the cross-cultural evidence concerning maternal treatment of male and female infants is inconclusive. Recently, Grossmann, Thane, and Grossmann (1980) using a German sample found no differences in maternal touching of male and female newborns. However, across a wide variety of age levels and cultures, there is considerable support for the hypothesis that adult *males* interact more with boys than girls.

Overview

The present study compares the early interaction of mothers and fathers with their newborn infants in both the United States and West Germany. This investigation permits (1) a comparison of these patterns across the two cultures and (2) an examination of the qualifying variables such as sex of infant that modify these early interaction patterns. Finally, the study permits us to tentatively evaluate the historical shifts in German child-care practices.

METHOD

Subjects

Eighteen American and nineteen German mother-father-infant triads were observed feeding during the mother's postpartum hospital stay. The infants (20 females, 17 males) were all full-term normal Caucasians. There were approximately equal numbers of primiparous and multiparous mothers. Twenty-nine of the infants (15 American, 14 German) were breastfed and eight (3 American, 5 German) were bottlefed. The German sample was selected from a small industrial German city in northern West Germany, whereas the American sample resided in a small midwestern American city with light industry. Both cities were sites of major universities.

As has been noted by other researchers, social class, as indexed by occupation, influences parent-child interaction both directly and indirectly by modifying family behavior, attitudes, and values (Caudill & Weinstein, 1969; Kohn, 1963; Moss & Jones, 1977). Tables 5.1 and 5.2 show the occupations of the fathers and mothers in our sample. Approximately 28% of the American fathers were em-

TABLE 5.1
Occupation of Fathers

American Fathers (n=18)		German Fathers (n=19)	
Occupation	Frequency	Occupation	Frequency
Technician	1	Clerk	3
Farmer	3	Grocer	1
Laborer	1	Technician	2
Grocer	1	Tavern Keeper	1
Firefighter	1	TV repairman	1
Sign painter	1	Lifeguard	1
Carpenter	1	Farmer	1
Salesperson	1	Salesperson	1
Maintenance worker	1	Metalworker	1
Store manager	1	Laborer	1
Truck driver	1	Gardener	1
Designer for florist	1		
Lawyer	1	Sociologist	1
Teacher	1	Economist	1
Student (preparing for advanced degree)	2	Student	3

TABLE 5.2
Occupation of Mothers

American Mothers (n=18)		German Mothers (n=19)	
Occupation	Frequency	Occupation	Frequency
Nurse assistant	1	Salesperson	4
Clerk-typist	1	Nurse	2
Secretary	2	Clerk-typist	2
Factory worker	1	Seamstress	1
Child care worker	1	Civil employee	1
Housewife	9	Secretary	1
		Factory worker	1
Speech therapist	1	Housewife	3
Teacher	1	Teacher	2
Student (preparing for advanced degree)	1	Student (preparing for advanced degree)	2

ployed as farmers, laborers, or workers compared with 21% of the German fathers. An additional 22% of the American fathers and 32% of the German fathers worked in positions associated with business. Twenty-two percent of the American fathers and 26% of the German fathers were in training for or functioned as professionals. Fifty percent of the American mothers identified themselves as housewives compared with 16% of the German mothers. Secretarial or clerical positions were occupied by 17% of the American mothers and 15% of the German mothers. Seventeen percent of the American mothers, compared with 26% of the German mothers were either in advanced training for or occupied professional positions.

PROCEDURE

The parents were observed feeding their infants in the mother's hospital room during regular hospital feeding periods. Each father-mother-infant triad was observed using a 15-second time-sampling method in which the observer watched the triad for the first 15 seconds of each 30-second period and in the second 15-second interval the observer recorded the behaviors that occurred during the previous 15-second period for 30 minutes per family (60 15-second intervals). The observers (the senior and second author in Germany and the senior and third author in the U.S.) coded the following parent and infant behaviors: (1) parent hold, which included (a) up front: baby is held facing the parent with the parent's arms extended (b) in arms (c) ventrally and (d) on the shoulder; (2) parent touch; (3) parent hand infant to spouse; (4) parent rock infant; (5) parent explore infant's body; (6) parent look at infant; (7) parent vocalize to infant; (8) parent smile at infant; (9) parent kiss infant; (10) parent feed infant; (11) parent stimulate infant feeding (e.g., stroking baby's cheek or gently moving bottle or breast); (12) parent burp infant; (13) parent imitate infant behavior; (14) infant move; (15) infant cry; (16) infant vocalize; (17) infant move mouth with object (e.g., eating, sucking thumb); (18) infant move mouth without an object, and (19) infant smile.

Interobserver reliability was calculated with the senior author acting as the criterion observer. Interobserver agreement, determined by the ratio of agreement divided by the sum of agreements and disagreements, was calculated separately for the American and German samples. Joint observations by two observers were obtained during four of the observations of the 18 American families and 7 of the observations of the 19 German families. The mean interobserver agreement across categories for the American and German observations was .79 and .73, respectively.

RESULTS

Mother-Father Comparisons

The pattern of our results can be best understood by posing and answering a series of questions about data. First, to what extent does mother and father behavior in relation to their newborn infants differ—regardless of culture? Table 5.3 presents the results of these mother-father comparisons. A series of analyses of variance (Huck & McLean, 1975) were executed to determine the significance of these differences. First, mothers clearly played a more active role in this early period: Mothers were more likely to hold their infants either in their arms or on the shoulder than fathers. Mothers displayed more affection as indexed by smiling and kissing and were more stimulating than fathers as assessed by vocalizing and touching. Role differentiation in terms of caregiving is evident at this early age period with the mothers assuming the major responsibility for feeding. Although this is hardly surprising in view of the large percentage of mothers who breastfed their infants, visual inspection of the few bottlefed infants indicated that a similar pattern was evident for these families as well, with mother assuming the more active role than father in feeding. As the main feeding agent, mothers also showed higher levels of "stimulate feed" and "burp"—part of a general feeding interaction pattern.

However, these differences between mothers and fathers do not suggest that fathers are inactive or inattentive. In spite of the fact that mothers were both holding and feeding more than fathers, fathers looked, rocked, imitated, walked with, and explored their infants just as much as mothers. Even in cases where the mother was more active than the father, father did play a significant role both in terms of stimulating the infant and in providing affection. For example, fathers touched their infants approximately one quarter of the total observation session ($\bar{X} = 15.5$) which, although significantly less than mothers' rate of tactile stimulation ($\bar{X} = 21.7$), was still a substantial portion of the time. Similarly, fathers

TABLE 5.3
Means and F-values for American and German Parental Behaviors

	Means									F-Values					
	Mothers				Fathers					Main Effects			Interaction Effects		
	American		German		American		German								
Parent Behavior	Males	Females	Males	Females	Males	Females	Males	Females	Parent Sex	Infant Sex	Culture	Sex of Parent X Culture	Sex of Infant X Sex of Parent	Sex of Infant X Culture
Hold Infant Up Front	1.50	5.13	8.70	6.56	3.90	.25	6.20	2.33	1.94	1.51	7.02**	.41	1.86	1.48
Hold Infant in Arms	42.20	42.25	31.40	37.56	5.00	10.25	12.20	13.11	52.56***	3.64**	.70	2.69	.01	.07
Hold Infant Ventrally	0	0	1.3	.11	1.0	0	0	0	.07	2.12	.07	2.58	.02	.02
Hold Infant on Shoulder	4.0	2.88	1.50	2.44	2.40	0	2.10	.11	3.42*	1.71	.80	.67	1.57	.51
Touch Infant	21.90	24.50	19.89	20.80	11.70	14.88	19.50	16.22	4.86**	.01	.05	1.75	.03	.43
Hand Infant to Spouse	.90	.50	.40	.78	.90	.63	.50	.56	.01	.07	.59	.24	.15	1.51
Rock Infant	12.10	7.88	.10	2.22	2.30	.50	4.00	4.67	2.06	.16	2.13	9.70***	.02	1.19
Explore Infant	1.90	2.00	1.50	.33	1.60	3.75	.90	.56	.10	.01	4.25**	.54	1.73	1.51
Look at Infant	59.80	59.00	53.80	59.89	58.20	51.75	59.90	59.00	.24	.07	.23	3.59*	2.90*	2.37
Vocalize to Infant	23.80	17.00	28.60	30.67	8.70	7.38	19.00	15.44	15.72***	.82	12.08***	.01	.01	.39
Smile at Infant	16.60	15.88	17.20	18.44	8.30	7.75	10.40	14.89	11.86***	.01	1.76	.01	1.01	.01
Kiss Infant	.10	.75	2.40	1.78	.10	0	.20	0	3.20*	.01	1.67	1.49	.02	.27
Feed Infant	25.70	25.88	20.40	18.44	2.60	5.63	7.50	1.56	52.15***	.25	1.63	1.79	.01	1.42
Stimulate Infant Feeding	12.10	9.13	9.70	6.44	1.30	1.75	4.60	.67	18.54***	1.91	.17	1.17	.17	.44
Burp Infant	3.80	3.50	2.00	4.67	2.30	2.13	.90	.11	8.43***	.25	2.04	.90	1.28	.69
Imitate Infant	0	0	.50	.56	.10	0	.40	.44	.05	.00	9.50***	.40	.05	.12

¹df = 1,33
*p < .10
**p < .05
***p < .01

vocalized ($\bar{X} = 12.7$) at nearly the same level as they touched—although significantly less than mothers ($\bar{X} = 25.2$). A similar pattern was evident for affectional behavior, such as smiling; mothers ($\bar{X} = 17.10$) smiled at their babies significantly more than fathers ($\bar{X} = 10.30$), but fathers still smiled a substantial amount.

A second question concerns the extent to which these patterns are modified by the sex of the infant. Analyses of variance indicated that there were no significant sex-of-infant main effects except an effect for holding the baby in their arms. Parents irrespective of their sex held females in their arms to a greater degree than they held boys in this position. Do mothers and fathers treat their sons and daughters differently? Generally not. Only in the case of the extent to which parents visually attend to their infants is there a borderline sex of parent × sex of infant interaction. Mothers look more at their girls than their boys while fathers show the opposite pattern—they visually attend more to their sons than their daughters. This pattern is similar to findings from studies summarized earlier, which indicated that both fathers and mothers in a wide variety of cultures stimulated their same-sexed infants more than their opposite-sexed infants.

Next, we turn to culture. Do German and American mothers and fathers differ in their treatment of their newborns? Although they hold their infants in their arms and on the shoulder to the same degree, German parents use the "up front" position more than American parents. Additionally, the patterns of stimulation used by parents in the two cultures differ. American parents are more physical in the style of their stimulation than German parents; they tactually explore and rock their infants more than their German counterparts. In contrast, German parents use more auditory-visual modes of interaction than American parents. They vocalize more and imitate more than American mothers and fathers. However, these patterns are qualified by the sex of the parent. In the case of rocking behavior, German fathers surpass German mothers while the opposite is the case for American families. Among American parents, American mothers rock more than American fathers. A similar pattern is present for looking at the infant: German fathers are more visually attentive than German mothers whereas American mothers look at their infants more than American fathers.

In the foregoing analyses, mother was holding the infant to a greater degree than father. Although this type of information is interesting as a source of how parents distribute the responsibility in this early period, it may lead to a biased picture of the differences in affectional and stimulatory behaviors of mothers and fathers. Many of these affectional (e.g., kiss, smile, vocalize) and stimulatory (touch, rock) behaviors are more likely to occur when the infant is being held. Although it was impossible to equate the amount of time that mothers and fathers held their newborns, it was possible to examine the behaviors of mothers and fathers with holding the infant held constant. Proportions for each parent behavior while the infant was being held by either mother or father were calculated to answer the question: "When fathers are holding their infant, is the rate of their display of these behaviors similar or different than the rate of these behaviors for mothers when they are holding their infant?" An analysis of variance was run in which sex of parent holding (2) and sex of parent behaving (2) were included as factors as well as sex of infant (2) and culture (2). This analysis confirmed our expectations that the differences in parent behavior are dependent on the identity of the parent who is holding the infant. As Table 5.4 shows, there was a significant sex of parent holding × sex of parent behaving interaction for all parent behaviors except exploration. Two series of analyses of variance were run to assess whether these differences between mother and father behavior while either father or mother was holding were significant. As seen in Table 5.5, when father and mother behaviors are compared for the situation in which mother or father are holding the infant, many of the previously observed differences between mothers and fathers are eliminated and in some cases reversed. When father is holding the infant he is significantly more likely than mother to be rocking ($p < .01$), vocalizing ($p < .01$), imitating ($p < .01$), and stimulating feeding behavior ($p < .05$). Touching, exploring, looking, and smiling were similar for both mother and father while father was holding. In sum, *when father is holding his infant* he plays a more active stimulatory role than mother and equals her in his display of affectional behavior. In contrast, *when mother is holding*, a picture emerges that closely parallels the earlier analyses. When the mother holds her infant, she engages in significantly higher frequencies of touching ($p < .01$), rocking ($p < .01$), vocalizing ($p < .01$), smiling ($p < .01$), and stimulation of feeding ($p < .01$) than the father. In the case of exploration and imitation, mothers and fathers did not differ while mother was holding.

These sex of parent differences in affectional and stimulatory behavior are *not* modified by the sex of infant. Nor were there any main effects for sex of the infant. Are there cultural effects yielded by this type of analysis? While mother is holding the infant, American parents rock their infants more than German parents; as the sex of parent × culture interaction suggests, American mothers rock their infants more than German mothers, while fathers in the two cultures rock equally. However, there were culture effects. Specifically, American parents explore more than their German counterparts, while German parents look at and imitate their infants more than American parents. Finally, there were a number of sex of infant × culture interactions. American parents look at and vocalize to their boys more than their girls, while German parents show the opposite pattern of looking at and vocalizing more to their female than their male infants. However, these were of borderline significance and therefore should be interpreted cautiously.

This type of analysis suggests that parents—regardless of their sex—interact in similar ways when they are holding their infants. Moreover, it underlines the importance of contextual variables in modifying the nature of interaction patterns and suggests the importance of controlling for such variables as who has the opportunity to interact with the infant.

TABLE 5.4
Means and F-Values for American and German Parental Behaviors As A Function of Mother Holding or Father Holding the Infant

	Means (Proportions)									F-Values[1]							
	Mothers				Fathers				Main Effects				Interaction Effects				
	American		German		American		German										
Parent Behavior	Males	Females	Males	Females	Males	Females	Males	Females	Culture	Infant Sex	Sex of Parent Holding	Sex of Parent Behaving	Culture X Infant Sex	Culture X Sex of Parent Holding	Culture X Sex of Parent Behaving	Infant Sex X Sex of Parent Holding	Infant Sex X Sex of Parent Behaving	Sex of Parent Holding X Sex of Parent Behaving
Touch Infant while Mother Holds	.43	.49	.48	.33	.19	.28	.41	.24										
Touch Infant while Father Holds	.25	.09	.10	.24	.27	.19	.14	.20	.01	.26	26.75***	5.56**	.01	.71	.57	.23	.01	5.87**
Rock Infant while Mother Holds	.24	.16	.02	.05	.01	.01	0	.01										
Rock Infant while Father Holds	.01	0	0	.02	.14	.11	.17	.24	.46	.01	1.33	1.00	.90	8.45***	7.00**	.29	.17	17.56***
Explore Infant while Mother Holds	.04	.05	.01	.01	.05	.06	.19	.01										
Explore Infant while Father Holds	.02	.01	.01	.01	.03	.02	0	0	.25	1.18	5.49	2.85	1.36	.28	.63	.57	1.23	2.12
Look at Infant while Mother Holds	.99	.96	.98	.94	.96	.80	.84	.91										
Look at Infant while Father Holds	.88	.70	.88	.98	.88	.90	.90	.96	1.17	.32	1.45	1.37	3.79*	2.31	1.53	.34	.80	5.08**
Vocalize to Infant while Mother Holds	.46	.27	.59	.59	.07	.06	.17	.24										
Vocalize to Infant while Father Holds	.28	.13	.14	.32	.45	.42	.55	.82	6.56**	.07	5.05**	0	3.10*	.43	.38	1.81	1.02	83.62***
Smile at Infant while Mother Holds	.29	.30	.37	.26	.14	.12	.18	.14										
Smile at Infant while Father Holds	.20	.20	.22	.33	.22	.16	.22	.47	1.39	.09	.60	4.71**	.31	1.54	.81	2.54	.36	23.95***
Stimulate Infant Feeding while Mother Holds	.26	.18	.16	.19	.01	.01	.03	.01										
Stimulate Infant Feeding while Father Holds	.01	.03	.03	.01	.04	.11	.17	.03	.06	.64	7.07**	6.32**	.97	.52	.69	.01	.07	32.49***
Imitate Infant while Mother Holds	0	0	.01	.01	0	0	0	.01										
Imitate Infant while Father Holds	0	0	.01	0	.01	0	.06	.03	4.33**	.40	2.75	2.65	.11	1.84	1.77	1.33	.77	4.42**

[1]df = 1,28
*p < .10
**p < .05
***p < .01

TABLE 5.5
Means for Sex of Parent Holding by Sex of Parent
Behaving Significant Interactions

(A) Touch

	Mother Hold	Father Hold
Mother Touch	.43	.28
Father Touch	.17	.20

(B) Rock

	Mother Hold	Father Hold
Mother Rock	.12	.01
Father Rock	.01	.17

(C) Look

	Mother Hold	Father Hold
Mother Look	.97	.86
Father Look	.88	.91

(D) Vocalize

	Mother Hold	Father Hold
Mother Vocalize	.48	.22
Father Vocalize	.14	.56

(E) Smile

	Mother Hold	Father Hold
Mother Smile	.30	.24
Father Smile	.15	.27

(F) Stimulate Infant Feeding

	Mother Hold	Father Hold
Mother Stimulate Feed	.20	.02
Father Stimulate Feed	.01	.09

(G) Imitate Infant

	Mother Hold	Father Hold
Mother Imitate	.004	.001
Father Imitate	.001	.03

DISCUSSION

This study extends our understanding of the universality of parent-infant interaction patterns and suggests that the cultural environment has a significant impact on family interaction behavior. As suggested earlier, studies of German parent-child interaction during the 1960s characterized German child-rearing behavior in a state of transition from a predominantly authoritarian approach to a more affectional and involved style. Our examination of German parent-infant interaction confirms this trend, and establishes its existence even in the very early days of life.

From a comparison of U.S. and German parent-infant interaction, we find very few differences, suggesting that parent behavior differences between the two cultures identified in the earlier studies reviewed above are not true for the first days of the infant's life.

One provocative set of findings that warrant further exploration concerns cultural differences in the parents' characteristic mode of interaction: American parents are more physical in their style of interaction, whereas German parents rely more on auditory-visual modes of interaction. Our data permit an evaluation of the role of mothers and fathers cross-culturally. In both American and German cultures, mothers and fathers are very similar in their distribution of responsibility for early care and stimulation of the infant. Mothers, in both cultures, not only assume a larger role in early feeding—a finding that is hardly surprising in view of the large percentage of breast-feeding families, but mothers also show more affectionate (kissing, smiling) and stimulatory behaviors (vocalizing, touching) than fathers. However, fathers still played a far from passive role in this early newborn period. Even though mothers were holding and feeding more than fathers, fathers looked, rocked, imitated, and explored their infants just as often as mothers. These data are consistent with the recently revised view of American fathers as active and interested participants in the newborn period (Parke, 1979; Parke & O'Leary, 1976), and suggests that this general picture may have some greater generality across Western culture.

Although it is of interest to determine which parent assumes primary responsibility for certain activities, such as feeding, our supplementary analyses in which parents' behavior was compared when they were holding the infant are revealing. These analyses suggest that holding places serious constraints on the interactive behavior of the nonholding parent and that it is necessary to examine parent behavior when the opportunity to hold is held constant. Fathers and mothers, in fact, are strikingly similar in the quality of their behavior when they are holding the baby, which, in turn, suggests that the differences in the opportunities to hold the infant—rather than differences in the quality of parent behavior—may, in part, account for previously observed mother-father differences.

A number of issues remain for future research. First, closer attention should be paid to social class and rural/urban differences across these two cultures in view of earlier studies demonstrating the importance of these variables in modifying interaction patterns. Second, are the patterns of interaction that were observed in this early newborn period predictive of parent-infant interaction at later developmental points for both cultures? The necessity of longitudinal studies is well illustrated by the results of a recent study of the development of infant attachment patterns in Germany (Grossmann & Grossmann, 1980). In contrast to our findings of marked similarity between the two cultures, these investigators found more insecurely attached infants in German than in previous American samples. By closer attention to individual differences among parent-infant pairs within each culture at a variety of time points beginning at the newborn period, the antecedents of these possible later cultural differences may be evident. Alternative methodological strategies, including sequential analyses, which permit assessment of variables such as sensitivity to infant cues, which are conceptually linked to later parent-infant behavior patterns may yield more meaningful relationships.

ACKNOWLEDGMENT

Thanks to the staffs of St. Franziskus Hospital, Bielefeld, West Germany and Burnham City Hospital and Mercy Hospital, Champaign-Urbana, Illinois, U.S.A. for their cooperation in the completion of this study. The senior author and second author were members of the Interdisciplinary Seminar on Early Development in Animals and Man at the Zentrum für Interdisziplinaere Forschung, University of Bielefeld, West Germany during the collection of the data in West Germany. Thanks to Professor Klaus Immelmann and the center staff for their generous support. The collection of the American data and analyses of the entire data set were supported, in part, by grants from the Office of Child Development, OHD 90-C-900, and National Institute of Child Health and Human Development, HEW PHS HD 05951. Thanks to Cathy Morris for her assistance with the data analyses, Thomas Power for his comments on the manuscript and Brenda Congdon for preparation of the manuscript.

REFERENCES

Ainsworth, M. D. S., Blehar, M. C., Waters, E., & Wall, S. *Patterns of attachment: A psychological study of the strange situation.* Hillsdale, N.J.: Lawrence Erlbaum Associates, 1978.

Arnold, R., Bulatao, R., Buripakdi, C., Chung, B. J., Fawcett, J. T., Iritani, T., Lee, S. J., & Wu, T. S. *The value of children: Introduction and comparative analysis* (Vol. 1). Honolulu: East-West Population Inst., 1975.

Bronfenbrenner, U. Socialization and social class through time and space. In E. E. Maccoby, T. M. Newcomb, and E. L. Hartley, (Eds.), *Readings in social psychology.* N.Y.: Henry Holt, Co., 1958.

Bronfenbrenner, U. The changing American child. *Journal of Social Issues,* 1961, *17,* 6–18.

Caudill, W., & Weinstein, H. Maternal care and infant behavior in Japan and America. *Psychiatry,* 1969, *32,* 12–43.

Coombs, C. H., Coombs, L. C., & McClelland, G. H. Preference scales for number and sex of children. *Population Studies,* 1975, *29,* 273–298.

Devereux, E., Bronfenbrenner, U., & Suci, G. Patterns of parent behavior in the United States of America and the Federal Republic of Germany. *International Social Science Journal,* 1962, *14,* 488–506.

Gewirtz, H. B., & Gewirtz, J. L. Visiting and caretaking patterns for Kibbutz infants: Age and sex trends. *American Journal of Orthopsychiatry,* 1968, *38,* 427–443.

Greenberg, M., & Morris, N. Engrossment: The newborn's impact upon the father. *American Journal of Orthopsychiatry,* 1974, *44,* 520–531.

Grossmann, K. E., & Grossmann, K. Parent-infant attachment relationships in Bielefeld: A research note. In G. W. Barlow, K. Immelmann, M. Main, & L. Petrinovich (Eds.), *Behavioral development: The Bielefeld interdisciplinary project.* Cambridge University Press: Parey Verlag, 1980.

Grossmann, K., Thane, K., & Grossmann, K. E. *Maternal skin-touching behavior of her newborn after various post-partum conditions of mother-infant contact,* Unpublished manuscript.

Hoffman, L. W. Changes in family roles, socialization and sex differences. *American Psychologist*, 1977, *32*, 644–658.

Huck, S. W., & McLean, R. A. Using a repeated measure ANOVA to analyze the data from a pretest-posttest design: A potentially confusing task. *Psychological Bulletin*, 1975, *82*, 511–518.

Kohn, M. L. Social class and parent-child relationships: An interpretation. *American Journal of Sociology*, 1963, *68*, 471–480.

Kotelchuck, M. The infant's relationship to the father: Experimental evidence. In M. E. Lamb, (Ed.), *The role of the father in child development*. New York: Wiley, 1976.

Levine, R. A. Cross-cultural study in child psychology. In Paul H. Mussen (Ed.), *Carmichael's manual of child psychology*, (Vol. II.) N.Y.: Wiley, 1970.

LeVine, R. A. Child rearing as cultural adaptation. In P. H. Leiderman, S. R. Tulkin, & A. Rosenfeld (Eds.), *Culture and infancy: Variations in the human experience*. New York: Academic Press, 1977.

Mackey, W. C., & Day, R. D. Some indicators of fathering behaviors in the United States: A cross-cultural examination of adult male-child interaction. *Journal of Marriage and the Family*, 1979, *43*, 287–299.

McGranahan, D. V. A comparison of social attitudes among American and German youth. *Journal of Abnormal Social Psychology*, 1946, *41*, 245–257.

Metraux, R. Parents and children: An analysis of contemporary German child-care and youth guidence literature. In M. Mead & M. Wolfenstein (Eds.), *Childhood in Contemporary Cultures*. Chicago: University of Chicago Press, 1955.

Moss, H. A., & Jones, S. J. Relations between maternal behavior as a function of social class. In P. H. Leiderman, S. R. Tulkin, & A. Rosenfeld (Eds.), *Culture and infancy*. New York: Academic Press, 1977.

Osofsky, J. D., & Danzger, B. Relationships between neonatal characteristics and mother-infant characteristics. *Developmental Psychology*, 1974, *10*, 124–130.

Parke, R. D. Perspectives on father-infant interaction. In J. Osofsky (Ed.), *Handbook of infant development*, New York: Wiley, 1979.

Parke, R. D., & O'Leary, S. E. Father-mother-infant interaction in the newborn period: Some findings, some observations and some unresolved issues. In K. Riegel, & J. Meacham (Eds.), *The developing individual in a changing world (Vol. 2): Social and environmental issues*. The Hague: Mouton, 1976.

Parke, R. D., O'Leary, S. E., & West, S. Mother-father-newborn interaction: Effects of maternal medication, labor and sex of infant. *Proceedings of the American Psychological Association*, 85-86, 1972.

Parke, R. D., & Sawin, D. B. Infant characteristics and behavior as elicitors of maternal and paternal responsivity in the newborn period. Paper presented at a Symposium of Society for Research in Child Development, Denver, April 1975.

Parke, R. D., & Sawin, D. B. The family in early infancy: social interactional and attitudinal analyses. In F. Pedersen (Ed.), *The father-infant relationship: Observational studies in family context*. New York: Holt, Rinehart, & Winston, 1980.

Poffenberger, T., & Poffenberger, S. B. The social psychology of fertility in a village in India. In J. T. Fawcett, (Ed.), *Psychological perspectives on population*. New York: Basic Books, 1973.

Rabbie, J. M. A cross-cultural comparison of parent-child relationships in the United States and West Germany. *British Journal of Social and Clinical Psychology*, 1965, *4*, 298–310.

Rainwater, L. Social status differences in family relationship of German men. *Journal of Marriage and Family Living*, 1962, *24*, 12–17.

Rapp, D. W. Childrearing attitudes of mothers in Germany and the United States. *Child Development*, 1961, *32*, 669–678.

Rohner, R. P. Why cross-cultural research? *Annals of the New York Academy of Science*, 1977, *285*, 3–12.

Rubin, J. Z., Provenzano, F. J., & Luria, Z. The Eye of the beholder: Parents' views on sex of newborns. *American Journal of Orthopsychiatry,* 1974, *43,* 720–731.

Schaffner, B. *Father Land: A study of authoritarianism in the German family.* N.Y.: Columbia University Press, 1948.

Thoman, E. B., Leiderman, P. H., & Olson, J. P. Neonate-mother interaction during breast feeding. *Developmental Psychology,* 1972, *6,* 110–118.

West, M. M., & Konner, M. J. The role of the father: An anthropological perspective. In M. Lamb (Ed.), *The role of the father in child development.* New York: Wiley, 1976.

6 A Comparison of Anglo, Hopi, and Navajo Mothers and Infants

John W. Callaghan
University of Chicago

The author has had the opportunity to administer the Cambridge Newborn Examination (Brazelton & Freedman, 1971) to infants in several cultures around the world: Japanese, Balinese, Australian Aboriginal, Punjabi, Hopi, and Navajo. This study is a preliminary attempt to demonstrate the importance of group differences and similarities in early infant behavior.

Three notions are pertinent to this study. The first is that mothers in different cultures (and subcultures) have different ideas about how infants should be handled. The second is that infants vary from group to group in the average behavioral tendencies that they exhibit (cf. Freedman, 1974). The third notion is that there then ought to be observable group differences in the ways in which mothers and infants interact.

In this study we describe and document behavioral differences between an Anglo sample (white, middle-class Chicago), a Hopi sample, and a Navajo sample of mothers and infants in face-to-face interaction. The potential effects of infants upon their mothers are stressed throughout the study.

METHOD

Data Collection

In order to test the hypothesis that there are behavioral differences between groups of mothers and infants, samples of elicited face-to-face interactions were videotaped in three different cultures: Anglo, Hopi, and Navajo. Anglo here refers to a white, middle-class Chicago sample that was part of the

Columbus Project (Kaye, 1979), Department of Education, University of Chicago (a longitudinal study of 50 mothers and infants under the direction of Dr. Kenneth Kaye).

The Hopi and Navajo populations were chosen as comparison groups as they are: (1) both fairly distinct from the Anglo population and each other, and (2) both fairly accessible to the investigator. The Hopi and Navajo data collection occurred during Autumn, 1974, Autumn, 1975, and December, 1975. The Hopi sample came from villages on all three of the Hopi reservation's mesas in northern Arizona. The Navajo homes visited were all in the outlying regions surrounding Keams Canyon, Arizona: Jeddito, Low Mountain, and White Cone.

Eighteen Hopi and 15 Navajo mothers and infants were visited in their homes; 19 Anglo homes were visited by members of the Columbus Project, of which the author was a member for a time (see Table 6.1).

For the purposes of this study, each mother was asked to "try to get and maintain your baby's attention." All of the Hopi and most of the Navajo mothers spoke English. In a few homes the field health nurse or translator would help with the instructions.

Mothers and infants were videotaped once the mothers began an attempt to get their babies' attention. Each was asked to sit on a comfortable chair or couch in such a way that both the mother's face and the infant's face were visible to the camera. With a minimal amount of "zooming," the cameraman attempted to keep the baby, mother's face and lap, and all interactive movement in full camera frame. In this way a consistency was achieved with regard to the location and recording of the task.

TABLE 6.1
Group Sample Characteristics

Anglo $n = 19$	Navajo $n = 15$	Hopi $n = 18$

Mean age:
Mothers = 25.1 yrs.
Infants = 14.9 wks.
8 female infants
11 male infants
Average birth
  order = 1.8 (10 first)
Overall infant
  state ratings:
  15 alert
  4 fussy
 	
Total time
  recorded:
  4092 seconds
  (68.20 minutes)
	Mean age:
	Mothers = 21.2 yrs.
	Infants = 12.9 wks.
	8 female infants
	7 male infants
	Average birth
	  order = 3.87 (2 first)
	Overall infant
	  state ratings:
	  10 alert
	  4 fussy
	  1 drowsy
	Total time
	  recorded:
	  2605 seconds
	  (43.42 minutes)
		Mean age:
		Mothers = 23.2 yrs.
		Infants = 16.1 wks.
		12 female infants
		6 male infants
		Average birth
		  order = 2.55 (7 first)
		Overall infant
		  state ratings:
		  14 alert
		  3 fussy
		  1 drowsy
		Total time
		  recorded:
		  3947 seconds
		  (65.78 minutes)

Coding Procedures and Rationale

Once the videotapes had been secured, coding of the interactions was begun. The coding was done by Darryl Banyacya—a local (New Oraibi, Az.) Hopi college student—and the author. The procedure was developed in part under the tutelage of Dr. D. G. Freedman and Dr. Kenneth Kaye in a seminar at the University of Chicago (1975) that explored various strategies for the coding of such interactions (microanalysis vs. macroanalysis). The procedure and rationale developed for these videotapes were as follows.

A videotape was first chosen at random. Both coders watched the interaction at least once through at real time—to get the "feel" of the sequence. Next, the interaction was viewed and the coders made note of *when* and for how long the mother and infant looked at each other. A stop watch and the pause mechanism on the videotape machine were used to do this. "Looking at each other" has come to be called *probable mutual gaze* in this study—abbreviated M.G. or mutual gaze. As the task was to "get your baby's attention," we wanted to know how successful each mother was at the task; that is, how often and for how long did she get her baby's attention?

Next we would code either all of the mother's behaviors or all of the infant's behaviors (see Table 6.2). Behaviors to be coded had been established primarily in a seminar on mother-infant interaction at the University of Chicago (1975); that is, discussions about interactions in each culture were held concerning the possible range of behavioral modes. If we chose to first code the mother's behaviors, several steps were taken.

All maternal behaviors that occurred in periods of mutual gaze were first coded. ("Coding" consisted of making frequency counts of the various behavioral modes.) Then all behaviors that occurred in periods of no mutual gazing ($\overline{\text{M.G.}}$)—when either the infant or the mother was not looking at their partner—were coded. Often a separate run through the videotape was necessary for certain modes that were either occurring rapidly or in unison with other modes (e.g., vocalizations). The distinction was made between behaviors in M.G. vs. $\overline{\text{M.G.}}$ as we were trying to determine what a mother might do to *get* her baby's attention—as opposed to what she might do to *keep* her baby's attention.

In the coding of behaviors, a count was kept of the frequency of each discrete behavior. Continuous behaviors (e.g., nonstop talking) were counted at the frequency of one per second.

After coding maternal behaviors, we would then code infant behaviors. Here "attention on" and "attention off" (M.G. and $\overline{\text{M.G.}}$) were again coded. At this point, the coders took the time to discuss and agree on every instance of mutual gaze. In this way mutual gaze was coded twice for each interaction.

Infant behaviors were then coded in the same fashion as maternal behaviors. One of the coders would observe and verbally note behaviors, while the other recorded occurrences on a score sheet. Whenever a mode was too "active" it

TABLE 6.2
Coded Behavior For Each Mother-Infant Pair

Maternal Modes	Infant Modes
Number of Mutual Gaze events	Attention on
Total Mutual Gaze Time	Attention off
Total Non-Mutual Gaze Time	
	Arm movement
Vocalizations (frequency)	Leg movement
Repositions (frequency):	Arching back/Tensing
Sits Infant	Crying/Whimpering
Stands I.	Sounds
Lays I. down	Finger movement
Holds I. under arms	Flops head
Pulls I. to sit	Head, side-to-side
Holds I. ventro-to-ventro	Reaching
	Grasping
Movement (frequency):	Hand to mouth (self)
Jiggles, bounces, sways,	Sticks tongue out
rocks, or turns I.	Frowns, grimaces
Tactual (frequency):	Yawns
Touches, pokes, strokes	Smiles
I. face	Eyes close
Holds or moves I. arms or	
hands	Obstructions
Holds I. behind head or neck	
Strokes I. behind head or neck	
Holds, strokes, pokes, or pats I. body	
Kisses I., face-to-face	
Claps I. hands	
Obstructions	

would be coded separately; likewise any particularly busy infant sequences would be observed several times in order to record the frequency of each mode being used.

Coder reliability was ascertained before any of the coding sessions were permanently recorded. Likewise, each day was begun with a check for coder reliability. Reliability scores for mother and infant behaviors ranged from 83% to 92%. Total behavior scores in any one mode were more reliable in that they were often correctly counted, but disagreement sometimes occurred in relation to the transition periods between mutual gaze and no mutual gaze. The coders felt very secure with the coding scheme—each mode was discussed to the extent that each coder agreed completely on what was meant by each behavior.

Statistical Analyses

Differences between group frequency counts were tested for mutual gaze and for all maternal and infant behaviors. Three types of statistics were used. For mutual gaze, infant behaviors, and maternal behaviors, group total frequency counts were first compared by means of the chi-square test statistic (a comparison of the observed group total with the expected). In this analysis, each group was treated as an aggregate sample, rather than as a collection of individuals, in order to establish overall behavioral frequencies. A basic assumption here was that within-group differences would be minimal.

Next, the group mean scores, standard deviations, and confidence limits based on the t-distribution were computed for mutual gaze, and infant and maternal behaviors. Here the population differences were not viewed as an accumulated group score as in the chi-square test; instead the central tendencies and the overlap of individual scores (i.e., the group variances) of the three groups were taken into account.

Finally, the Mann-Whitney U Test was employed as a test of the possible differences between several of the infant behavioral modes. Ranking was used here as a nonparametric means of distinguishing the populations in that the scores in some modes were skewed to the extent that the normal curve was not a safe assumption.

In general, significance levels were set at the $p < .10$ level in order to allow trends in the data to be visible.

Mutual gaze scores, infant behavior scores, and maternal behavior scores will now be reported.

RESULTS

Mutual Gaze

Mutual gaze scores were computed for: (1) total time in mutual gaze, (2) number of mutual gaze events, that is, how often mother and infant looked at each other, (3) number of mutual gaze runs—a *run* being defined as any period of interaction where there are consecutive mutual gaze events occurring with no in-between pauses of no mutual gaze for more than 5 seconds, and (4) mean length of runs of mutual gaze.

The length and number of mutual gaze runs were computed in order to study the pattern of "looking at" and "looking away" over long time periods, i.e., whole sessions. Individual M.G. events were found to be numerous and variable; it will perhaps take a sophisticated computer program to determine significant sequential differences in patterns of M.G. events. By grouping together mutual

TABLE 6.3
Comparisons of Group Mutual Gaze Scores

Mode	Groups	Scores (adjusted for time)		χ^2	p
M.G.: Total Time	A × H	A = 982.0	H = 908.0	2.90	<.10
in seconds	A × N	A = 982.0	N = 940.0	.92	n.s.
(duration)	H × N	H = 908.0	N = 940.0	.55	n.s.
M.G.: Number of	A × H	A = 160.4	H = 122.3	5.13	<.03
Events	A × N	A = 160.4	N = 143.0	1.00	n.s.
	H × N	H = 122.3	N = 143.0	1.62	n.s.
M.G. *Runs:*	A × H	A = 98.3	H = 77.4	2.51	n.s.
Number of	A × N	A = 98.3	N = 66.6	6.12	<.02
Events	H × N	H = 77.4	N = 66.6	.81	n.s.

gaze events that occur within at least 5 seconds of each other, we feel that we have gotten a preliminary, if somewhat primitive, sense of the patterns of mutual gaze.

Mutual gaze results in Table 6.3 and Fig. 6.1 show the following differences between the groups. In terms of the number of mutual gaze events, the Anglo group totals are significantly higher than the Hopi ($\chi^2 = 5.13$, $p < .03$). And, when the events are grouped according to the number of mutual gaze *runs*, the Anglo group exhibits more runs than the Navajo (AxN: $\chi^2 = 6.12$, $p < .02$). That the Anglo group has more M.G. runs is also evident in the mean scores and confidence limits in Fig. 6.1. The Anglo and Navajo scores are significantly different with the Hopi in the middle overlapping each group ($p < .09$).

The final significant mutual gaze result is the group differences in mean length of M.G. runs. The mean length of the Anglo M.G. runs ($\bar{X} = 6.53$ seconds) is significantly smaller ($p < .05$) than the Navajo ($\bar{X} = 14.28$ seconds). Again the Hopi overlap each.

Infant Behavior

Infant group total scores for various behaviors demonstrate several consistent patterns (behavioral modes not included are few in number, e.g., yawns). The Anglo group is significantly different from both the Hopi and the Navajo in all modes except Head Movement (See Table 6.4). Interestingly, the Hopi and Navajo groups are quite similar in over half of all infant modes. Comparing the Hopi and Navajo total kinesthetic behavior scores (totals excluding vocalizations), there is no significant difference. In general, the Hopi and Navajo infants tend to demonstrate much less activity.

The Mann-Whitney *U* Tests in Table 6.5 give significant nonparametric comparisons between the three groups with regard to infant behaviors. The Anglo

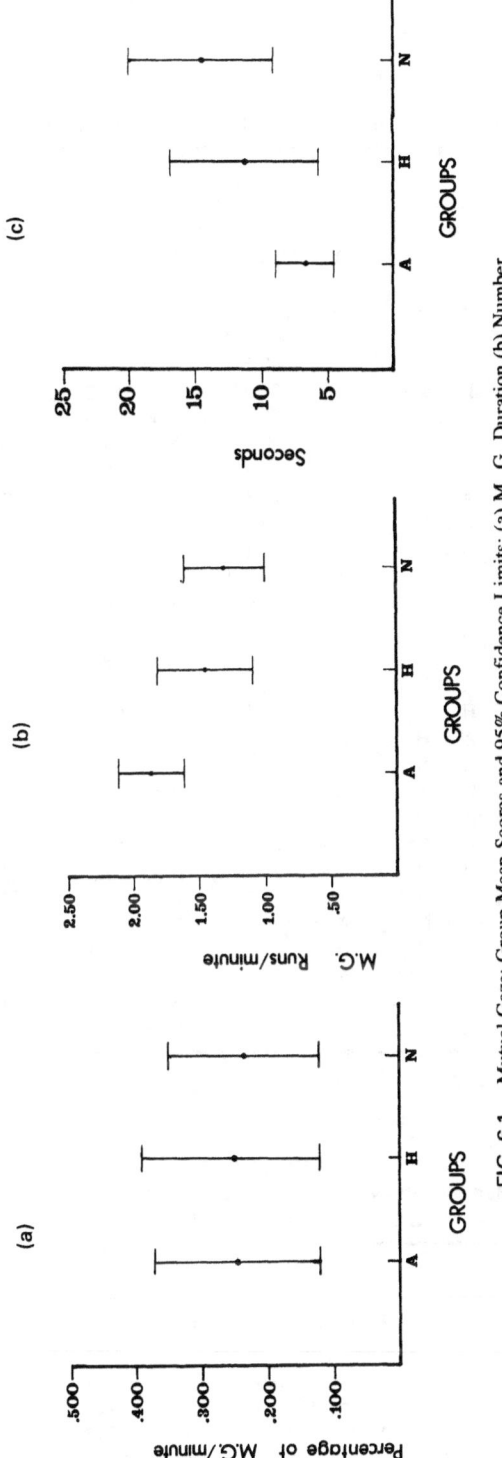

FIG. 6.1. Mutual Gaze: Group Mean Scores and 95% Confidence Limits: (a) M. G. Duration (b) Number of M. G. Runs (c) Mean Length of M. G. Runs.

TABLE 6.4
Comparisons of Group Infant Behavior Scores

Mode	Groups	Scores (adjusted for time)		χ^2	p
Total behaviors	A × H	A = 1313.7	H = 900.7	77.03	<.001
Total behaviors	A × N	A = 1313.7	N = 995.1	43.96	<.001
Total behaviors	H × N	H = 900.7	N = 995.1	4.70	<.04
Total behaviors excluding vocalizations	A × H	A = 1040.6	H = 709.2	62.76	<.001
	A × N	A = 1040.6	N = 653.2	88.60	<.001
	H × N	H = 709.2	N = 653.2	2.30	n.s.
Total arm movement	A × H	A = 620.3	H = 449.6	27.23	<.001
	A × N	A = 620.3	N = 438.9	31.07	<.001
	H × N	H = 449.6	N = 438.9	.13	n.s.
Arm movement: non-directed random activity	A × H	A = 529.1	H = 337.4	42.41	<.001
	A × N	A = 529.1	N = 378.7	24.92	<.001
	H × N	H = 337.4	N = 378.7	2.38	n.s.
Reaches/Grasps	A × H	A = 64.8	H = 90.8	4.34	<.05
Reaches/Grasps	A × N	A = 64.8	N = 29.4	13.30	<.001
Reaches/Grasps	H × N	H = 90.8	N = 29.4	31.36	<.001
Leg movement	A × H	A = 156.6	H = 99.5	12.73	<.001
Leg movement	A × N	A = 156.6	N = 61.7	41.26	<.001
Leg movement	H × N	H = 99.5	N = 61.7	8.86	<.006
Arches Back/ Tenses	A × H	A = 105.8	H = 45.0	24.51	<.001
	A × N	A = 105.8	N = 31.3	40.48	<.001
	H × N	H = 45.0	N = 31.3	2.46	n.s.
Head movement	A × H	A = 79.8	H = 67.4	1.04	n.s.
Head movement	A × N	A = 79.8	N = 54.5	4.77	<.04
Head movement	H × N	H = 67.4	N = 54.5	1.37	n.s.
Cries/Grimaces	A × H	A = 160.4	H = 70.1	21.48	<.001
Cries/Grimaces	A × N	A = 160.4	N = 219.3	9.14	<.005
Cries/Grimaces	H × N	H = 70.1	N = 219.3	76.92	<.001
Smiles	A × H	A = 45.1	H = 20.4	9.31	<.005
Smiles	A × N	A = 45.1	N = 10.8	21.05	<.001
Smiles	H × N	H = 20.4	N = 10.8	2.95	<.09

TABLE 6.5
Mann-Whitney U Tests for Differences Between Group Infant Behavior Scores

Mode	Groups (n)	U	p
Leg movement	Anglo (15); Navajo (14)	148	= .07
Arches back/ Tenses	Anglo (19); Hopi (18)	251	<.02
	Anglo (19); Navajo (15)	219	<.01
Cries/Grimaces	Anglo (19); Hopi (17)	221	<.07
Sounds	Anglo (19); Navajo (13)	192	<.01

6. FACE-TO-FACE INTERACTION STYLES   123

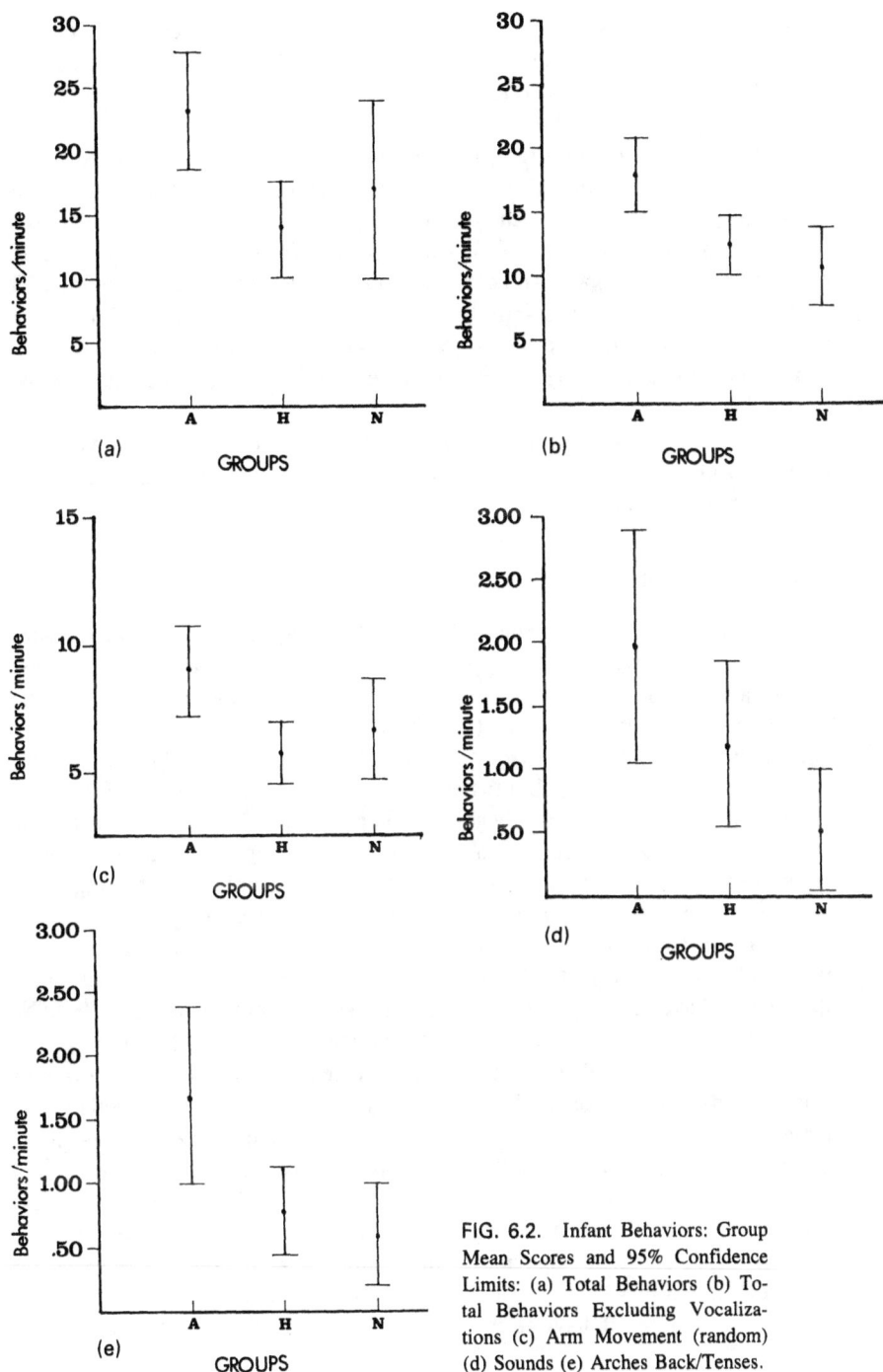

FIG. 6.2. Infant Behaviors: Group Mean Scores and 95% Confidence Limits: (a) Total Behaviors (b) Total Behaviors Excluding Vocalizations (c) Arm Movement (random) (d) Sounds (e) Arches Back/Tenses.

group is still distinguished from the Hopi on rankings of Arches Back/Tensing ($p < .02$) and Cries/Grimaces ($p < .07$). Likewise, the Anglo group is significantly different from the Navajo in Leg Movement ($p < .07$), Arches Back/Tensing ($p < .01$) and Sounds ($p < .01$).

Finally, Fig. 6.2 demonstrates the group mean scores and confidence limits for various significant infant modes. The Hopi and Navajo groups both have significantly lower scores than the Anglo group in terms of total infant behaviors excluding vocalizations ($p < .05$). Likewise the Navajo emitted significantly fewer Sounds ($p < .05$) and Arches Back/Tensing ($p < .05$) than the Anglo, with the Hopi infants showing a definite trend toward low scores in both of these modes. And, lastly, the Hopi infants show a significantly lower amount of Arm Movement than the Anglo ($p < .05$), with the Navajo having a more modest low score.

All of these test statistic measures and results demonstrate, to varying degrees, a pronounced passivity among the Hopi and Navajo infants when compared to Anglo infants.

Maternal Behaviors

Maternal group scores for various behaviors show highly significant differences (χ^2, $p < .001$) between all three groups in Total Behaviors and Vocalizations. The Navajo mothers score low in these modes, the Anglo mothers high, and the Hopi are significantly in between (see Table 6.6).

In addition to Total Behaviors and Vocalizations, the Anglo mothers use Repositions (χ^2, $p < .001$) significantly more than the Hopi mothers. Likewise, the Anglo mothers score significantly higher than the Navajo in Repositions (χ^2, $p < .001$). On the other hand, the Anglo and Navajo mothers are quite similar in the use of Tactual and Movement modes—Hopi mothers using these two modes significantly more than either of the other two groups.

Figure 6.3 shows significant group mean scores with confidence limits for maternal behaviors. At $p < .09$, the three groups distinguish themselves in terms of Total Behaviors. Anglo mothers ($\bar{X} = 48.86$) emit significantly (AxN, $p < .005$) more behaviors than the Navajo mothers ($\bar{X} = 26.87$), with the Hopi again in the middle. Likewise, the groups distinguish themselves in terms of Vocalizations: Anglo mothers have extremely high scores, Navajo mothers extremely low, and the Hopi fall significantly in the middle (AxHxN, $p < .07$). And the Anglo and Navajo mothers are significantly different in terms of the number of Repositions observed ($p < .05$)—the Hopi, with a trend toward few repositions, falling between the high Anglo group and the low Navajo group.

When expected Total Behaviors within mutual gaze periods (expected Total Behaviors in M.G. = % of sessions in M.G. × Total Behaviors) are compared with expected Total Behaviors in periods of no mutual gaze (expected Total

TABLE 6.6.
Maternal Behaviors
Comparisons of Group Maternal Behavior Scores

Mode	Groups	Scores (adjusted for time)		χ^2	p
Total behaviors	A × H	A = 2708.5	H = 2226.8	47.02	<.001
Total behaviors	A × N	A = 2708.5	N = 1539.1	321.95	<.001
Total behaviors	H × N	H = 2226.8	N = 1539.1	125.58	<.001
Total behaviors	Anglo	M.G. = 888.0	$\overline{\text{M.G.}}$ = 2236.0	.82	n.s.
within groups:	Hopi	M.G. = 710.0	$\overline{\text{M.G.}}$ = 1767.0	12.12	<.001
M.G. × $\overline{\text{M.G.}}$	Navajo	M.G. = 325.0	$\overline{\text{M.G.}}$ = 805.0	2.97	<.09
Vocalizations	A × H	A = 1377.7	H = 720.1	206.14	<.001
Vocalizations	A × N	A = 1377.7	N = 302.4	688.22	<.001
Vocalizations	H × N	H = 720.1	N = 302.4	170.63	<.001
Vocalizations	Anglo	M.G. = 535.0	$\overline{\text{M.G.}}$ = 1054.0	28.29	<.001
within groups:	Hopi	M.G. = 332.0	$\overline{\text{M.G.}}$ = 469.0	105.52	<.001
M.G. × $\overline{\text{M.G.}}$	Navajo	M.G. = 58.0	$\overline{\text{M.G.}}$ = 164.0	.02	n.s.
Repositions	A × H	A = 213.3	H = 129.5	36.93	<.001
Repositions	A × N	A = 213.3	N = 104.9	20.49	<.001
Repositions	H × N	H = 129.5	N = 104.9	2.58	n.s.
Repositions	Anglo	M.G. = 57.0	$\overline{\text{M.G.}}$ = 189.0	2.52	n.s.
within groups:	Hopi	M.G. = 17.0	$\overline{\text{M.G.}}$ = 127.0	14.38	<.001
M.G. × $\overline{\text{M.G.}}$	Navajo	M.G. = 25.0	$\overline{\text{M.G.}}$ = 52.0	1.07	n.s.
Tactual	A × H	A = 617.3	H = 723.7	8.44	<.007
Tactual	A × N	A = 617.3	N = 582.9	.99	n.s.
Tactual	H × N	H = 723.7	N = 582.9	15.17	<.001
Tactual beh.	Anglo	M.G. = 133.0	$\overline{\text{M.G.}}$ = 579.0	28.92	<.001
within groups:	Hopi	M.G. = 222.0	$\overline{\text{M.G.}}$ = 583.0	1.65	n.s.
M.G. × $\overline{\text{M.G.}}$	Navajo	M.G. = 99.0	$\overline{\text{M.G.}}$ = 329.0	2.49	n.s.
Movement	A × H	A = 500.3	H = 653.6	20.37	<.001
Movement	A × N	A = 500.3	N = 548.9	2.25	n.s.
Movement	H × N	H = 653.6	N = 548.9	9.12	<.005
Movements	Anglo	M.G. = 163.0	$\overline{\text{M.G.}}$ = 414.0	.09	n.s.
within groups:	Hopi	M.G. = 139.0	$\overline{\text{M.G.}}$ = 588.0	16.03	<.001
M.G. × $\overline{\text{M.G.}}$	Navajo	M.G. = 138.0	$\overline{\text{M.G.}}$ = 265.0	12.41	<.001

Behaviors in $\overline{\text{M.G.}}$ = % of sessions in $\overline{\text{M.G.}}$ × Total Behaviors), the Hopi mothers use significantly more behaviors in periods of mutual gaze (χ^2, $p < .001$); the Navajo mothers show a trend in that direction (χ^2, $p < .09$); and the Anglo mothers do not appear to distinguish periods of mutual gaze from periods of no mutual gaze (i.e., Total Behaviors, χ^2, M.G. × $\overline{\text{M.G.}}$: n.s.).

In terms of particular behaviors, the Anglo and Hopi mothers stress vocalization in periods when their babies are looking at them. Also, Anglo mothers use the Tactual mode—whereas Hopi mothers use the Movement mode—more often than chance in periods of $\overline{\text{M.G.}}$ (χ^2, $p < .001$). Only the Hopi mothers distinguish

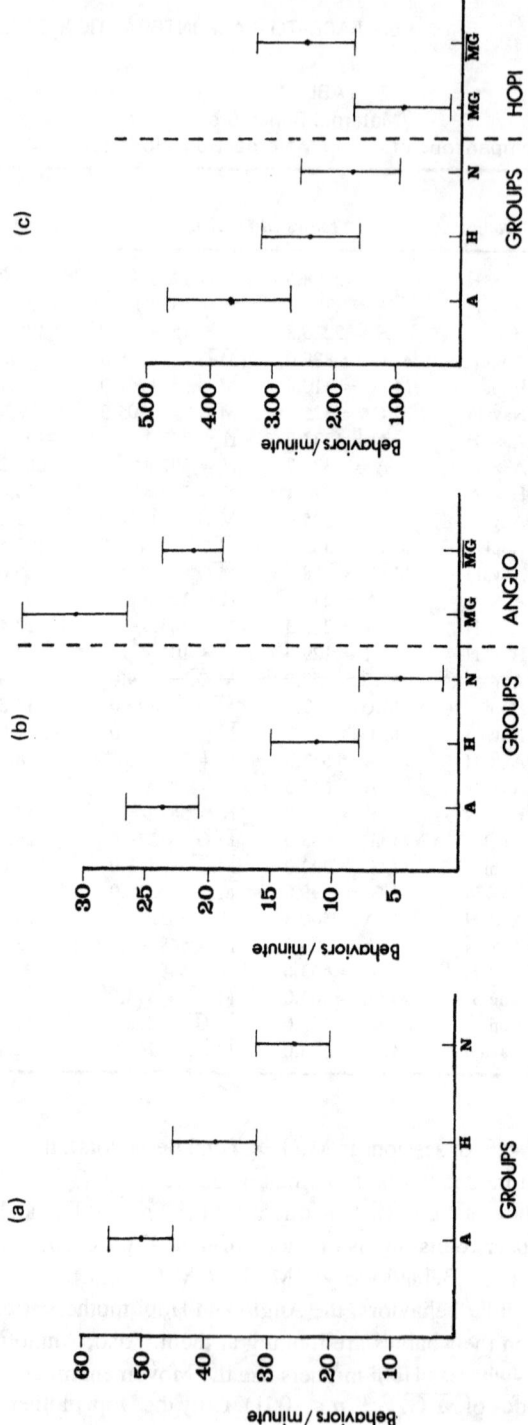

FIG. 6.3. Maternal Behaviors: Group Mean Scores and 95% Confidence Limits: (a) Total Behaviors (b) Vocalizations (c) Repositions.

between M.G. and $\overline{\text{M.G.}}$ when they use the Reposition mode (χ^2, $p < .001$)—that is, they do not reposition their infants while in mutual gaze.

The Navajo mothers do not distinguish between M.G. and $\overline{\text{M.G.}}$ in terms of the Vocalization, Reposition, and Tactual modes. However, group total scores demonstrate that they significantly use the Movement mode when their infants are looking at them (χ^2, $p < .001$).

Figure 6.3 also demonstrates the significant mean differences concerning Anglo Vocalization in M.G. vs. $\overline{\text{M.G.}}$ and Hopi Repositions in M.G. vs. $\overline{\text{M.G.}}$. The Anglo mothers have a significant preference for the use of vocalizations while their infants are attending them (M.G. × $\overline{\text{M.G.}}$; $p < .025$). Contrariwise, the Hopi mothers reposition their babies more often than chance in periods of no mutual gazing (M.G. × $\overline{\text{M.G.}}$; $p < .06$).

In summary, the Anglo mothers emit significantly more Total Behaviors than the Hopi or Navajo—particularly Vocalizations and Repositions. However, the Hopi group has a significantly higher score than either group in the Tactual and Movement modes. And, in terms of when behaviors are used, the Hopi appear to most clearly differentiate between periods of mutual gaze and no mutual gaze.

DISCUSSION

The analysis of the interactions was begun with certain hunches about the groups in mind. It was suspected that the Anglo mothers would use the greatest number of behavior modes—and use each mode more often. On the contrary, it was thought that the Navajo mothers would use the fewest number of modes. The Hopi were believed to fall somewhere in between.

As the task presented to the mothers was to get their babies' attention, how successful each group was—and for what reasons—will now be discussed. It is of utmost interest that the three groups scored almost exactly the same on the amount of time mothers and infants spent looking at each other (based on group mean statistics). There was initial speculation that two things might affect how mothers responded to the task. The presence of a camera could possibly have altered how a mother—and infant—behaved (i.e., made them more or less active). Field (1977), for example, has shown that activity level among white mothers may increase in manipulated attention getting situations. And likewise, how mothers in the different groups perceived the task might have changed their behavior; that is, mothers could have differed depending on whether they thought it was the baby who was to "perform" or whether it was they who were to be in the spotlight. However, the fact that the mutual gaze totals are almost identical for each group leads to a belief that each group did understand the instructions in essentially the same way. This, in turn, makes the data from the three groups comparable.

The infants in each group are different in ways similar to Freedman's (1974) newborn scores: Total Behaviors are less among the Hopi and Navajo infants than the Anglo; and particularly, Leg movement, Arm movement, Arching back/Tensing, and Sounds emitted are fewer. These lower group averages present a culturally average infant to the Hopi and Navajo mothers, which doubtless affects the manner in which mothers behave with their infants.

An initial prediction was that the quieter infants would correspond with less active mothers. We felt that the Navajo infants and mothers would show the most quiet interactive patterns, the Anglo group the most active, with the Hopi being in between. This trend held among maternal behaviors. The Anglo mothers are considerably more active than the Hopi and Navajo mothers—especially in Vocalizations and Repositions. However, this is not to say that the Hopi and Navajo mothers are inactive: upon close inspection of the interactions, the Hopi mothers are quite active in the Tactual and Movement modes—they bounce, jiggle, and poke at their infants more than the Anglo and Navajo mothers. The Anglo and Navajo mothers use these modes to about the same degree.

These results have shown that mothers in each group are doing things to get their infants' attention. The Anglo mothers are dealing with more active infants. This infant activity may reflect the aforementioned group newborn qualities or it may be the result of the higher activity levels of the mothers—or, what is most likely, both; cause aside, both mother and infant are demonstrably more active than the Hopi and Navajo groups.

On the basis of the macroanalyses made in a seminar at the University of Chicago, (1975) an additional set of predictions had been developed: The Anglo mothers would tend to "overstimulate" their infants; that is, do so much with their infants so as to overlook messages that the infants themselves might be sending. On the other extreme it was felt that the Navajo mothers would perhaps be more "ideal" mothers; that is, they would let their infants act according to their own agenda—looking "at" and looking "away" at will. The Hopi mothers were expected to fall somewhere in between—moderately talking and stimulating while at the same time attending to the infants' cues.

We were influenced in these predictions by certain studies of the interaction of individual mothers and infants within our own culture. Brazelton et al. (1974), in their sequential analysis of 60 second portions of ongoing interactions, suggested that interactions may be maintained for longer periods by a mother who reduces the intensity and frequency of her responses as infant attentive behavior decreases, i.e., one who allows her infant to attend at his own pace. It is therefore noteworthy that the Navajo mothers managed to get their infants' attention to the same extent as did other mothers but with a less active approach. As Navajo mothers are dealing with infants who, indeed, score low on almost all behavioral modes, might it not be that Navajo mothers have adapted their strategies to their infants' behavior? And that their strategy enables them to maintain attentive infants without a high degree of overt stimulation (through the process that Brazelton et al. describe)?

Upon a detailed analysis of these interactions, some predictions have proven wrong. Although it appears to be true that the Anglo and Navajo groups represent the extremes, the Hopi mothers represent more than a mere mix of the two. As one Hopi mother commented as she watched a set of the videotapes, the Hopi mothers "seem to be having more of a conversation with their infants than the Chicago and Navajo mothers." We can see this in the analysis of behaviors in mutual gaze vs. behaviors in no mutual gaze: in group Total Behaviors, and in all modes except Tactual (Vocalizations, Repositions, Movement), the Hopi made a significant distinction between mutual gaze on and mutual gaze off (see Table 6.6; M.G. × $\overline{\text{M.G.}}$). The mean scores and confidence limits (Fig. 6.3) for Hopi Repositions in M.G. vs. $\overline{\text{M.G.}}$ demonstrated the most significant use of any mode during periods of no mutual gaze.

The Navajo mothers, overall, showed somewhat less of a concern for when they used modes, although they did jiggle (Movement) significantly more while in mutual gaze. The Anglo group showed no *overall* significance in terms of when a behavior occurs (M.G. or $\overline{\text{M.G.}}$), although they tended to use the Tactual mode more often when infants were not looking and to vocalize more often to their infants when they were looking.

In terms of quantity the Hopi also seem to have reached a happy medium. They did stimulate their infants. They talked to their infants—not as much as Anglo mothers but more than twice as much as the Navajo. The Hopi repositioned their infants infrequently, like the Navajo, and mostly to bring the infant into mutual gaze. They used the Tactual and Movement modes more than both the Anglo and Navajo mothers. In general they seemed to use a variety of modes—but not to an overbearing degree—and this appeared to facilitate active and communicative infants that were not particularly irritable or excitable.

As the Anglo infants smiled and vocalized to a greater degree than the other groups, the Anglo mothers can be seen as most successful in communicating with their infants. However, the Arching back/Tensing mode, as well as Arm and Leg movement, point to infants who are "moving" at a comparatively high rate; this may mean they are out of synchrony with their mothers' behaviors, or it may reflect dispositional uniqueness in the infants themselves.

On the other extreme, the Navajo mothers failed perhaps to "converse" with their infants. They allowed their infants to "come and go," but at the same time they appeared to do less to maintain their infants' attention; that is, there was little active encouragement to vocalize or smile. This may be evidence of having little traditional need, and therefore experience, in the management or coercion of unattending infants.

Although the behaviors were not coded according to infant state (other than the global assessments presented in Table 6.1), several speculative observations can be made. The Navajo mothers, and to a lesser degree the Hopi mothers, appear to be more concerned with infant state than the Anglo mothers; only after the baby was in a contented mode did the Hopi and Navajo make attempts to get their babies' attention. The Anglo mothers seemed more intent on getting their infants' attention—breaking through rather than awaiting infant states that were more conducive to mutual gaze.

The analysis of mutual gaze runs (Table 6.3 and Fig. 6.1) seems to corroborate these ideas. The Hopi and Navajo have respectively fewer mutual gaze events and runs, and longer periods of mutual gaze, than the Anglo. Thus it appears that: (1) the Navajo mothers do not overstimulate; that is, they allow their infants to come and go at their own rate—thereby creating longer periods of mutual gaze. (2) The Hopi mothers communicate and respond to their infants, keeping the infants interested; this strategy, too, makes for longer periods of mutual gaze. (3) The Anglo mothers more often demand that their infants look at them—to the point of being intrusive. That the Anglo group has more numerous but shorter bursts of mutual gaze probably reflects a high rate of both infant activity and infant aversion to maternal stimulation.

CONCLUSION

Comparisons of the behaviors emitted by three different groups of mothers and infants in face-to-face interaction revealed the following:

    1. Although all three groups scored the same in total mutual gaze, the Anglo mothers and infants had significantly more, and therefore shorter, mutual gaze runs than the Navajo group; likewise, the Anglo group had more mutual gaze events than Hopi.

    2. The Anglo mothers and infants scored significantly higher than than both the Hopi and Navajo groups in Total Behaviors as well as in the majority of the coded behavioral modes.

    3. The Navajo mothers similarly scored significantly lower than the Anglo and Hopi mothers.

    4. The behaviors of the Hopi mothers were more closely related to their infants' attention (M.G. vs. $\overline{M.G.}$) than either the Anglo or Navajo groups.

In conclusion, differences (as well as similarities) between groups in mother and infant behavior have been demonstrated. In order to isolate the input of each participant in the dyadic interaction, it remains for more sophisticated research techniques to be developed. Future efforts need to emphasize the cultural and familial contexts as well as the biological factors that influence specific mother-infant interaction patterns.

ACKNOWLEDGMENTS

The author would like to thank the many persons who have assisted in the various aspects of this study: Alan Fogel, Marilyn De Boer, Danny Sage, Beth Lee, Darryl Banyacya, Ken Kaye, D. G. Freedman, Martina Callaghan, and the mothers and families whose cooperation made the entire study not only possible but enjoyable.

REFERENCES

Brazelton, T. B., Koslowski, B., & Main, M. The origins of reciprocity. In Lewis and Rosenblum, *The effect of the infant on its caregiver,* New York: Wiley, 1974.

Brazelton, T. B., & Freedman, D. G. *The Cambridge Neonatal Scales.* In J. J. van der Werff ten Bosch, (Ed.), *Normal and abnormal development of the brain.* Leiden, Netherlands: Leiden University Press, 1971.

Field, T. M. Effects of early separation, interactive deficits and experimental manipulations on infant-mother face-to-face interaction. *Child Development,* 1977, *48*(3), 763–771.

Freedman, D. G. *Human infancy: An evolutionary perspective.* N.Y.: Wiley, 1974.

Kaye, K. *The social context of infant development.* Final report to the Spencer Foundation. University of Chicago, 1979.

7
Maternal Rhythmicity in Three American Cultures

Barbara Fourcher Fajardo
Dysfunctioning Child Center
Michael Reese Hospital

Daniel G. Freedman
Committee on Human Development
University of Chicago

Research questions are ultimately formulated because the investigators are curious about something, and there is frequently a practical (or personal) motive for the curiosity, in addition to a formal theoretical one. These things are rarely discussed or mentioned in research reports; the usual course is for the authors to assume that readers will share their enthusiasm and will quickly recognize the significance of the questions addressed by the investigation. One danger of this is that the readers or listeners will become bored and frustrated, and another more significant danger is that the investigators themselves will become confused and frustrated. Cross-cultural research in particular has many exotic tinges to it, which can appeal to one's own social prejudices, and it is too easy to forget the question in the excitement aroused by the complex social contrasts observed. In the research reported here, we found it invaluable to return repeatedly to the original questions and purposes of the study, and to be continuously articulate about their formulations. Beyond simply reporting our research and findings, one objective of this chapter is to illustrate the history of the process of our inquiry.

We began with a practical problem emerging from a hospital-based intervention project for prematurely-born infant–mother dyads. The population includes both black and white patients of diverse social class. Clinically, it has become increasingly apparent that black and white mothers are very different with their babies. If we are to intervene with premature mothers to assist them in developing mothering skills, what is considered "skilled mothering" may be different for different sociobiological/ethnic populations. In order to recognize troubles the mother of a premie is having, we should know what is typical for mothers of full-term infants of the same biocultural group. It would be inappropriate to evaluate the interaction in a black dyad by standards of typical white behavior, and vice versa.

With the practical objective of discerning some dimension of "typical mothering" for black and for white dyads, the authors looked at videotapes of face-to-face interaction in white and black dyads. To add depth to the group comparison, a third group, the Navajo dyads, was added. In all of these tapes, mothers had been asked to "get the baby's attention" and were face-to-face with their 3- to 5-month-old infant.

Approximately 4 dyads of each group were scrutinized repeatedly, and two classes of graduate students also observed and commented on the salient difference among these groups: Among the many observations and speculations made, there was a concurrence that the degree of *maternal rhythmicity* varied between groups. Black mothers seemed to have a steady and regular "beat" regardless of the infant's state; white mothers' rhythms were more variable and there were more pauses in them that seemed to be related to the infants' responses; Navajo mothers seemed to have almost no "beat" at all, and were very passive and silent with their infants. The babies in all groups were equally alert.

Maternal rhythmicity was chosen for systematic cross-group study because it related to the practical purposes of the research (finding a baseline of typical mothering for evaluating premature infant–mother interaction), because it is a variable that has been studied in other research with Caucasian dyads, and because it is a variable that can be made behaviorally specific and can be reliably observed.

The choice of "maternal rhythmicity" has a further advantage in that there is literature that gives it rich connotations as an early influence on the child's development. Its significance has been proposed and substantiated in work by various investigators, notably Brazelton, Koslowski and Main (1974); Brazelton, Tronick, Adamson, Als, Weise (1975), Stern (1975), Stern and Gibbon (1979), and Stern, Beebe, Jaffe and Bennet (1977). These studies showed that during face-to-face play, mothers approach and engage their infant with rhythmic behaviors. Although definitions of rhythmicity differ somewhat among investigators, the general consensus is that regularity and predictability of maternal responses are a prerequisite for synchrony and mutuality in interaction between infant and mother. In the clinical psychiatric literature, Kestenberg (1977) describes her therapeutic interventions with pathologically interacting infant–mother pairs. She is explicit about the importance of a predictable rhythmic maternal response in providing the infant with necessary external regulation and a focus for internally organizing his own responses. Kestenberg's interventions with the mother are intended to restore or introduce "fitting" maternal rhythm so normal mutual cuing can occur between infant and mother. There is some evidence that there is a lack of successful mutual cuing in many premie infant–mother pairs (Field, 1977), and our observations suggest that this difficulty is related to irregularities in maternal rhythmicity similar to the problems described by Kestenberg in her pathological dyads.

Throughout this literature, maternal rhythmicity is considered a *sine qua non* for emergence of complex mutual cuing, for language functions, and for the development of internal regulatory functions within the infant. In the clinical literature, maternal rhythmicity is an important way that a mother conveys her steady reliable presence to her infant; by cuing her rhythmic cycles to her infant's, she sets the stage for communicative interactions (Modell, 1976) and the experience of mutuality.

The universality attributed to the importance of maternal rhythmicity in infant development is not necessarily challenged by our initial observations of biocultural differences in maternal rhythmicity. Without being inclined to dispute the developmental impact of maternal rhythmicity, it seemed worthwhile to take a more careful look at our group differences, and to more formally define and observe rhythmicity. Our impressionistic observations of biocultural group differences had to be systematically established; also, we expected that a closer examination of the nature of the differences would enrich our understanding of rhythmicity in mothering and infant development.

GROUP DIFFERENCES IN MATERNAL RHYTHMICITY

Our first hypothesis was that there would be group differences in degree of maternal rhythmicity, comparing normal full-term mother–infant pairs of American black, white and Navajo Indian groups.

Methods

"Maternal rhythmicity" came to be defined as *vocal* rhythmicity, because as we watched the tapes, other maternal behaviors such as touching and presentations of visual stimuli appeared to follow the same rhythms as maternal vocalizations. We chose to limit our coding of rhythmic behavior to vocalizations because these are more reliably coded than other behaviors. Since we wanted to score the "beat" of the vocal stimuli, the time of *peak of emphasis* was recorded. By *peak* we mean the point of greatest accentuation in vocal pitch, loudness, or inflection. Each mother received a rhythmicity score that was based on the intervals between *peaks*. This constituted the vocal "beat," which was a measure based on the frequency of peaks and the variance between them. This measure was statistically defined as the *coefficient of variation* of the intervals between peaks. It is the ratio of the standard deviation of peak-to-peak intervals to the mean peak-to-peak interval.

Subjects

There were 9 white, 9 black and 10 Navajo mother–infant pairs. The black and white infants were all 4 months of age and the Navajo infants ranged from 3- to

5-months. All pairs were videotaped in face-to-face interaction for 3 minutes or more. All tapes of each group had been made for separate studies, but were appropriate for this study because we felt they were comparable in most significant respects. Mothers were all in the same age range of about 18- to 28. Educational levels of the mothers were between 10 and 14 years. Parity and sex of infants were fairly evenly distributed. All infants had normal full-term births. Subjects were volunteers for longitudinal research projects, and all mothers knew the investigators from several previous contacts and seemed comfortable and familiar with them.

The observational setting differed for the subject groups: The white and Navajo dyads were videotaped in their own homes, whereas the black dyads were taped in an informal studio, with the infants in an infant seat. The effects of different observational contexts on dyadic interaction are not well understood, particularly for cross-cultural comparisons. However, it was our belief that the particular data we chose were not affected by these differences in observational setting.

One sampling bias was deliberately introduced by the authors. The 10 Navajo dyads in this study were not selected randomly from the available tapes; they were chosen instead on the basis of their having *some* maternal vocalization. About 25% of the videotaped Navajo dyads, from which we selected our sample, were totally *silent* with their infant, and manifested few other stimulating behaviors. They represented the extreme end of a continuum among Navajo mothers. This characteristic of our sample is consistent with observations of Navajos made by others (Freedman, 1979 & Callaghan, 1977). We felt it was justifiable to exclude the silent mothers on the basis that we are concerned not with total *amount* of vocalization, but rather with consistency of the *intervals* between peaks.

All mothers were given the same instructions, to "get your baby's attention in whatever way you wish."

Procedures

An on-line event recorder was used for coding the peaks of maternal vocal phrases. "Vocalization" was defined as *any* sound emitted from the mother's mouth. The raters observed the 3 minute tape segments in real time, and pushed a recording button each time a *peak of emphasis in voice inflection* occurred. The signal from the event recorder directly entered the computer where it was stored as raw data. Each mother received a score for rhythmicity, which was the coefficient of variation (C.V.) of the intervals between vocal peaks or "beats." (The coefficient of variation is the standard deviation divided by the mean of the intervals. The higher the C.V., the less rhythmicity.) Before calculating the coefficient of variation, the computer excluded every interval that exceeded 2 standard deviations about the mean, because we felt the irregularly lengthy intervals occurred when the mother was distracted from her infant, e.g., by another child entering the room and talking to the examiner. This actually happened rarely, but it could have distorted the scores had these events not been identified and excluded in some way.

All the tapes (N = 28) were scored by one rater, and a second rater scored 13 of them to establish reliability. Interrater reliability consisted of the correlations between the two raters' rhythmicity scores (coefficient of variation) for each mother. Interrater reliability was high (.95). Test retest (intrarater) reliability, using nine tapes, was also very high (.99).

Results

An analysis of variance, applied to mean maternal rhythmicity for the three groups, was significant ($p < .001$). The ordinate axis of the scatterplot, Fig. 7.1, shows the distribution of rhythmicity scores. It is clear that the Navajos are different (less rhythmic) from either the black or white mothers ($p < .001$). Table 7.1 shows the group means of maternal rhythmicity, and Table 7.2 shows the comparisons among the groups for maternal rhythmicity.

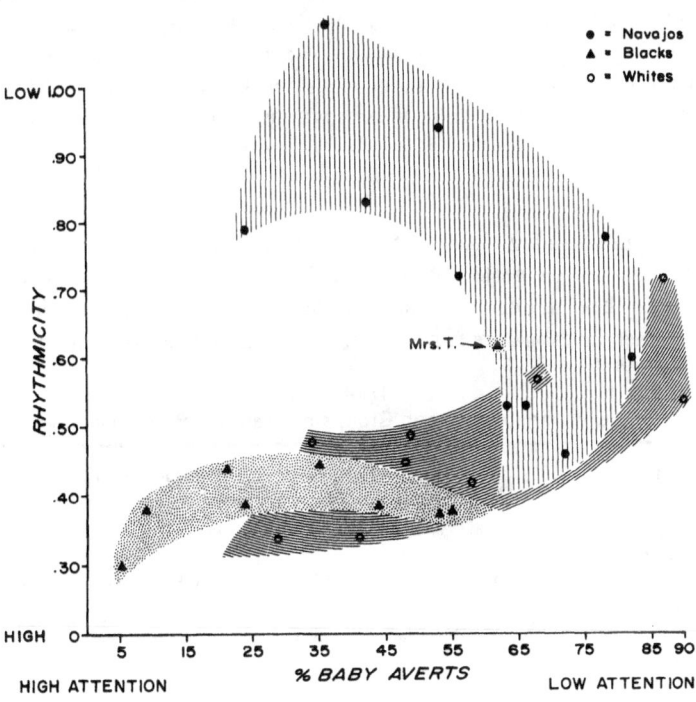

FIG. 7.1. Maternal rhythmicity and baby averting

TABLE 7.1
Means and Standard Deviations for Mother's Rhythmicity and Infant's Averting

	Mothers' Rhythmicity (CV)		Infants' Averting	
Group	Mean	S.D.	Mean	S.D.
Black (n = 9)	.41	.09	.33	.19
Black (excluding Mrs. T) (n = 8)	.39	.45	.30	.18
White (n = 9)	.48	.12	.56	.22
Navajo (n = 10)	.73	.20	.57	.19

The difference between the black and white groups was not significant. However, the scatterplot of Fig. 7.1 shows a strong trend toward a difference. The distribution of scores within the black group shows one mother (noted as Mrs. T. in Fig. 7.1) as an exception to the rest of the black mothers. This particular mother is much less rhythmic than other black mothers, and less rhythmic than all but one white mother. If Mrs. T. is excluded, then the variance of the black group is reduced by 74%, a significant decrease of variance ($F = 3.81, p < .05$). The whites have almost seven times as much within-group variance as this reduced black group ($F = 6.86, p < .01$). A comparison (done in isolation of the Navajo group) of this more homogeneous black group with the white group shows a significant difference in mean rhythmicity ($t = 2.08, p < .03$).

Discussion

The Navajo mothers are clearly different than the black and the white mothers. The interpretation suggested here is that Navajo mothers do not make active efforts to get their infants to interact with them. This is consistent with observations by other investigators (Freedman, 1979). Callaghan presents data in this

TABLE 7.2
Comparisons Among Groups on Maternal Rhythmicity

Comparison	Name of Test	Test Statistic Value	p value
C.V.'s of 3 groups	ANOVA	$F(2,29) = 12.25$	.001
Blacks (including Mrs. T) vs. Whites	ANOVA (variance ratio)	$F(8,8) = 1.80$	n.s.
Whites vs. Blacks (excluding Mrs. T)	ANOVA (variance ratio)	$F(8,7) = 6.86$	.01
Blacks (excluding Mrs. T.) vs. Whites	t-test	$t(15) = 2.08$	.03

volume and reviews other studies indicating that Navajo mothers have a low level of maternal activity compared to mothers of other biocultural groups.

As mentioned earlier in this chapter, there is a widely-held notion that optimal maternal stimulation of the infant is basic for his or her development. According to this notion, during an interaction the mother's steady and consistent stimulation of the infant provides an interesting but nonjarring context for the infant to tune into and to use as an external focus for regulating his own states. These ideas need refinement in view of the silent and passive Navajo mothering patterns. There is evidence (reviewed by Freedman & DeBoer, 1979) that Navajo and other Oriental newborns, and Navajos especially, are born with greater capacities for self-soothing and self-regulation than infants of other biocultural groups. These data lead to the speculation that the Navajo mothers' silence and lack of rhythmic stimulation are suited to her infant's greater congenital capacities for self-regulation. Silent passive Navajo maternal behavior could interact with the self-soothing, well-regulated infant in a comfortable optimal fashion. In face-to-face paradigms, Navajo infants spend the same total amount of time gazing at mother as do Caucasian infants (Callaghan, J. W., reported by Freedman, 1979), but their attending to mother does not require the mothers to stimulate them. This "fit" is perhaps an important ingredient in producing notable Navajo characteristics of "coolness" and reluctant eye contact in adult interpersonal interaction. Apparently the Navajo infant learns to use something other than deliberately presented maternal rhythms as organizing stimuli, and instead must use more subtle aspects of maternal behavior as a basis for interpersonal mutuality. The voiceless, relatively impassive maternal face is as attractive (measured by total time gazing at mother) for a Navajo infant as are the talkative mobile faces that white and black infants experience.

Regarding the black and white comparison, we wondered why the black mothers were so much more homogeneous than the white mothers, and why the one black mother (Mrs. T.) was an outlier. When we reviewed the tapes again, it appeard that Mrs. T's infant was less attentive to her than other black infants were to their mothers, and Mrs. T. appeared bored and restless. However, when we looked at the white tapes, many of those babies seemed as low or lower in attentiveness than Mrs. T.'s baby. In these cases as well as in others where there was more infant attentiveness, the white mothers' rhythmicity and involvement with their infants were not apparently as affected by infant inattentiveness. We speculated that perhaps rhythmicity for both black and white groups of mothers was positively correlated with infants' attentiveness, but that black and white mothers may respond differently with a baby who has a high level of averting. Further, it seemed, because of much greater homogeneity of maternal rhythmicity among black mothers, that the relationships between mother's and baby's behavior would be less strong for the black than for the white groups.

To explore these questions the next step was to code the tapes for infant averting.

RELATIONSHIPS BETWEEN INFANT AVERTING AND MATERNAL RHYTHMICITY

Our second hypothesis was that maternal rhythmicity would be negatively correlated with infant averting from mother, and that there may be no differences between groups on the magnitude of correlations. We deliberately speak here of a correlation, avoiding hypotheses about the direction of effect (as to whether mother's behavior was causing baby's or vice versa).

Method and Procedure

Infants' "averting" from mother was chosen as the variable, rather than "attentiveness," because as we coded the infants' behavior, "averting" was a more easily recognized behavior. Averting was defined as the infant turning eyes away from mother's face or from the activity or object she was presenting to him.

Coding the tapes for infant averting was done by the same raters as before, and the same computer system and push-button apparatus was used. There were 5 buttons, each of which corresponded to the 5 possible mutually exclusive behaviors of the infant:

1. infant brightly regards (visually) mother's face,
2. infant neutrally regards mother's face,
3. infant brightly regards or responds to an activity or object presented by mother (e.g., patty-cake game, during which the infant could be looking away from mother and delightedly laughing),
4. infant neutrally regards an activity/object presented by mother (e.g., he indifferently gazes at mother's fingers snapping),
5. infant averts from mother's face or things she is doing and presenting to him by actively turning away.

The rater pushed the button that corresponded to the proper category as soon as he or she judged the infant to have shifted into another behavior. The total time the infant spent in each behavior category was computed, and then was converted to percent of total interaction time to correct for some differences in tape length. Interrater reliability was high for all categories, based on the correlation of each rater's scores for percent time in each category (12 tapes were coded by both raters for the interrater reliability check). The reliability for percent time averting (total scored for each infant) was .94. The final data were the scores based on the coding by the one rater who had coded all 28 tapes (B.F.).

For the study reported here, only the scores of percent averting (category #5) have been used. Each infant received a score of percent time averting mother as an indicator of his typical state of attention during the 3-minute taped sequence.

Results

Black vs. White groups. Figure 7.1 is scatterplot of the data from the dyads showing the relationship between maternal rhythmicity and infant averting. (Note that high infant attention is to the left of the horizontal axis, and high maternal rhythmicity is the bottom of the vertical axis.) Table 7.3 presents the correlation and *t*-test values for the significant group comparisons.

The correlations are positive for both black and white groups, as predicted (black group $r = +.55, p < .062$; white group $r = +.80, p < .007$), suggesting that there is *less* infant averting (i.e., more attending) in the presence of more maternal rhythmicity. (A high number for rhythmicity translates as *low* rhythmicity, because as the ratio of the mean and standard deviation (C.V.) approaches 1, the variance is less regularly proportionate to the mean.) Although both correlations are positive, the magnitude of the relationship is different for each group (see Table 7.3). The correlation between mother and infant behavior for black dyads is not significant whereas it is for the white dyads. Compared to white infants, black infants avert from mother with less dependence on the mother's vocal rhythmicity. Considering the infant behavior, black infants do less averting (33%) than white infants (56%), and the difference is significant ($t = 2.37, p < .02$).

Navajo group. Navajo dyads are clearly different from both white and black groups; the correlation between Navajo maternal rhythmicity and infant averting is significant and *negative* ($r = -.63, p < .03$). The more rhythmic Navajo mothers have *more* averting infants, whereas among the black and white groups the more rhythmic mothers have *less* averting infants. This is the most striking group difference found so far, along with the result that Navajo mothers are significantly lower in rhythmicity than the other two groups. It is noteworthy also that the total amount of averting by Navajo infants (57%) is almost the same as

TABLE 7.3
Comparisons Among Groups on Infant's Averting

Comparison	Name of Test	Test Statistic Value	p – value
Black Maternal Rhythmicity and % baby avert	Pearson r (n = 7)	r = .55	.06
White Maternal Rhythmicity and % baby avert	Pearson r (n = 7)	r = .80	.007
Navajo Maternal Rhythmicity and % baby avert	Pearson r (n = 8)	r = –.63	.03
Black baby avert vs. White baby avert	t-test	t (16) = 2.37	.02

among white babies (56%) who, in contrast, have mothers who are much more rhythmic and stimulating. It seems that what Navajo mothers do that is successful in engaging babies' attention is to be quiet and *not* be rhythmic.

Discussion

Black and white dyads are more similar to each other, in that for both groups, the highly rhythmic mothers have the *less* averting babies. Navajo dyads are different in that the more rhythmic mothers have babies who avert *more*. Faced with this great discrepancy between Navajos and the other two groups, it would be tempting to interpret our findings to mean that black and white dyads are from a homogeneous population and that the Navajo dyads are from another population. However, there is cause to doubt whether the black and white groups are really homogeneous; it seems more congruent with more detailed examination of the findings to think these are three quite distinct groups as far as the covariance of maternal rhythmicity and infant averting.

Black vs. White dyads. Just as Mrs. T. stands out from the rest of the black group on the measure of maternal rhythmicity, she and her infant also stand out from the rest of the otherwise relatively homogeneous group on the scatterplot of Fig. 7.1, where correlations between maternal rhythmicity and baby's averting are shown. All the other black mothers resemble each other by manifesting high maternal rhythmicity, with Mrs. T. apart from the group with the least rhythm. Her baby is also the most averting baby of the group. Possible interpretations of this outlier are as follows:

1. This may be a spurious random variation (individual differences, etc.) not related to biocultural group membership. Because of small sample size, it is difficult to assess this.

2. Alternatively, Mrs. T. and her baby's position regarding the rest of the black group can be interpreted as a meaningful variation; Mrs. T. might be representative of a sub-group of black mothers who are faced with an infant who is especially unresponsive and inattentive to efforts to engage them. Mrs. T. may have "turned off" (became nonrhythmic) to her infant when he became inattentive, compared to other black mothers whose rhythmicity continued despite their infants' (albeit much less) averting. Mrs. T.'s infant averted her 57% of the time, compared to other black mothers whose babies averted a mean of 30%. Mrs. T.'s "turning off" could have been a reaction to her infant's high averting.

We wondered if black mothers more than white mothers generally persist in rhythmic stimulation *in spite* of infant averting; however, if it goes beyond a certain point of difficulty for mother to engage her infant, i.e., when the infant averts too much, a black mother will "give up," resulting in lowered rhythmicity. Mrs. T.'s infant may have been so highly averting that it exceeded mother's capacity to sustain her own rhythmicity.

The suggestion that black and white mothers differ in their persistence with averting babies is given weight by the greater homogeneity in maternal rhythmicity among blacks compared to whites, and by the greater magnitude of relationship between rhythmicity and baby averting in whites compared to blacks. Black mothers are highly rhythmic with less regard for their babies attentiveness. Maybe black mothers in our experimental task are more involved with "being an interesting mother," i.e., their *own* performances, than with responding to the baby and *his* cues. White mothers are more concerned with getting the *baby* to perform, and hence are more responsive to the baby's cues. White mothers often try *harder* (become more rhythmic) to engage their infants when the infant averts; on the other hand, the black mothers do *not* change their approach when the infant averts, unless the infant is so extremely averting that mother (e.g., Mrs. T.) gets discouraged. Black mothers' initial persistence could have a payoff in often eventually capturing the infant's attention when at first he showed minimal attentiveness. White mothers, on the other hand, are more deterred from rhythmicity by their infant's averting, and "give up" sooner than black mothers do, thereby losing some opportunities to eventually capture the infant's attention.

Speculating about direction of effects between our measures of mothers' and infants' behaviors, it seems that black and white mothers are affected differently by their infants' averting, which is tantamount to saying that they respond differently to "failures" in engaging their babies. Black mothers display a rhythmicity that does not fluctuate significantly with variations in infant responsiveness, until a point where the infant is exceedingly averting. They will continue trying to engage their infant in spite of his manifesting great disinterest. In contrast, white mothers are more likely to sooner interrupt their approach to the infant and to become less rhythmic when their infant is unresponsive. White mothers, in this sense, are more sensitive to their failure to engage the infant, and while this may result in losing some opportunities for engagement, it also permits the infant more initiative to disengage.

These interpretations must remain in the realm of hypotheses for further testing. They require sequential analysis of the mother–infant interaction, and these matters of sequence and timing of mutually-cued behaviors cannot be addressed with the present data.

Navajo dyads. The major findings for the Navajo were the low maternal rhythmicity, and the negative correlation between maternal rhythmicity and infant averting. Attempting to find a suitable explanation for this, we looked again at our tapes. We noticed that for Navajo dyads, a "successful" interaction, manifested by longer periods of infant attentiveness to mother, occurred when both partners were silently looking at each other. A "successful" interaction, for black and white dyads (especially black dyads) was when there was more excitement, where both partners were noisy and expressing lots of emotion. In Navajo dyads, there is a tendency for rhythmicity to take place when the infant is averting from the mother. However, when the infant attends, the mother stops her rhythmic behavior. Efforts made by Navajo mothers to engage their infants' attention are very low-key and sometimes seem nonexistent; i.e., they typically do not speak at all, or make nearly inaudible sounds.

Summary and Discussion

Our comparison of black, white and Navajo mothers substantiates the initial hypothesis that there are biocultural differences in how mothers act with their babies. Combining our findings reported here with our informal observations, we will now summarize the characteristics of mother–infant interaction for each group:

White mothers appear to use rhythm or peak voice inflections to prod the infant into engagement and to sustain interaction with her, but when their infants persistently avert, the mothers pause, perhaps to permit their infants a "rest" before returning again to their rhythmic behavior. White mothers try to get the infant to perform, and will try lots of things to get this to happen. Sometimes these mothers are intrusive, and white infants seem to have a lower tolerance for intrusive stimulation than infants of the other two groups, and spend much time looking away from mother, as if to reduce the impact of her stimulation.

Black mothers, like white mothers, also use rhythm to prod the infant into engagement with her and to sustain it. Unlike white mothers, black mothers will continue their rhythmic approach despite their baby's turning away, until the infant's averting becomes especially pronounced. At this point, black mothers may disengage, stop rhythmic approaches, and lose interest in the interaction entirely. Unlike white mothers, black mothers are less easily discouraged by the infant's averting, and do not permit so many "rest periods" initiated by the infant. But the black mother's loss of interest does occur with an infant who is *highly* averting, and then her loss of interest is more abrupt and complete than the white mother's. Black mothers seem to put on a performance for the infant, and invite him to join. If the infant is not a responsive audience, the mother loses interest and leaves the baby alone. Whereas the black mothers are highly stimulating, they do not seem as intrusive as white mothers because their rhythmicity is not as much a response to infant nonattentiveness as to their *own* interest and pleasure in performing for the baby. Black infants seem to have a high tolerance for stimulation, and do not turn away from their mothers' intensified rhythmic displays like white infants sometimes do. Instead, they appear to find it interesting.

Navajo mothers use rhythm as a device to get baby's attention, but not nearly as consistently as white and black mothers do. In contrast to black and white mothers, Navajos do not use rhythm to sustain an interaction; once the baby is engaged, mother stops any rhythmic stimulation and lets the baby be entirely "in charge" of the interaction. Navajo mothers are much more tolerant of their baby's not attending to her, and will less often distract him from his other-directed interests in order to get his attention on herself. Navajo mothers' respect for baby's initiative and choices of what to focus interest upon far exceeds such respect among black and white mothers. Navajo infants appear very easy-going and seem to attend to things more steadily and for longer periods of time than infants of either of the other groups. This observation is congruent with Callaghan's findings, reported in this volume, that Navajo infants have extended periods of attending and averting to mothers, compared to Caucasian infants who have short bursts of attending and averting.

Turning to the literature on congenital differences among infants of these three groups (Freedman, 1974; Hopkins, 1976), there is evidence that suggests a "good fit" is made between typical maternal and typical newborn behaviors for each biocultural group. According to the findings reported by these authors, Caucasian neonates have a lower tolerance for stimulation, and are more irritable. Black neonates are more mature, have a higher tolerance for stimulation and are less irritable. Navajo neonates are of a more placid disposition, are less irritable, and more capable of organizing their own responses (self-soothing) without structuring by the caretaker. These group differences observed in infants' inborn capacities for tolerating and organizing stimulation fit optimally with the differences in maternal rhythmicity and styles reported in this paper.

We have spoken here as if maternal rhythmicity is the same thing as maternal stimulation. This is clearly an oversimplification of a very complex matter; *what is stimulating* for one infant may be soothing for another, and what is optimally interesting (and organizing) for some may be overwhelming to others. Perhaps if we assume that the above ethnic differences consist largely of mothers adapting to differences in their babies, consistent rhythm is optimally stimulating for black infants, whereas shifting rhythms might be optimally stimulating and interesting for white infants. Further complicating the matter, the *source of maternal stimulation* does not have to be in the context of a directed mutual interpersonal exchange, where mother and infant become engaged and disengaged in a back-and-forth "dialogue." The source of stimulation may not be mother herself at all, but instead a variety of other things (that may include mother) that the infant fixates on. Thus, among Navajos, the mother's function may not be to stimulate, but to support and facilitate the infants' initiative in seeking other environmental stimulation.

Optimal stimulation is that which is interesting to the infant, so that he does not avert in the frustration of too much or too little stimulation. Optimal stimulation provides the infant with a context for organizing himself. "Maternal rhythmicity," as we have used it in this chapter, is one way a mother has of expressing her sense of what is optimally stimulating and organizing for her baby. It is a way of helping him be interested and engaged.

Among other things, these findings, questions and issues have implications for learning more about what is problematic for premature infant–mother dyads. What mothers do to encourage engagement or to permit disengagement of their full-term infants will tell us something about how similar mothers manage an infant who might be immature and physiologically and socially poorly organized. Given the fact that a premature infant is especially sensitive to being under or over-stimulated, our findings about biocultural group differences in maternal rhythmicity lead us to expect biocultural group differences in problems mothers may have with premature infants. It would be predicted that black mothers will be initially persistently rhythmic in an interaction, but will soon become disinterested themselves when the infant cannot respond by "watching" or joining their "performance." White mothers will be initially rhythmic and, like the black mothers, will pause when the infant is unresponsive, but then will return quickly to a rhythmic approach to begin a new attempt to engage the infant. The black mother runs a greater risk of *understimulating* her premature infant, leaving him alone when he is unresponsive (to her performance). The white mother runs the risk of being intrusive and *overstimulating* when her infant is incapable of responding (by performing himself). Field (1980), comparing black and white premature infant-mother interactions, reported differences compatible with our predictions. The Navajo mother of a premature infant is predicted to *understimulate,* perhaps not providing the infant with enough opportunities to experience her as soothing and organizing, relying on his still underdeveloped self-organizing capacities. This is but one example of the possible implications of such ethnic contrasts for various developmental issues.

ACKNOWLEDGMENTS

The authors gratefully acknowledge Kenneth Kaye, Ph.D., University of Chicago, for the use of his videotaped data for the Caucasian group. We also acknowledge the participation of Nell Logan, Ph.D., University of Illinois Medical Center, in the collection of videotaped data for the black group.

REFERENCES

Brazelton, T., Koslowski, B., & Main, M. The origins of reciprocity: The early mother–infant Interaction. In M. Lewis & L. Rosenblum (Eds.), *The effect of the infant on its caregiver.* New York: Wiley, 1974.

Brazelton, T., Tronick, E., Adamson, L., Als, H., & Weise, S. Early mother–infant reciprocity. In M. A. Hofer (Ed.), *Parent–Infant Interaction,* Ciba Foundation Symposium #33, New York: Elsevier, 1975.

Callaghan, J. W. *Anglo, Hopi and Navajo mothers' face-to-face interactions with their infants.* M. A. Thesis, University of Chicago, 1977.

Field, T. Effects of early separation, interactive deficits and experimental manipulations on infant–mother face-to-face interaction. *Child Development*, 1977, *48*, 763–771.

Field, T. M. Interactions of preterm and term infants with their lower and middle class teenage and adult mothers. In T. Field, S. Goldberg, D. Stern & A. Sostek (Eds.), *High-risk infants and children: Adult and peer interactions.* New York: Academic Press, 1980.

Freedman, D. *Human infancy: An evolutionary perspective.* Hillsdale, New Jersey: Lawrence Erlbaum Associates, 1974.

Freedman, D. *Human Sociobiology.* New York: The Free Press, 1979.

Freedman, D. G., & DeBoer, M. Biological and cultural differences in early child development. *Annual Review of Anthropology*, 1979, *8*, 579–600.

Hopkins, B. *Considerations of comparability of measures in cross-cultural studies of early infancy from a study on the development of black and white infants living in Britain.* Paper presented at the Third International Association of Cross-Cultural Psychology Congress, Child Development Symposium, Tilburg, July 1976.

Kestenberg, J. Prevention, infant therapy, and the treatment of adults. *International Journal of Psychoanalytic Psychotherapy*, 1977, *6*, 339–396.

Modell, A. The holding environment and the therapeutic action of psychoanalysis. *Journal of the American Psychoanalytic Association*, 1976, *24*, 285–308.

Stern, D. Vocalizing in unison and in alternation. *Annals of New York Academy of Science*, 1975, *263*, 89–100.

Stern, D., & Gibbon, J. Temporal expectancies of social behaviors in mother–infant play. In E. Thoman (Eds.), *Origins of the infant's social responsiveness.* Hillsdale, New Jersey: Lawrence Erlbaum Associates, 1979.

Stern, D., Beebe, B., Jaffe, J., & Bennet, S. L. The infant's stimulus world during social interaction. In R. Schaffer (Eds.), *Studies on interactions in infancy.* New York: Academic Press, 1977.

8 Mother-Infant Interaction Among the Gusii of Kenya

Suzanne Dixon
University of California, San Diego

Edward Tronick
University of Massachusetts, Amherst

Constance Keefer
T. Berry Brazelton
Children's Hospital Medical Center, Boston

INTRODUCTION

The daily interaction between an infant and his caregivers has been hypothesized as the process through which the infant develops a sense of himself as a separate person of family and of culture (Kohut, 1971; Whiting & Whiting, 1975). Caudill and Weinstein (1969) demonstrated how cultural values infused and shaped the interactions of Japanese and American mothers and their infants. Japanese mothers saw their infants as independent biological beings that had to be incorporated into the culture and made interdependent. American mothers saw their infants as dependent beings who had to be helped to become independent. Specific infant-mother interactions during the course of daily caretaking reflected these cultural expectations. For example, Japanese mothers slept with their infants, fed them and performed caretaking activities on a sleeping infant while American infants most often slept alone. Sleep, as a sign of independence, was seldom interrupted. In both cultures the infants were the unknowing focus of the universal process of gaining a culture-specific sense of self.

One segment of caretaking patterns that has become the focus of recent research is infant–caretaker face-to-face playful interaction (Brazelton, Koslowski, and Main, 1974; Stern, 1974b). Face-to-face interaction makes up only a small proportion of an infant's experience but it is thought to be a particularly significant and intimate form of interaction. There are several reasons for this:

Firstly, because of its intimacy, it becomes the earliest and most basic form of communication and one in which the infant can develop the capacity to regulate the behavior of others. He or she learns the rules of joint regulation of interchanges with people in general, providing him with an expectancy for social responsiveness to his own behavior (Tronick, Als, and Brazelton, 1977). Secondly, speech and conversation are thought to be based on face-to-face interaction and becomes a developmental product of it (Tronick, Als, & Adamson, 1979). Sophisticated capacities essential to affective and cognitive development are built upon the structure that can be seen in the face-to-face situation. Finally, the infant in the enface position learns the language of emotional expression, his own and others'. Most importantly (Tronick et al., 1977) the infant grows to understand the mutual effects of these emotional expressions, and upon these mutual exchanges his or her sense of attachment is first formed.

The structure of infant–adult exchanges has been described in some detail (Als, Tronick, & Brazelton, 1979; Tronick, Als, & Brazelton, 1980). Positive states of dyadic interaction characterized by smiles and vocalizations cycle and alternate among neutral and negative states; the latter are exemplified by fusses, pouts, frowns and cry faces for the infant, and neutral or sober expressions for the adult (Brazelton et al., 1974). The rhythmic nature of these interactions is seen in the behavior of both infant and caregiver. Furthermore, the movement within the interaction is characterized by both partners changing state together in order to achieve greater synchrony of affective states rather than by one partner leading or following the other (Brazelton, Tronick, Adamson, Als, & Wise, 1975). This mutual regulation of the interaction can be seen when the structure of the interaction is examined microscopically. The structure has been characterized as dialogic, conversational, or synchronous. Infants as young as one month can participate in this mutuality in interaction with familiar adults. Even within the caretaking unit, the infant can participate in the specific joint regulation of the interaction with different partners in accordance with the goals and expectations for these differing interactions (Dixon, Yogman, Tronick, Brazelton, in press; Yogman, 1977). Interactions with unfamiliar people lack this essential conversational quality.

Prior to this volume, almost all of the studies of face-to-face interaction had been of American, English and other Western European mother–infant pairs. Exceptions might be the ethological descriptions of caretaker infant interaction, for example, the observational studies of Konner (1977) on the !Kung and Goldberg (1972) on the Zambians. But these descriptive studies were not subjected to detailed microbehavioral analyses of the structure of the interactions.

The study reported here on the mother–infant face-to-face interaction among the Gusii is aimed at beginning to decipher the structure within these cross-cultural observations. This attempt to bring these basic observations under more careful scrutiny was designed to answer specific questions on both universal and culture-specific aspects of early mother–infant interaction: Would such interactions show a cyclic structure? Would they have both dialogic and synchronous structural elements, and which would predominate? Would the systems of analysis designed in this culture allow complete analysis of the interactions in another (how ethnocentric is the system itself)? What was the nature of the mutuality achieved in the interaction and how was it achieved? Who led and who followed? Could one see from the elements of the interaction the goals of the partners? In what way might these goals reflect culture-specific expectations for infants and the socialization of children in general? Our thoughts were that the structural elements—the nature of the behavioral displays, the cycling of affective states, the dialogic and synchronous structure—would all be found in these interactions and would represent their universality, whereas their quantity and the signal value of the elements of negotiation—who leads, who follows, the signal behaviors represented, the evidence of goal direction—would reflect culture-specific elements.

The Gusii

The Gusii are a Bantu-speaking agricultural minority tribe living in the densely populated highlands of southwestern Kenya. Ethnographic material has been collected over the past 50 years and provides some detail on all aspects of life (LeVine & LeVine, 1966; Mayer, 1951). Clan affiliation is the basis of patrilineal, patrilocal patterns of living and allows for the cultivation of small plots of land in cooperation with members of an extended family. Tribal survival and the smooth functioning of clan units is monitored by elders working under traditional systems of rules for the settlement of disputes, the inheritance of land, the enforcement of moral behavior, and the adherence to ritual (LeVine & LeVine, 1966). The goal for each person is to fit into the modal role of a hard worker in tilling the soil, to meet the expectations of the kinship system of obligations and to raise children with these same expectations (LeVine, 1980a).

The patterns of social interchange are governed by implicit rules for every situation. These serve to make clear age and sex divisions among tribe members and to avoid the display of any intense affect, as it is seen as a possible disruptive force. The face-to-face situation may call up strong feelings, hence it is particularly regulated. Conversation can be uncoupled from gaze in the enface position and often is. A typical adult-adult interaction often occurs with completely averted gaze. Conversations occur with the participants at a 90° or greater angle to each other. Interactions of adjacent generations and cross-sex partners (e.g., mother-son, father-in-law/daughter-in-law) call up the most strict restrictions on face-to-face interaction. The buildup of either positive or negative feeling is avoided in this manner.

The power of gaze in interpersonal relationships is seen in the elaborate Gusii belief system built upon concepts of the "evil eye" and the danger of being seen at vulnerable periods of life (S. LeVine, 1979). Some individuals, usually women, are said to be afflicted with the capacity to bring illness or misfortune to children by simply looking upon these young ones, and thereby affecting incorporation of small particles normally present on the skin. Children can be protected from this "evil eye" by certain practices such as wearing small charms, etc. (LeVine, 1963). Although only a few people are unfortunate enough to inflict this specific injury on children, the danger in being looked at directly by anyone seems to be a constant theme behind many beliefs and practices (S. LeVine, 1979; R. A. LeVine, 1980).

Rituals among the Gusii reflect the dangerous aspect of gaze. For example, practices proscribed at the birth of premature infants, ceremonies of circumcision for young boys and girls, reconciliations and rituals of funerals, all include seclusion of a vulnerable person, protecting that individual from being seen during an important life transition. Interestingly, the danger for the weakened person is thought to be most severe from close relatives and neighbors. These individuals may harbor jealousness and resentments, leading them to invoke sorcery or witchcraft directed at their kin. One requires the most protection from persons most closely related by kinship and physical proximity.

Greeting behavior among the Gusii is also strictly governed, with proscribed forms and sequences demanded in any encounter, no matter how familiar the person or how frequent the meeting. "Slips" or "mistakes" in the regularity of these exchanges would lead to interpersonal tension, embarrassment, and apprehension. There is some suggestion that this greeting behavior as well as other ritualistic practices are increasing in importance among the Gusii rather than decreasing (R. A. LeVine, 1980b).

These practices and beliefs among the Gusii are in marked contrast to our own culture's emphasis on face-to-face encounters. We believe that eye-to-eye contact is universally and absolutely necessary for affective communication. In fact, in our culture, gaze avoidance is seen as a violation of mutual trust and arouses suspicion of malintent or insincerity.

Early parent–child relationships among the Gusii are characterized by avoidance of eye-to-eye contact and restraint in playful interactions. The almost continuous physical contact between the mother and her infant does not encourage other kinds of social intimacy, because the infant is rarely held in a face-to-face posture and, therefore, does not often achieve eye-to-eye contact (R. A. LeVine, 1979). Affectionate and social behaviors are rarely directed toward the baby, nor is the infant regarded as capable of communicative intent other than to signal hunger or distress (LeVine & LeVine, 1966; New, 1979). The mother sees her job as one to respond to these signals appropriately, and to safeguard the cleanliness and health of her infant. Enhancing social development or cognitive growth are not part of her culture-specific parental goals. The long-term adaptiveness of these norms in late childhood and adulthood can be seen in maintenance of incest taboos and strict discipline. Extended to infancy and early childhood, these practices may be protective for both partners in a culture where infant mortality has been high. Mothers may have needed a ritualized method to dampen the intensity of their feelings for infants they may lose. These deeply engrained beliefs are absorbed by young children early in life and are manifest in their own behaviors. In their extensive comparative analysis of the behavior of children from six cultures, the Whitings (Whiting & Whiting, 1975) found the Gusii children to be the least attention seeking of all children studied. The regulation and diffusion of direct face-to-face contact becomes part of their behavioral repertoire very early.

In a series of "naturalistic" observations (coded in the home by trained native observers with a technique adapted from Clarke-Stewart (1973), insights into the social environment of the infant have been summarized. Gusii infants with a median age of 12 months or less are held on an average of 58% of the time (Hitchcock, 1979). The mean level of holding drops to 18% when the median age is 12- to 20-months. Before 5 months mothers held their babies over half of the time, but after that less than half of this holding was attributed to mothers; the rest to child-caretakers of 5- to 8-years of age (omereri). Young children are assigned care for infants in order to allow mothers to return to crop cultivation or housework. Only in families where the father's income was low and there was little land for the mother to till, was the mother the sole caretaker; in these cases she held her baby 70–80% of the time (Hitchcock, 1979).

Looking directly at their infants was represented in a range of 2–21% of the mothers' behaviors at 3 months, but by 6 months it represented less than 10% of all interactional behaviors (New, 1979). Talking to infants at 3 months was even less and varied from 0–10% seen in all responses. A mother is likely to respond to cries or demands of an infant but not to initiate or to respond to contented vocalizations. Using as a comparative base, the mean proportion of all caretaker behaviors in response to contented infant behaviors, mothers at both 3 and 6 months appeared to initiate less than did other caretakers. However they did respond more to their infants' cries and demands than did other caretakers. Maternal responsiveness to less than 10% of 3-month-old infant vocalizations as opposed to 50% responses to fret or cries, conforms to the Gusii belief that infants are not regarded as capable of social interactions (LeVine, 1963; New, 1979). As infants are held on the hip or back most of the time, this allows for little enface interaction. Communication appears to be mediated through touch rather than gaze. The infant's social experience is bounded by the demands of external circumstances (e.g., mother's work) and is based on the child's vegetative needs rather than his need for social stimulation. Mutual regulation of social interaction is seen as neither possible nor desirable.

In short, Gusii babies were not being exposed to the same type of social experience, nor do the mothers have the same goals as are present in our culture. Gusii babies were rarely played with in a face-to-face situation. This caretaking pattern then, seems to be a way of visualizing cultural norms for interpersonal communication, as well as of defining the particular expectations for mothers and their infants.

METHOD OF STUDY

Videotapes of face-to-face interactions of Gusii infants and their mothers from a single market area were analyzed. These mothers and infants were part of a larger multifaceted, longitudinal study of parenting and early child development.

Because of the semitropical climate and living arrangements of the Gusii, most of the taping was done out-of-doors at the homes of the subjects. In a typical outdoor filming arrangement, the infant was seated in an American infant seat with the mother seated or kneeling on the ground in front of him (Fig. 8.1). An assistant held a tarpaulin curtain to "contain" the interaction and to decrease distracting stimuli. Another assistant held up a mirror with which to reflect the mother's image on the camera. This allowed one video camera to record a face-to-face image of both mother and infant. The video camera and microphone were placed about 15 feet from the interacting pair. Figure 8.2 demonstrates the resultant video image.

The mothers were instructed in this situation, as in the American laboratory situation, to "talk to your baby," "play with your baby," "get your baby's

FIG. 8.1. Infield situation for taping of mother–infant social interaction.

8. MOTHER-INFANT INTERACTION AMONG THE GUSII OF KENYA   155

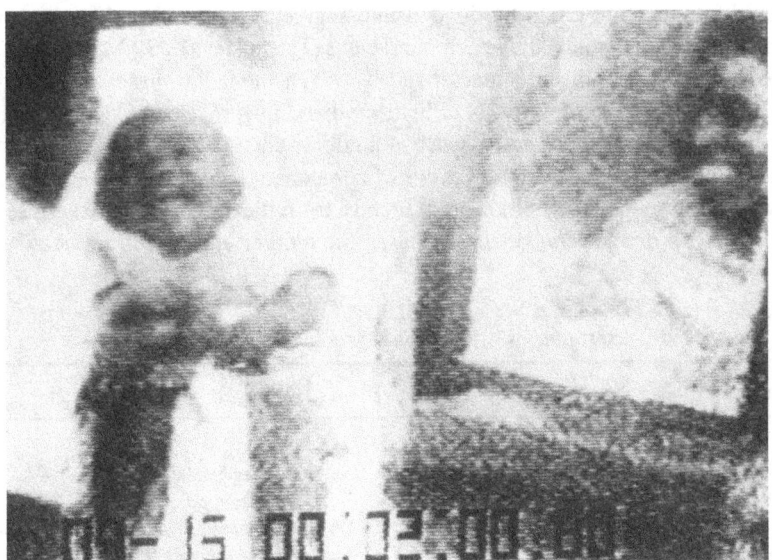

FIG. 8.2. Image recorded by videotape of Gusii mother-infant interaction. Digital timer superimposed prior to analysis.

attention." Two and a half minutes of this playful interaction were recorded. Infants were taped biweekly from 2- to 12-weeks and at monthly intervals till 6 months of age. The final data set includes sequential sessions of nine mother-infant pairs with a mean duration of 2 min 22 sec (Range: 1 min 22 sec to 3 min 10 sec).

The taping was done when the infant was in a quiet, alert state and all distracting elements (e.g., chickens, older children) had been cleared from the area. Mothers were allowed to see the tapes after each session. Mothers (and infants) became accustomed to the situation and participated eagerly. However, they continued to preserve their own judgment as to the value of such observations, considering them a pleasant waste of time. They specifically said it was silly to talk to a baby.

In order to understand the meaning of the face-to-face data, we had also gathered medical, social and psychological information on the mothers while pregnant, pediatric and Brazelton Neonatal Behavioral Assessments (Brazelton, 1973) in the newborn period, as well as naturalistic observations in the homes and cognitive testing over the next 15 months. The face-to-face data then can be understood within this context in order to allow us to make meaningful interpretation of its goals within this culture. The mother-infant pairs as well as the whole market population were well known to the authors.

The videotapes are analyzed by scoring behavioral phases for mother and infant. American studies have led to the development of a system of analysis by which the interaction could be divided into segments of identifiable behavioral clusters or phases displayed by each interactant (Tronick et al., 1977). Individual behavioral clusters can be characterized by seven monadic phases: (1) Avoid/Protest, (2) Avert, (3) Monitor, (4) Elicit (mother only), (5) Set, (6) Play, and (7) Talk. Each monadic phase has specific mutually exclusive behavioral descriptors built upon the microscopic observations of component behaviors. The composite cluster can be reliably ($> .85$) scored directly from the videotapes. Examples of the descriptors for several of these phases for mother and infant are shown in

TABLE 8.1
Examples of Criteria for Monadic Phase Coding

Infant	Mother
A. *Aversion (2)*	
Neutral to negative affect, but not crying or fussing;	Neutral to negative affect;
	Gaze away from infant;
	Distance medium to far back;
Gaze away from mother;	Head position variable, toward to part-side away;
Posture neutral to slumped;	
Head position variable:	Vocalizations variable:
a) fully to part-side away with or without focused attention elsewhere;	a) none to infant;
	b) may or may not vocalize to another adult;
b) any position, totally involved in object or hand play.	
	Contact with infant variable, none to simple touch.
B. *Monitor (3)*	
Affect slightly negative;	Affect neutral to slightly negative;
Head and/or gaze predominantly toward the mother;	Gaze intermittant or lidded;
	Body in neutral position;
Posture slumped to neutral.	No contact of infant;
	Head may be partially turned away.
C. *Set (5)*	
Affect neutral to positive;	Affect neutral to positive;
Bright look to simple smile;	Face bright or with simple smile;
Head & gaze toward mother;	Vocalizations of all types except abrupt and/or negative;
Eyes open & alert;	
Body upright;	Body and head orientation toward infant in medium to close position;
Vocalizations positive or none.	
	Touches may include containment or none.
D. *Play (6)*	
Affect greater than neutral;	Affect greater than neutral;
Head and gaze totally oriented to mother;	Body, head and gaze fully oriented to infant;
Posture upright;	Vocalizations variable, from none to low burst-pause narrative, playful-stern or non-verbal sounds and laugh;
Face variables, from simple smile to coo face;	
Vocalizations variable, from none to positive vocalization to laugh;	
	Contact with infant variable, from none to simple touch or tapping.
Movement variable, from none to large limb movements.	

Table 8.1. The phases constitute the continua in the degree of attention to the other in the dyad (7 to 1). It is scored as positive to negative in affect (7 to 1), and in this way provides an ordinal scaling system. This system was used to analyze the Gusii tapes by identifying the monadic phase for mother and infant for each ¼ sec of interaction. Technical problems including lighting difficulties and marginal resolution account for the exclusion of 6% of the time of the taped material. Scrutiny of these missing data verifying that there is no systematic bias in these exclusions; these reflect random events in the field conditions of the study.

RESULTS

Global Description of the Interactions

Gusii mothers entered the interaction with their infants by sitting at a medium close distance from the child's seat. They appeared relaxed and comfortable within the interaction. They gave the prescribed stylized greeting with a simple smile followed by a short pause. The infant would attend brightly and may or may not have smiled. Mothers often would initiate a repetitious verbal pattern using single words or phrases, ones we often heard them use in the course of daily caretaking, (e.g., "kira, kira, kira"; be quiet, don't complain, be content; or "issi, issi, issi"; you see, attend here; or "seca, seca, seca"; smile). Their repetitive phrases may or may not have been accompanied by tapping of the infant's arm, leg, or occasionally chin, or very prominently, the face. These taps would typically occur in short clusters of four rapid beats followed by a pause. Although reminiscent of the mother–infant "game" as defined by Stern (1974b), these sequences did not vary upon each repetition, nor were they elaborated upon during the course of the interaction. These sequences were repeated unchanged for several repetitions. They seemed to be used to maintain steady attention from the infant rather than as elicitations.

"Baby talk" in its most exaggerated form was not heard. However, mothers did use dialogue broken by long pauses to interact with the infants. Some mothers did raise the pitch of their usually low voices, but dramatic changes in inflections were not used. The action for the mothers' part, then, was carried along steadily using voice and through touch. Facial expression had little variation. The mothers smiled pleasantly or had an alert, open expression throughout most of the interactions. Gaze was generally toward the infant but appeared to have a grossly distracted quality. Slow motion and stop-frame review of the tapes indicated that the mothers' gaze was broken by brief glances away from the infant and was frequently directed at some part of the infant's body other than the face. Movement of the mother was very limited and was generally restricted to small head movements rather than large shifts of body position. The overall intensity of the interaction seemed less than those seen in the American sample;

one had the feeling that there was less of a sense of hovering by the African mothers.

Infants responded to their mothers' attentions with pleasure. Dramatic aversions of gaze or posture were very rare. Cooing vocalizations were accompanied by big kicks of the legs and large smiles. Uniformly positive affect was present. Infants were usually content and interested in the interaction. Occasionally an infant would wiggle in the chair with arms extending out or up. This behavior appeared to signal that the infant wanted or expected to be picked up by the mother. When mothers left at the end of the designated time, few infants showed the dramatic change in affect common in similar American sequences. They seemed quite competent to redirect their attention toward objects in the surrounding environment. Their affect remained neutral to positive as they casually scanned the environment.

Some of the infants laughed out loud, with lots of movement and vocalization. These peaks in affective display produced a mixed response in mothers: some giggled nervously; others' faces became devoid of expression and turned away. The infant would then display less dramatic, though still positive behaviors. Even these abrupt shifts in mothers' attention produced little change in the infant's affective level; positive affect, only slightly dampened prevailed. The cyclic nature of the interactions was not immediately apparent. In the field the sessions seemed very flat and in certain ways monotonous. It is only upon review that the rhythmic quality was seen. The cyclic modulation is smooth and regular but much more subtle than in American interactions. At first inspection the mothers momentary gaze aversions appeared random and seemed to give the whole interaction a distracted quality. Only after closer scrutiny does one see that these are closely linked to the infant's peaks of affective display and as such are important junctures in the interactions.

Individual differences in pacing and style were apparent among the African mother-infant pairs. Temperamental characteristics of the infants themselves seemed to be the basis of some of that variation. For example, one very large, placid infant vocalized frequently and smiled often; body movements were very rare. His affective peaks or periods of withdrawal were signaled by cessation of vocalization. His mother, a relaxed, older woman with many children, responded by participating in the dialogues. She extended the rhythm of that interchange to touch by moving slightly forward and tapping the infant with each vocalization in a very pleasant, moderately excited way. In this case, the infant seemed to determine the pacing of the interaction, and the mother its complexity. In another case, the infant seemed vigilant, quiet and relatively stoic throughout the interactions. His mother gave repeated, stylized greetings as if she too sensed his reticence to engage in the interaction. When initiated, the dialogue was carried by gentle tapping games and quiet reciprocal vocalizations. His mother had an unwavering, broad smile and a low pitched voice that she used to gently draw him out. In addition to the gaze aversion, this mother used her hands to hold

8. MOTHER-INFANT INTERACTION AMONG THE GUSII OF KENYA   159

down the child's arms if his movements became large or tremulous. The whole interaction was dampened by these maneuvers.

Another mother was more dramatic in her response to the slightly withdrawn infant; she readjusted the infant's head when she attempted to turn away. Although she would not accept disengagement, within an attentive state she was very nonintrusive. Long dialogues with the infant were present but were modulated by a flurry of eye blinks by this mother. She did not turn away herself but did avert gaze by blinking when the intensity of the interaction began to build.

One of the interactions with a temperamentally negative and irritable infant was quite uncomfortable to watch. The child's mother used taps and an unusual hissing sound to get the attention of a solemn, slumped over infant. This sound coupled with the child's name appeared to be a greeting. recognized as such by both participants. Several short-lived engagements followed these greetings, but were terminated by the infant turning away. The mother then repeated this greeting behavior to begin the cycle again. Finally, the infant put up her hand in a real avoidance posture and made some swipes towards the mother's face. The mother's forthright and relatively aggressive personality was clear in her persistence and insistence with this very difficult infant. The interaction appeared uncomfortable to the onlooker as these two negotiated their patterns of early communication.

Although almost all the Gusii mothers appeared relaxed and calm, two of the mothers seemed very calm and slightly distanced from the interaction. Their style outside the face-to-face situation was consistent with this mode. The shifts and modulations in these interactions were slow and smooth and the whole sessions were more obviously rhythmic on even casual inspection.

The observations of these individual differences only serve to highlight how the more generalized influence of culture is modified but not suppressed by the specific temperamental and situational characteristics of the mother and infant pairs. There was no Gusii stereotype but rather a range of behavioral displays and patterns that were clearly different from the American mother-infant pairs interacting within the same structure.

Microanalysis of the Interaction

I. *Proportion of Time and Duration of Each Phase for the Gusii Infants.* The monadic phase system is used to describe the infants' performance during the interaction. Table 8.2 presents the percentage of time each phase occurs in an interaction and the duration of each phase. The relatively large standard deviations and ranges indicate large individual differences. Except for infant protest, each phase made up a significant proportion of the interaction with monitor and set being the modal state. Monitor also had the largest mean and median

TABLE 8.2
Behavioral Phases of Gusii Infants

Percent of Time	Mean	S.D.	Range	States
Phase: 1 Protest	5.1	11.1	0–33	Disengaged
2 Avert	20.8	19.7	0–50	25 ± 17
3 Monitor	19.0	28.4	0–90	Neutrally engaged
5 Set	21.1	17.9	0–53	40 ± 23
6 Play	19.5	16.3	0–47	Positively engaged
7 Talk	13.3	14.1	0–41	32 ± 16

Duration in Seconds	Mean	S.D.	Range
Phase: 1 Protest	7.0	2.3	4.5–9.1
2 Avert	6.4	.5.7	0.7–17.0
3 Monitor	8.2	11.2	0.2–37.0
5 Set	5.2	5.5	1.8–18.0
6 Play	3.0	1.9	0.5–6.5
7 Talk	1.7	0.6	1.1–2.7

duration. Talk and play had the shortest durations, and next to protest, the smallest proportion of total time. Avert and protest had relatively long mean durations (6.4 and 7.0 seconds, respectively).

Combining phases shows that the infants spend 25% disengaged (phases 1 and 2), 40% neutrally engaged (phases 3 and 5) and 32% positively engaged (phases 6 and 7). Periods of high attention and positive affect are brief and few in number. Infants spend longer periods in phases at the midportion of the range of possible behaviors.

II. *Infant Transitions.* The ordering of transitions from one state to another was examined to determine how the infants change among the phases over the course of the interaction. Figure 8.3 gives examples of a graphing of these interactions. In each, the phase is plotted on the ordinate and time intervals of ¼ second along the abscissa. A horizontal line indicates the phase and its duration and a vertical line indicates a phase transition. The phases are ranked from positive to negative along an affective dimension to allow for sequential relationships in the data but not to imply any judgment of the behaviors scored.

Figure 8.3 shows the cycling among the negative, neutral and positive phases that have been described for infants in interactions in our own country. This cyclic quality was seen in all the Gusii mother–infant interactions. The infants cycle from neutral or positive engagement and back to negative an average of 3.3 times per min. Two other significant features of the infants' transitions among phases were noted: Only 2% of the transitions were from phases 1/2 to 6/7 or vice versa, the extremes of the scale. Seventy-six percent were from within the neutral to positive range. The usual transitions were in a narrow range along the atten-

8. MOTHER-INFANT INTERACTION AMONG THE GUSII OF KENYA

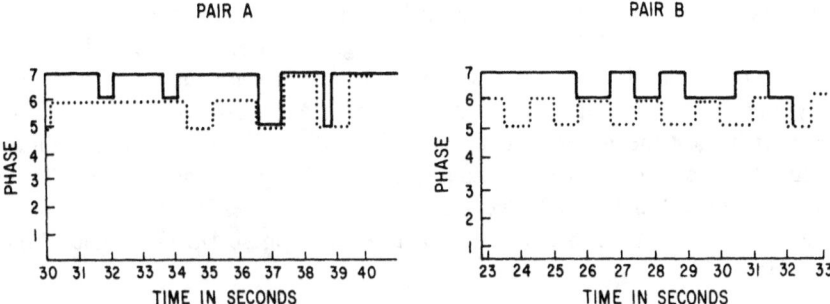

FIG. 8.3. Examples of mother-infant interaction laid out sequentially using sequential monadic phases.

tional continuum, one-step transitions. Secondly, infants typically changed from one phase to the next adjacent phase. For example, Gusii infants moved from Play to Talk, and Play to Set, but seldom from Talk to Monitor or Avert. One step transitions (i.e., modulations from one phase to adjacent one) constituted 51% of infant changes; two step transitions, 32%; and three and four step transitions a total of only 8%. Thus, regardless of an infant's predominant phase, transitions took place within a narrow range.

III. *Proportion of Time and Duration of Each Phase for the Gusii Mothers.* Table 8.3 presents the data on proportion of time spent in each phase and the duration of each phase. The relatively large standard deviations and ranges indicate that there were large individual differences. However Gusii mothers

TABLE 8.3
Behavioral Phases of Gusii Mothers

Percentage of Time	Mean	S.D.	Range	State
Phase: 1 Avoid	4.1	3.3	1–11	Disengaged
2 Avert	3.8	3.3	2–12	7 ± 3
3 Monitor	13.6	9.3	14–27	Neutrally
4 Elicit	11.1	11.3	1–35	engaged
5 Set	34.0	14.9	11–58	47 ± 13
6 Play	20.5	11.7	0–41	Positively engaged
7 Talk	11.7	12.1	0–37	31 ± 11
Duration, seconds	Mean	S.D.	Range	
Phase: 1 Avoid	1.1	0.5	0.5–2.0	
2 Avert	3.0	1.9	1.3–7.6	
3 Monitor	2.5	1.3	1.2–5.0	
4 Elicit	1.7	0.8	0.9–3.7	
5 Set	2.1	1.0	0.7–3.6	
6 Play	1.4	.4	0.8–2.0	
7 Talk	1.2	.2	0.8–1.6	

spent the greatest proportion of time in Set (.34) and next in Play (.20). They spent a total of only 7% of the time disengaged (Phases 1 and 2). The mean duration of Avert was 3.0 sec, representing the longest phase duration. This was a very long behavioral unit in our experience with American tapes. Monitor had the next longest mean duration, 2.5 sec. Play and Talk were relatively short-lived, (1.4 sec, and 1.2 sec, respectively). Combining the phases into "disengaged" (phases 1 and 2), .07; "neutrally engaged" (phases 3 and 5), .47; "positively engaged" (phases 6 and 7), .31; and "elicit" (phase 4), .11 completed the analysis.

IV. *Maternal Transitions.* Maternal transitions among the phases were analyzed in the same manner as the infant fluctuations. Examples are plotted in Fig. 8.3. These again show the cyclic pattern of transitions along the affective and attentional continuum. This is again, the modal pattern of the Gusii mothers. On the average Gusii mothers cycled from being neutrally or positively engaged to negatively engaged 4.4 times a minute. Mothers tended not to go directly from the extreme negative phases (1 and 2) to positive phases (6 and 7). The largest proportion of their transitions were 1 step transitions. These accounted for 71% of transitions, even a greater proportion than the 1 step infant fluctuation. Two step transitions constituted 17% of the total. Three and four step changes accounted for only 9% of changes. Again, the fluctuations were, by and large, within a narrow range. Sixty-four percent were within the neutral to positive category. When in the disengaged phases (1 and 2), the transition was to the positive states 1% of the time, and to neutral 4%. Two percent of the time, the mother went to the other of the disengaged states.

V. *Relational Aspects of the Interaction.* Examination of the behavior of both partners in the interaction simultaneously provides some understanding of the amount of synchrony in the interactions. Table 8.4 represents the proportion of time that infant and mother are in joint phases. Both partners were simultaneously in positive monadic phases 18.6% of the time (phases 6 and 7) and were in mutually negative states only 2.1% (phases 1 and 2). Patterns were in the neutral categories synchronously (phases 3 and 5) 20.6% of the time. When the specific patterns of the "conjoint" state are examined in detail, it can be seen that the infant more frequently displayed behavior characteristics of a more affectively positive state than does his mother at that time. For example, the percentage of time when the mother was in a neutral state while the infant was in a positively engaged state is 15.2%. The portion of time when the reverse occurred (i.e., mother positively engaged and infant neutral) was .5% of the time. Overall, the proportion of time the infant had a more positive affective state than the mother was 40%; the mother was more positive 31% of the time.

Dyadic Transitions

Two additional analyses were made to determine the nature of the changes that define the cyclic quality in the interaction. The first is an assessment of events

TABLE 8.4
Percent of Time in Joint Phases for Gusii Mother-Infant Pairs[a]
(matched pairs are highlighted on the diagonal)

		Maternal Phase							
		1 Avoid	2 Avert	3 Monitor	4 Elicit	5 Set	6 Play	7 Talk	Total
Infant Phase	1 Protest	0	0	0.8	1.5	1.1	.9	.2	4.5
	2 Avert	1.6	0.5	3.6	4.2	5.6	2.2	2.1	19.8
	3 Monitor	0.8	0	1.0	2.0	7.2	1.4	1.6	14.0
	5 Set	0.6	1.6	4.9	1.1	7.5	3.8	2.7	22.2
	6 Play	0	0.6	1.1	0.5	5.9	7.7	4.3	20.1
	7 Talk	0	0.4	1.7	0.2	6.5	5.2	1.4	15.2
	Total	3.0	3.1	13.1	9.5	33.8	21.2	12.3	

[a]Truncation of the matrix during calculations accounts for the discrepancy of values of infant and maternal percentages of time in phases on this table in comparison with Tables 8.1 and 8.2.

when mother and infant are both in the same state (about 40.3% of interaction time). Using the occurrence of this "match" state as a marker, this analysis looked at the transition to the "conjoint" or "disjoint" states. Sixty percent of the time the mother initiated the move out of the matched joint state and only 40% of the time was the infant responsible for this change. Mothers initiated the alterations more frequently, and further adjustments were then necessary to return the interaction to the "match" state. If the infant made the initial transition, the mother followed this change in level of attention or affect and returned to a joint state of match 34% of the time; the infant, however, followed her change only 5.8% of the time. Mothers appear to be responsible for the readjustment towards the synchronous state six times more frequently than are the infants. The second analysis examines how the mother responded to the infant as he changed into a positive phase (6 or 7). Fifty-six percent of the time she followed the infant by altering her behavior into positive engagement (phases 6 or 7). However, 39% of the time, she changed to the less positive states of 5 or 3. Five percent of the time she turned away from the interaction, behavior characterized in the "Avoid" phase, phase 1.

DISCUSSION

Gusii mother–infant face-to-face interaction was seen to be organized in a cyclic flow of affective behaviors similar to interactions described in our own culture (Brazelton et al., 1975). This organization suggests an underlying universal form. The monadic phase scoring system, a descriptive system developed within our culture, described the behaviors seen in the Gusii mother–infant interactions as well. The range and quality of affective behaviors were similar across the different cultures, but were used differentially. The emergence of play and talk episodes, with the modulation of voice effective for sustaining infant attention, were seen in this cultural setting as well as our own. Adult behavior, including speech in all cultures described to date, had an infantalized form when interacting with young infants. This seems to reflect the universal awareness of the capacities of young infant. The infants displayed a full range of behaviors within our system in spite of a very different social experience.

Brazelton, Koslowski and Main (1974) have hypothesized that the cyclic acceleration and deceleration of affective behavior during interactions becomes basic to the organization of the interaction. Such cycles of affect and attention were clearly evident in the Gusii interaction. Additionally, as has been described in American interactions, there is a high degree of predictability as to both the change of affective direction and the size of that change for infant and mother. Infants and mothers moved among the states in a regular fashion, i.e., rarely from Avert to Play or vice versa, and the changing between states in one step apart predominating. The orderliness of each participant's behavior permitted or resulted in the successful negotiation of frequent joint interactive states. These were evident in large proportion of matched states and in synchronous ("chorusing together") interchanges and transitions.

Yet, some of these features showed culturally specific features. Comparisons to American infant–mother interactions highlight differences in the behavior of the Gusii mother (Tronick et al., 1980).[1] We think these differences reflect Gusii cultural regulations of face-to-face interaction and the expression of intense emotions. Gusii mothers Play and Talk a similar proportion of time to their infants as do American mothers, 31% vs. 32%, but the duration of these two phases among the Gusii (1.4 sec and 1.2 sec, respectively) is shorter than for the American mothers (3.6 sec and 3.4 sec). Gusii mothers look away from the infant a greater proportion of time than do American mothers (7% of the time vs. 4.8% for phases 1 and 2). Both of these comparisons suggest a different investment in sustaining affectively charged episodes, because "avert" behaviors serve to dampen and diffuse any buildup of affective display and to limit its duration. Play sequences of short duration do not allow time for this buildup of affect to occur either. A smooth, even interaction appears to be the goal for the Gusii mothers. This contention is supported by the fact that Gusii mother–infant interactions achieve a Match state 40% of the time whereas American interactions achieve it only 19.8%. The interactions are in steady balance between partners most commonly, and as a result, there is a certain monotony or evenness to them. They do not show the peaks of affective excitement seen in interaction in this country. Only 8.1% of the time are the Gusii interactions in joint positive states (Talk or Play) as compared to 17% in joint positive states in American interactions. Synchrony is achieved most frequently in the neutrally engaged states (12% American vs. 20.6% Gusii).

[1] American mother-infant interactions have been described using the monadic phase system and this study is presented descriptively here as a contrast to the Gusii data only. The data are published in detail elsewhere (Tronick et al., 1980).

Differences do not appear to be related to the availability of the Gusii infants. The infants' behavior on the tapes and as analyzed by the microscoring system looks like that of American infants. Fully 32% of the time they are in Play or Talk as compared to 19% of the time for American infants. Talk, the more excited of the two phases, accounts for most of this difference, 13% vs. 3%. Of critical importance is that 39% of the time when the infant goes to Play or Talk, the Gusii mother goes to Set or Monitor, (phases 3 and 5), and 5% of the time she goes to Avert/Avoid (phases 1 and 2). The mother's response to these displays of positive affect seem to be to dampen, diffuse or diminish the affective level of the interaction. In the U.S. the goal for mothers seems to be to build upon or amplify or extend these infant behaviors. Every attempt is made to sustain Play and Talk episodes up to the limits of the infant's capacities.

Expansion and elaboration of the infant's displays is the usual response for U.S. mothers. Gusii mothers do not appear to want this high intensity in the interactions with their infants; their behavior reflects this difference. They have a repertoire of repetitive vocalizations, taps, head nods and fixed facial expressions. These stylized behaviors give an evenness, a flatness to the interactions. The analysis of the size of state transitions supports and specifies those clinical impressions of the steadiness and regularity of the Gusii interactions. American mothers change among phases in one step units 38% of the time and in two step units 51% of the time. The two step changes serve to heighten and exaggerate the interaction, to turn up the "gain." Gusii mothers change 71% of the time in one step units and only 17% of the time in two step units. This would seem to lessen the exaggerated quality of their behavior and the affective intensity of the interaction. The interaction remains contained within a narrow range of affect and attention. This containment reflects the mothers' underlying concern about the experience as well as the expression of intense emotion in any interpersonal exchange. Such intensity may be dangerous and the anxiety that is produced by this buildup demands to be quickly diffused. The narrow range of the state transitions represents a very automatic fine tuning of the interaction in response to culturally determined rules for interpersonal exchange. These observations do not imply that the Gusii mothers are unresponsive to their own individual infants. They respond sensitively to their infants' behaviors as shown by the frequency with which they match their own behavior to that of their infant and the frequency with which they alter their behavior after the infant makes a transition in the interaction (34% of the time). Even the occurrence of negative phases (1 and 2) seems to be linked to the infant's behavior episodes of positive display rather than either random or as markers of disinterest. The mother's modulation of the interaction speaks to a sensitivity to the infant within a matrix of culture-specific expectancies and goals.

These comparisons add clarification to the goals of American mothers' face-to-face interactions. American mothers behave in a fashion that intensifies the level of affect expressed; they share the infant's most excited behaviors. Intensity of interaction may represent a prototype of expectations for our children's interactions with other people and events in their environment. We value an individualistic, dynamic and aggressive approach to life in general and to interpersonal experience in particular. The interactions we have with our children appear to reflect these goals and to prepare our children to be ready for this intensity. A strong sense of self as a separate, autonomous individual is built within these early interactions with sensitive caretakers (Kohut, 1971). This may be appropriate for a culture dependent on individual initiative and assertiveness. The interactions of mother and infant can be seen as uniquely suited to the cultural goals and expectations.

The long-term adaptiveness of the Gusii behavior in social encounters can be seen by looking at it in context. Tribal solidarity is essential for the survival of a small tribe surrounded by unrelated neighbors. Close living situations for an extended family, with sons, their several cowives and their children, all living off the same land, put many stresses on the interpersonal sphere. Extremes of negative affective display could cause family disruptions and even tribal divisions; extremes of positive affect set up jealousies or reveal dangerously sensitive areas of the self. Both extremes are to be avoided. One's self must be defined not by unique characteristics, but rather by participation in the kin system and good worker in one's expected role (LeVine, 1980a). The elaborate set of implicit and explicit rules that govern social interaction are designed to protect the Gusii from those dangerous extremes and to reinforce compliance with role expectation. They serve to preserve a constancy and evenness in all the affairs of life that is clearly economical and advantageous to all members. Greater self-assertiveness or even conspicuous self-esteem do not meet these societal needs.

The Gusii infant is learning these lessons in his own culture at a very young age. In the earliest interactions with his mother, he is shown how to ration the periods of intense affective display carefully, to keep them under control and to avoid the dangerous extremes. Individual initiative is contained within firm boundaries. The definition of self is made within an implicit set of rules that give clear messages as to the expectations of those around him. Repetitiveness and formality safeguard interactions within safe limits.

Face-to-face interaction appears to have an underlying universal structure that is modified by specific cultural goals and expectancies. As in Caudill and Weinstein's (1969) studies, it is striking how early these cultural aspects begin to permeate the infant caregiver interaction. It is our feeling that the interaction does not simply reflect the developmental process but rather forms the base of that process. That is, the infant's cumulative and iterative daily experiences of engagement in a culturally specific universal form shapes the infant's development of self.

ACKNOWLEDGMENTS

We would like to express our thanks to R. A. LeVine, Ph.D. for inspiration and facilitation of all aspects of this work; to Anna Getoi, Driscilla Ombui, Agnes Nyabeta, Teresa

Monari and Joseph Obongo for participation in data collection, to Sarah LeVine for insights and support while in the field; to P. H. Leiderman, M.D. for his critical review of these observations; to the Bureau of Educational Research, University of Nairobi for help and cooperation.

We would like to thank particularly the Gusii mothers and their infants who with patience and good humor allowed us a window into their early life together.

This work was supported in part by grants from the National Science Foundation, the William T. Grant Foundation, The Robert Wood Johnson Foundation and the Spencer Foundation.

REFERENCES

Als, H., Tronick, E., & Brazelton, T. B. Analysis of face-to-face interaction in infant–adult dyads. In M. E. Lamb, S. J. Suomi, & G. R. Stephenson (Eds.), *The study of social interaction: Methodological problems.* Madison: University of Wisconsin Press, 1979.

Argyle, M., & Cook, M. *Gaze and mutual gaze.* Cambridge: Cambridge University Press, 1976.

Brazelton, T. B. Neonatal behavioral assessment scale. *Clinics in Developmental Medicine,* No. 50, Philadelphia: J. B. Lippincott, 1973.

Brazelton, T. B., Koslowski, B., & Main, M. The origin of reciprocity: The early mother–infant interaction. In M. Lewis & L. Rosenblum (Eds.), *The effect of the infant on its caregiver.* New York: Wiley, 1974.

Brazelton, T. B., Tronick, E., Adamson, L., Als, H., & Wise, S. Early mother–infant reciprocity. In *Parent–infant interaction.* Ciba Foundation Symposium 33, Amsterdam: Elsevier, 1975, 137-154.

Caudill, W., & Weinstein, H. Maternal care and infant behavior in Japan and America. *Psychiatry,* 1969, *32,* 12-43.

Clarke-Stewart, A. Interactions between mothers and their young children: Characteristics and consequences. *Monographs of the Society for Research in Child Development,* No. 6 & 7, 1973.

Dixon, S., Yogman, M., Tronick, E., & Brazelton, T. B. Early infant social interaction with mothers, fathers, and strangers. *Journal of the American Academy of Child Psychiatry,* 1981, *20,* 32-52.

Goldberg, S. Infant care and growth in urban Zambia. *Human Development* 1972, *15,* 77-89.

Hitchcock, J. *Infant holding.* Unpublished manuscript, Harvard University, 1979.

Keefer, C. *A cross-cultural study of face-to-face interaction: Gusii infants and mothers.* Paper presented at the Society for Research in Child Development, New Orleans, March 1977.

Kohut, H. *The analysis of self.* New York: International Universities Press, 1971.

Konner, M. Infancy among the Kalahari Desert San. In P. H. Leiderman, S. Turkin, & A. Rosenthal (Eds.), *Culture and infancy: Variations in the human experience.* New York: Academic Press, 1977.

LeVine, R. A. Witchcraft and sorcery in the Gusii community. In J. Middleton & E. Winter (Eds.), *Witchcraft and sorcery in East Africa.* London: Routledge & Kegan Paul, 1963.

LeVine, R. A. *Culture, behavior and personality.* Chicago: Aldine Publishing Co., 1973.

LeVine, R. A. *Gaze in an African society: Looking and being looked at.* Preliminary Report, 1979.

LeVine, R. A. The self and its development in an African society: A preliminary analysis. In B. Lee (Ed.), *New approaches to the self.* Norwood, N.J.: Ablex Publishing Co., 1980. (a)

LeVine, R. A. Adulthood among the Gusii of Kenya. In N. Smelser & E. Erickson (Eds.), *Themes of love and work in adulthood.* Cambridge: Harvard University Press, 1980. (b)

LeVine, R. A., & LeVine, B. *Nyansongo: A Gusii community in Kenya.* New York: Wiley, 1966.

LeVine, S. *Mothers and wives: Gusii women of East Africa.* Chicago: University of Chicago Press, 1979.

Mayer, P. *Two studies in applied anthropology in Kenya.* Colonial Research Studies No. 3. London: His Majesty's Stationary Office, 1951.

New, R. *Mothers and others: A review and preliminary analysis of infant-caretaker interaction.* Unpublished monograph, Harvard University, 1979.

Stern, D. N. The goal and structure of mother-infant play. *Journal of the American Academy of Child Psychiatry,* 1974, *13,* 402-421. (a)

Stern, D. N. Mother and infant at play: The dyadic interaction involving facial, vocal and gaze behaviors. In M. Lewis & L. Rosenblum (Eds.), *The effect of the infant on its caregiver.* New York: Wiley, 1974. (b)

Tronick, E., Als, H., & Adamson, L. Structure of early face-to-face communicative interactions. In M. Bullowa (Ed.), *Before speech: The beginnings of human communication.* Cambridge: Cambridge University Press, 1979.

Tronick, E., Als, H., & Brazelton, T. B. Mutuality in mother-infant interaction. *Journal of Communication,* 1977, *27,* 74-79.

Tronick, E., Als, H., & Brazelton, T. B. Monadic phases: A structural descriptive analysis of infant-adult face-to-face interaction. *Merrill-Palmer Quarterly,* 1980, *25,* 3-24.

Whiting, B. B., & Whiting, J. W. M. *Children of six cultures.* Cambridge: Harvard University Press, 1975.

Yogman, M. W. *The goals and structure of face-to-face interaction between infants and fathers.* Paper presented at Society for Research in Child Development, New Orleans, 1977.

IV GROWTH AND DEVELOPMENTAL STATUS OF INFANTS

9 Infant and Caretaker Behavior as Mediators of Nutritional and Social Intervention in the Barrios of Bogotá

Charles M. Super
John Clement
Lea Vuori
Niels Christiansen
José O. Mora
M. Guillermo Herrera
Harvard School of Public Health

American behavioral scientists have traditionally been interested in early social interaction in foreign cultures for its comparative value, that is, in broad comparison with the American pattern. Most often, the comparison takes the form of a thematic contrast and is used to illuminate the influence of adult values on early socialization, and the influence of early socialization on the adult psyche (e.g., Caudill & Weinstein, 1969). Less frequently the emphasis is on aspects of early interaction that are universal to our species (e.g., Lewis & Ban, 1977). In this report we put observations of early behavior to a third use by examining the role of early interaction as a mediating factor in the development of children at risk of malnutrition, under two conditions of experimental intervention: nutritional supplementation and maternal education concerning child development. The results speak not only to the particular purposes of our applied research, but also to larger issues in understanding the complexities of early social interaction.

Pathways of Influence for Moderate Malnutrition

Studies of malnutrition in human populations have drawn heavily and profitably from experimental studies with animals. With complete control over experimental conditions, the laboratory approach can attempt to isolate the necessary and specific sequelae of severe nutritional deficit. The results of such work strongly suggest that severe protein–calorie deprivation early in life, when the proliferation and elaboration of brain cells are most rapid, causes permanent biological damage and related cognitive deficit (see, for example, Dobbing, 1970, 1974).

Extrapolation of this work to common public health concerns, however, is problematic. With the exception of acute famine caused by natural disaster or war, most malnutrition in children does not involve massive deprivation; neither does it occur independently of other health factors, social and economic conditions, or patterns of child care. If, as seems likely, the pathways of influence for chronic, moderate malnutrition are tied to these other, non-nutritional factors, then modeling the process for laboratory study becomes virtually impossible. To understand the systematic impact of inadequate nutrition during childhood as it occurs in the real word, it is necessary to study it in the real world in its naturally occurring relationship with other factors. Although such a natural history approach cannot replace the causal precision of the laboratory experiment on biological aspects of nutrition, it is a necessary complement for examining the multitude of possible causal pathways as they actually occur in particular human populations.

When, in addition, experimental interventions in a field setting interrupt an existing pattern of development that includes nutritional deficit, growth retardation, and social and cognitive deficiencies, functional features of the existing pattern may be revealed. The model that emerges is likely to be, not one of linear cause and effect, but rather one of a system of mutual influences and adaptations. Understanding this system will shed light not only on the nature of early development, but also on approaches to intervention in situations of human suffering.

Although the "ecology of malnutrition" (Pollit, 1969) has concerned researchers and policy makers for over a decade, field reports more frequently provide information on the general correlates of malnutrition, such as family income, than on specific pathways of effect. Of the exceptions, several address the importance of moderate malnutrition in lowering infants' level of activity, exploration, and social interaction (Chavez, Martinez, & Yachine, 1974; Dasen, Inhelder, Lavallee, & Retschitzki, 1978; Graves, 1976; Klein, Lasky, Yarbrough, Habicht, & Sellers, 1977; Pollit, 1975). The behavioral apathy is thought to have two kinds of effects on development. First, reduced levels of activity should have a direct negative effect on cognitive development, since exploration and experience with the physical and social world are considered essential ingredients of intellectual development (e.g., Piaget, 1952). At the group level, there are several reports of both low activity and delays in cognitive development in moderately malnourished children, compared to well nourished peers (Chavez et al., 1974; Graves, 1976; Klein et al., 1977).

In addition, less demanding and responsive infants may fail to call forth from their caretakers optimal kinds of encouragement and stimulation. For example, Brazelton and his associates found newborns in Guatemala who were undernourished during pregnancy to be less active and appealing than healthy babies; they speculate that this could begin a cycle of less and less supportive interaction with the mother (Brazelton, Tronick, Lechtig, Lasky, & Klein, 1977; see also

Lester, 1979). Chavez et al. (1974) report from Mexico that better nourished infants are seen as more demanding by their parents, and that this greater activity is engaging and eventually results in parental pleasure and pride.

The destructive effect of moderate malnutrition, then, may rest more on the infant's apathy toward engaging the physical and social world than on direct biochemical insult to the central nervous system. It would be an error, however, to focus on the infant as the sole source of causation in a cycle of nutritional deficit. The process of eliciting, or failing to elicit, particular caretaking behaviors necessarily involves the parents' values and beliefs about child development, and their pattern of adaptability in providing care. To take seriously the introduction of behavioral mediation into an understanding of the dynamics of nutritional deficit, therefore, requires attention to the patterns of caretaking behaviors and their sociocultural means of integration. Intervention studies in America have often worked through mothers as a means of influence, teaching them to encourage and respond to greater activity and exploration by their infants. The intended changes in caretaker and infant behavior appear in many ways to be an antidote to the apathy effects of moderate malnutrition. To focus on behavioral factors, in short, brings one quickly to appreciate the importance of understanding the contextual mechanisms of early development. At the same time, the complexity of the interactive mechanisms between infant and caretaker suggests a variety of possible routes of intervention.

The project reported in this chapter was designed to evaluate the effects of two different kinds of intervention into the development of infants known to be at risk for early malnutrition in Bogotá, Colombia. One experimentally administered intervention consisted of nutritional supplementation; the corresponding research question, in the present context, is whether supplemented infants are more active and more interactive with their physical and social environment. The second intervention was a program of maternal education in early development conducted by trained home visitors. In this case, the hypothesized effects focus on changes in the mothers' attitudes and behavior toward the baby, presumably of a kind that promote greater interaction and support for social and cognitive growth. The results confirm the effectiveness of the interventions but also point to complexities in the self-regulating system of infant and caretaker behavior.

DESIGN OF THE BOGOTÁ STUDY

Sample

Barrios on the southern edge of Bogotá display an urban poverty that is recognizable in most of the rapidly growing cities of the Third World (Christiansen, Mora, & Herrera, 1975). Housing and sanitation are poor, jobs are scarce, and nutrition and medical care are expensive enough (compared to income) to put families at serious risk. For many families, the southern barrios are a staging ground for migration from rural areas to the city. Family networks and personal enterprise provide a foothold; relatives and friends follow. Some families prosper and move to better quarters; others continue a struggling existence; a few return to the countryside.

Four door-to-door demographic surveys of the zone were carried out at sixmonth intervals starting in 1974 in order to identify pregnancies at risk of nutritional deficit. The criteria used for selection were: (1) the mother was in the first or second trimester of pregnancy with one or more other children under 5 years of age; and (2) at least 50% of her other children were found to suffer mild-to-moderate malnutrition as indicated by 85% or less of standard weight for age (using Colombian standards).

Five hundred fifty-two cases were found. Seventeen percent of these families were not enrolled in the study due to migration (39), spontaneous abortion (34), or refusal (23). Examination of available sociological indices (income, housing, neighborhood, maternal age, and maternal education) and nutritional information on over half of these families revealed no significant differences from the 83% who were enrolled.

Treatments

The 456 participating families were all provided free medicines and obstetric and pediatric care. Families were randomly assigned to one of six groups, after clustering by city block of residence where necessary in order to minimze communication among families in different experimental groups. Four experimental treatments were created by independent nutritional and educational interventions. They are:

1. nutritional supplementation: The 82 families in this group were given local foodstuffs in an amount sufficient to raise the consumption by each member above the recommended daily allowances. Pregnant and lactating women were provided daily with 856 calories (39% RDA), 38.4 g protein (60% RDA), 6024 IU vitamin A (100% RDA) and 18 mg iron (100% RDA), through dry skim milk, enriched bread, vegetable oil, and vitamin and mineral supplements. Supplementation began at approximately 6 months of gestation. Despite instructions to the mothers to continue consuming their usual diet in addition to the supplements, comparison of actual intake (as indicated by 24-hr recall) before supplementation and in the eighth month of pregnancy indicated that the average increase consisted of only 133 calories and 19.6 g protein per day. The relatively small net effect resulted from both substitution of supplementation for part of the normal diet and less than full consumption of the supplementation (Mora, de Navarro, Clement, Wagner, de Paredes, & Herrera, 1978).

2. maternal education: The 58 mothers in this group were informed late in their pregnancy that they would be visited twice a week by a home tutor who

would help them learn ways to facilitate their infants' physical and intellectual growth. Actual visits were begun within a week or two following birth. The home visitors, Colombian women with the equivalent of an American high school degree, were trained in an adaptation of the Infant Education Curriculum initially developed by the High/Scope Educational Research Foundation in Ypsilanti, Michigan (Lambie, Bond, & Weikart, 1974). This curriculum, based primarily on Piaget's theory of the development of intelligence, contained several important and explicit features. The home visitor presented a view of the child as an intrinsically motived learner, for whom interaction with people and objects are the stuff of growth. She emphasized that the mother could play an important role as her baby's teacher, providing appropriate materials, encouraging initiative, responding to needs, and evaluating rate of progress. Specific activities were explained and demonstrated, using readily available materials such as cloth and sticks. The visitors encouraged the mothers to continue the curriculum activities between the twice-weekly visits and to share her new perspective with other family members. A detailed analysis of the teaching sessions has been presented by Ortiz, Florez, Clement, Mora, and Cuellar (1979).

3. supplementation and maternal education: 58 families received both the interventions described above.

4. controls: Ninety families received no interventions beyond the health care program and the repeated assessments of health, growth, development, and sociocultural factors that were common to all groups.

There were two further groups, which differed in the timing of nutritional supplementation and did not participate in the maternal education program, but they are not considered in the present report.

Observational Method

One of two home observers, who did not know the group assignment of individual families, visited the homes at prearranged times to record the naturally occurring behavior of the infants and caretakers. The observational method was adapted from previous work by Clarke-Stewart (1973), Lewis and Lee-Painter (1974), and Moss (1967). As the mother goes about her normal daily routines, the observer notes discrete infant and caretaker behaviors (such as looking, vocalizing, and touching) and records them on a checklist divided into sequential 10-second blocks of time. When possible, the observed behaviors are noted not only for their occurrence, but also their sequence within a block (for example, baby frets, then mother looks and speaks, then baby vocalizes).

Each infant was observed for 54 minutes of real time. This elapsed time was divided into nine periods of 6 minutes, each period consisting of 30 10-sec blocks (the basic unit of recording) followed by a 1 min break during which the observer completed several summary rating scales concerning the previous 5 minutes.

Actual recorded time, therefore, totaled 45 min. In 80% of the cases, the observation was completed in one visit. For the others, two and occasionally three visits were needed to accumulate 45 min of observed time, primarily because the infant fell asleep.

Four kinds of intermediate measures are available from these observations. First, the frequency of each discrete behavior was added up from the observational protocols (range = 0 to 270); second, summary counts were made of the 5-min ratings (e.g., infant predominantly carried vs. free; range = 0 to 9); third, measures of infant–caretaker interaction were derived from the protocols, such as proportion of infant vocalizations to which the caretaker responded, and the frequency and duration of "chains" or sequences of infant and caretaker behavior and response; and fourth, several indices of the observational situation were available, including ratings of the infant's state at the outset, length of time since sleeping and feeding, and the number of people present.

Data Transformation and Scale Construction

Comparison of the data collected by the two observers indicated a number of significant differences in average scores; as the observers were not assigned in a balanced fashion to the experimental groups we adopted the following procedure to adjust for this confounding. Each behavioral variable and rating (but not situational facts such as the number of people present) was regressed onto dichotomous dummy variables representing the experimental conditions of Nutritional Supplementation and Maternal Education, as well as Sex of Infant and all possible interactions of these three indices. After the dummy variables had been forced into the regression, in the order listed, an additional variable representing one of the two observers was introduced. The resulting beta weight for this observer thus represented a "correction" to be subtracted for her scores, and unaltered scores were used for the other observer. In order to adjust for skewed distributions, all frequency variables were transformed by taking the square root, and proportion scores were transformed by the arc sine function. The transformations were found to improve modestly but not alter qualitatively the final results.

Given the large number of interrelated observational variables, nine summary scales were derived for analysis. One measures infant behavior, five reflect different aspects of infant–caretaker interaction, and three indicate caretaker behavior in response to infant behavior. Each represents a meaningful and statistically identifiable cluster of behaviors, although there is some covariation among Scales 1, 3, and 5.

Scale 1 is derived from factor analysis of the 9 individual infant behaviors, and it reflects the infant's overall level of positive activity. At both 4 and 8 months, the principal component accounted for about 23% of the total variance. All behaviors with loadings greater than .40 (absolute value) were used in making the summary scale, which was defined as the sum of standardized scores (within age) of the frequency of infant smiles, positive vocalizations, quiet play with objects, and gross body movement (not included at 8 months), minus standard scores of the frequency of fretting (including crying), closing eyes (indicating drowsiness), and "blank stare" (eyes open with no activity or apparent interest in looking).

Individual scores on this positive activity scale were found to be correlated with a number of other variables. Not surprisingly, the caretakers of active infants were more positively active themselves (more smiling, for example, but not more rocking or feeding). In addition, the correlations indicated that the more active infants had been fed more recently. Scale 1, in short, is not a pure and generalizable measure of the infant. An infant may display more or less positive activity during an observation because of hunger or drowsiness, or because of stimulating caretakers and visitors. Five more scales were developed, therefore, in a way that permitted such features to be included. Again factor analysis was used, but the pool of variables included, in addition to infant behaviors, caretaker behaviors (such as vocalization and picking up), interactive measures (such as the proportion of infant behaviors that were sequentially chained with caretaker behaviors, but not including redundant measures such as caretaker responses to infant fret), and setting variables (such as the number of people present and the infant's initial mood at the beginning of the observation). This procedure assumes, in effect, that no general judgment can be made about a particular infant solely on the basis of his or her behavior because of uncontrolled variation in the setting, but that useful measures can be derived of infant–caretaker-behavior-in-a-context. (An additional adjustment for setting is described at the end of this section.)

Interpretation of the factor solution to this larger data set was facilitated by a Varimax rotation. The resulting factor structure was similar enough at the two ages for five matching scales to be constructed at 4 and 8 months. At both ages the same items are included by using (with only minor exceptions) .40 as the criterion loading. The five scales are:

Scale 2. High scores on this scale indicate happy babies who organized a large percentage of their activity in consort with an active and stimulating caretaker. Standard scores of the following items were summed for the scale: infant smile, number of chains proportional to the total of infant behaviors, and caretaker look at baby, give toy to baby, play with baby, smile at baby, and vocalize to baby.

Scale 3. Fussy, tired babies received high scores. The scale consisted of a rating of infant mood at the beginning of observation, 5-minute judgments of infant drowsiness and (negatively) alertness, and frequency of infant fretting.

Scale 4. The dull baby ("blank stare") who was picked up by the caretaker and did little independent playing (minus play alone) scored high.

Scale 5. Interaction with many people other than the mother is reflected in this scale. It is a sum of standard scores of the amount of interaction with people other than the caretaker, the number of people present, ratings of the noncentrality of the mother as caretaker, and (negative) the amount of interaction with the mother.

Scale 6. This scale identifies a quiet baby often held by a caretaker who is socializing with someone else. It consists of standard scores for caretaker socialize, caretaker pick up baby, minus infant vocalize, and minus the proportion of chaining to caretaker behavior.

Three other scales were constructed on the basis of factor analysis of the derived measures of caretaker responses:

Scale 7. The proportion of infant vocalizations and frets to which the caretaker responded.
Scale 8. The proportion of caretaker responses to vocalizations and frets which were themselves vocalizations (in contrast to only looking).
Scale 9. The proportion of caretaker responses to vocalizations which were smiles (in contrast to vocalizations), combined with nonfeeding responses to frets.

Only for Scale 5 did a situational feature of the setting (number of people present) qualify for inclusion. Nevertheless, several scales were found to be significantly correlated with situational features. In order to further adjust for such effects, therefore, the 9 summary scales were regressed on three situational measures (time since last feeding, time since last sleep, and number of people present), and the residuals were saved for further analysis. These residual scores can be conceptualized as adjusted scales for which potential confounding of the observational setting has been statistically controlled. Although statistical adjustment of this sort can be problematic, the results presented below suggest the adjustment was effective and the residual scales are meaningful measures.

THE EFFECTS OF INTERVENTION

Nutritional Supplementation and Maternal Education are crossed factors in a true experiment. Classical analysis of variance is therefore appropriate and a causal interpretation of group differences is possible. Sex is included as a third factor in the analyses because of its known effects in behavioral interaction (e.g., Moss, 1967) and its statistical independence from group assignment. Tables 9.1–9.6 present the results of analysis of variance on the nine scales and the corresponding residual scales.

At Four Months

Effect Maternal Education. The effects of Maternal Education were straightforward and consistent with the goals of the intervention. Mothers enrolled in the home visiting program were observed to be especially active and stimulating with their babies who, in turn, responded with happy interaction (Scale 2, Table 9.1); this was especially true for mothers with daughters (significant interaction of Education × Sex). The home visit program also increased the probability of mothers' responding to their infants' vocalizations and frets, and their responses were especially likely to be vocalizations (Scales 7 and 8).

Analysis of the setting of the observations indicated that more people were present in the homes of the mothers in the education program. As there was no average difference in family size, it appears the occasion of the observation attracted neighbors in the same way as the weekly educational visits. Situational analysis also indicated that there was more positive interaction (Scale 2) when more people were present; the rate of responding to infant positive and negative vocalizations was also higher (Scale 7), but the caretaker responses tended not to be vocalizations (Scale 8). Analysis of variance of the residuals of the situational regressions, however, which adjusted for the number of people, revealed that the

TABLE 9.1
Results of Analysis of Variance at 4 Months:
Scale Scores

Scale	n	Nutritional SUPP F	p	Maternal EDUC F	p	SEX F	p	SUPP × EDUC F	p	SUPP × SEX F	p	EDUC × SEX F	p	SUPP × EDUC × SEX F	p
1 activity	198	4.58	.03	2.01	ns	3.36	.07	4.35	.04	1.18	ns	0.14	ns	0.45	ns
2 happy interaction	198	1.60	ns	10.05	.002	0.75	ns	0.22	ns	1.03	ns	7.86	.006	0.38	ns
3 tired fussy baby	198	3.14	.08	0.39	ns	0.04	ns	2.34	ns	3.23	.07	1.09	ns	0.30	ns
4 dull baby, picked up	198	0.37	ns	0.44	ns	2.86	.09	3.29	.07	0.06	ns	0.19	ns	3.14	.08
5 caretaker not mother	198	0.02	ns	0.09	ns	1.36	ns	0.08	ns	0.63	ns	2.28	ns	0.05	ns
6 quiet baby social caretaker	198	1.67	ns	1.23	ns	5.35	.02	0.85	ns	0.01	ns	0.78	ns	0.23	ns
7 caretaker respond	198	0.80	ns	16.57	.001	0.00	ns	2.05	ns	1.07	ns	0.09	ns	0.13	ns
8 vocalization responses	184	1.91	ns	4.95	.03	1.90	ns	0.01	ns	0.10	ns	0.21	ns	1.87	ns
9 smile responses	184	0.12	ns	0.77	ns	0.19	ns	0.28	ns	0.00	ns	2.16	ns	2.05	ns

effects of the home tutoring program cannot be attributed only to the situational effect. The main effect of Maternal Education on happy interaction remained significant (Table 9.2), and caretaker responsiveness remained high and verbal in the tutored groups (Scales 7 and 8).

Effect of Supplementation. Nutritional Supplementation influenced infant behavior both directly and in interaction with Maternal Education and Sex. Supplemented infants, in general, were seen to have higher levels of positive activity (Scale 1, Table 9.1). In addition, supplemented babies were especially active if their mothers participated in the home education program (Supplementation × Education interaction). Supplementation had a marginal effect on Scale 3, decreasing the amount of tired fussing, but in fact it was significant only for males.

TABLE 9.2
Results of Analysis of Variance at 4 Months:
Adjusted Scores (Residuals)

Scale	n	Nutritional SUPP F	p	Maternal EDUC F	p	SEX F	p	SUPP × EDUC F	p	SUPP × SEX F	p	EDUC × SEX F	p	SUPP × EDUC × SEX F	p
1res positive activity	194	2.16	ns	2.11	ns	3.41	.07	6.93	.01	3.05	.08	0.34	ns	0.25	ns
2res happy interaction	194	0.67	ns	5.38	.02	0.54	ns	0.15	ns	0.33	ns	0.17	ns	0.40	ns
3res tired, fussy baby	194	3.11	.08	0.11	ns	0.01	ns	2.99	.09	2.95	.09	1.45	ns	0.02	ns
4res dull baby, picked up	194	0.16	ns	0.87	ns	1.99	ns	5.83	.02	0.89	ns	0.01	ns	1.85	ns
5res caretaker not mother	194	2.15	ns	4.30	.04	2.81	.10	0.49	ns	0.08	ns	4.98	.03	0.02	ns
6res quiet baby social caretaker	194	0.64	ns	0.41	ns	5.61	.02	1.52	ns	0.43	ns	0.54	ns	0.04	ns
7res caretaker respond	194	0.25	ns	11.73	.001	0.02	ns	2.01	ns	1.60	ns	0.11	ns	0.05	ns
8res vocalization responses	181	1.14	ns	6.79	.01	2.33	ns	0.08	ns	0.03	ns	0.04	ns	1.51	ns
9res smile responses	181	0.03	ns	1.54	ns	0.65	ns	0.37	ns	0.01	ns	1.91	ns	2.10	ns

Regression of these two scales on the situational measures yielded significant results on Scale 1, indicating that positive activity was higher in infants who were more recently awakened and fed, and when many people were around. Analysis of the residual scores, therefore, gives an indication of whether or not the supplementation effects described above are primarily mediated by these factors or whether they hold independent power. This test of direct effects is in fact a very conservative one, for Supplementation had an effect on time since last sleep: babies without supplementation had been awake longer when the observation began (F (1/196) = 9.09, p = .003). The regression therefore removed as well that portion of the variance in the dependent variables which is shared by the situational and experimental indices.

The regression procedure eliminated the main effect of Supplementation (Scale 1, Table 9.2). The interaction with Maternal Education persisted, however, so that even controlling for time since sleeping and eating, supplemented infants were more active if their mothers were in the home visiting program, while unsupplemented infants were not affected by maternal education.

The marginal influence of Supplementation on tired fussing (Scale 3) remained in the adjusted scores, and became more visible in interaction with Maternal Education: Education marginally increased tired fussing for the unsupplemented infants, presumably because it increased at least momentary demands on limited energies, while it decreased fussing for the better nourished babies, probably because the infants' behavior was more positively organized in response to the stimulating caretakers. In addition, Supplementation decreased tired fussing for males, but not for females (again at a marginal level of statistical confidence).

At Eight Months

Effect of Education. The home visiting program continued to have a significant effect when the infants were 8 months old, but the nature of the effect changed. Apparently, the novelty of the home visits diminished for the neighbors, for the number of people present was no longer affected. Mothers in the program were more likely than those not tutored, however, to retain exclusive charge of their babies instead of sharing the responsibility with another caretaker (usually an elder daughter). This is reflected in the fact that they were more often within sight of the baby than were the nonprogram mothers and that there were fewer people actually interacting with the baby ($F(1/171)$ = 11.31, p = .001; $F(1/179)$ = 5.70, p = .02). The mothers, in fact, were often holding their babies, resulting in a greater frequency of interaction ($F(1/180)$ = 7.16, p = .009). On the other hand, the babies were also more likely to play by themselves for a short period ($F(1/180)$ = 2.80, p = .10). This complex picture is summarized by Scale 6 (Table 9.3), indicating the tutored mother socialized

TABLE 9.3
Results of Analysis of Variance at 8 Months:
Scale Scores

Scale n	Nutritional SUPP F	p	Maternal EDUC F	p	SEX F	p	SUPP × EDUC F	p	SUPP × SEX F	p	EDUC × SEX F	p	SUPP × EDUC × SEX F	p
1 180 positive activity	0.06	ns	0.03	ns	1.08	ns	2.23	ns	0.03	ns	2.72	ns	1.09	ns
2 180 happy interaction	0.34	ns	0.82	ns	0.08	ns	0.01	ns	2.20	ns	0.06	ns	0.98	ns
3 180 tired, fussy baby	0.20	ns	1.21	ns	0.10	ns	1.65	ns	0.00	ns	0.53	ns	0.64	ns
4 180 dull baby picked up	0.23	ns	0.54	ns	1.19	ns	2.40	ns	1.46	ns	0.17	ns	3.63	.06
5 180 caretaker not mother	0.22	ns	12.05	.0007	0.38	ns	0.01	ns	0.73	ns	1.12	ns	0.59	ns
6 180 quiet baby social caretaker	0.35	ns	8.66	.004	5.32	.02	1.45	ns	0.02	ns	0.36	ns	8.04	.005
7 173 caretaker respond	0.50	ns	15.77	.001	0.64	ns	1.95	ns	2.21	ns	0.48	ns	0.01	ns
8 173 vocalization responses	0.00	ns	1.52	ns	0.38	ns	0.07	ns	3.27	.07	1.78	ns	0.00	ns
9 173 smile responses	0.11	ns	1.02	ns	0.02	ns	0.85	ns	2.37	ns	1.97	ns	0.19	ns

while the baby was quiet and content, but she picked the baby up rather frequently; and by Scale 5, indicating the tutored mother was more likely than the untutored mother to be the central caretaker.

The caretakers in the maternal education groups were also more likely to respond when the babies vocalized or fretted (Scale 7). As already noted, however, the baby whose mother was not in the program was more likely to be in the care of a sister. The sister was not socializing with others, apparently, but was in fact providing a socially active, if not equally responsive, environment. Overall, infants not in the home-tutoring condition received and gave more smiles (caretaker smile, $F(1/180) = 8.60$, $p = .004$; infant smile, $F(1/180) = 5.28$, $p = .02$).

As is the case at 4 months, and as indicated by the description just offered, the pattern of care is related to features of the situation observed. In this case, Scales 5, 6, and 7 are related to the number of people, and Scale 6 to the time since sleep as well. Controlling for these factors, however, does not eliminate the main effects of Maternal Education (Table 9.4).

Effect of Supplementation. At 8 months, Nutritional Supplementation no longer had any main effects on the summary scales, and only one interaction reached standard confidence levels (supplemented girls of women in the tutoring program were especially high on Scale 6). The adjusted residual scores yield a similar picture (Table 9.4). This overall result, however, masks a continuation of the effect of supplementation for those babies who were still breast-fed.

TABLE 9.4
Results of Analysis of Variance at 8 Months:
Adjusted Scores (Residuals)

Scale	n	Nutritional SUPP F	p	Maternal EDUC F	p	SEX F	p	SUPP × EDUC F	p	SUPP × SEX F	p	EDUC × SEX F	p	SUPP × EDUC × SEX F	p
1res positive activity	178	0.01	ns	0.02	ns	0.85	ns	1.54	ns	0.02	ns	2.58	ns	1.04	ns
2res happy interaction	178	0.26	ns	0.59	ns	0.02	ns	0.31	ns	1.72	ns	0.23	ns	2.11	ns
3res tired, fussy baby	178	0.26	ns	1.03	ns	0.16	ns	2.14	ns	0.00	ns	0.66	ns	0.36	ns
4res dull baby, picked up	178	0.27	ns	0.34	ns	0.67	ns	2.01	ns	0.74	ns	0.10	ns	2.91	.09
5res caretaker not mother	178	0.68	ns	10.84	.001	0.09	ns	0.42	ns	0.02	ns	2.34	ns	0.01	ns
6res quiet baby social caretaker	178	0.59	ns	8.66	.004	4.37	.04	2.35	ns	0.10	ns	0.24	ns	5.64	.02
7res caretaker respond	173	0.53	ns	15.32	.0001	0.89	ns	1.27	ns	1.87	ns	0.42	ns	0.02	ns
8res vocalization response	173	0.06	ns	0.75	ns	0.52	ns	0.19	ns	3.26	.07	1.88	ns	0.01	ns
9res smile response	173	0.06	ns	0.71	ns	0.01	ns	0.76	ns	2.46	ns	2.00	ns	0.11	ns

The median age at weaning for the full sample was 5.4 months, or midway between the two observation points. Age at weaning was not affected by experimental group, except for a significant interaction of Sex and Maternal Education: being in the home-visited group slightly hastened the average weaning for the females and delayed it for the males ($F(1.192) = 4.69$, $p = .003$). This effect seems to account for the three-way interaction noted earlier. Up until the point of weaning, the major portion of the infant's nutrition came through the mother who, in some groups, was herself receiving nutritional supplementation. After weaning, adequate nutrition was available for children in the experimental groups, but actual ingestion of the food depended on a new set of parental and infant behaviors. It seems reasonable that the group differences seen at 4 months might be disrupted around the point of weaning as parents started their children on solid foods with an effectiveness unrelated to experimental group.

TABLE 9.5
Results of Analysis of Variance at 8 Months:
Breast-Fed Only: Scale Scores

Scale	n	Nutritional SUPP F	p	Maternal EDUC F	p	SEX F	p	SUPP × EDUC F	p	SUPP × SEX F	p	EDUC × SEX F	p	SUPP × EDUC × SEX F	p
1 positive activity	47	3.79	.06	0.39	ns	0.09	ns	0.02	ns	0.00	ns	0.57	ns	0.99	ns
2 happy interaction	47	0.05	ns	0.36	ns	0.21	ns	0.69	ns	0.01	ns	3.48	.07	0.15	ns
3 tired, fussy baby	47	0.33	ns	0.79	ns	0.01	ns	1.01	ns	0.26	ns	0.42	ns	0.21	ns
4 dull baby, picked up	47	2.62	ns	0.19	ns	0.57	ns	0.17	ns	0.01	ns	0.31	ns	3.19	.08
5 caretaker not mother	47	0.05	ns	2.37	ns	0.79	ns	0.00	ns	1.87	ns	0.92	ns	1.05	ns
6 quiet baby, social caretaker	47	6.17	.02	0.29	ns	0.14	ns	0.09	ns	0.01	ns	0.04	ns	6.06	.02
7 caretaker respond	47	3.20	.08	3.56	.07	1.67	ns	1.08	ns	7.76	.01	0.92	ns	0.02	ns
8 vocalization response	47	1.12	ns	2.00	ns	0.43	ns	0.40	ns	0.47	ns	0.03	ns	0.16	ns
9 smile response	47	1.15	ns	4.06	.05	0.45	ns	0.41	ns	1.16	ns	0.08	ns	2.34	ns

TABLE 9.6
Results of Analysis of Variance at 8 Months:
Breast-Fed Only: Adjusted Scores (Residuals)

Scale	n	Nutritional SUPP		Maternal EDUC		SEX		SUPP × EDUC		SUPP × SEX		EDUC × SEX		SUPP × EDUC × SEX	
		F	p	F	p	F	p	F	p	F	p	F	p	F	p
1res positive activity	46	3.22	.09	0.44	ns	0.00	ns	0.01	ns	0.00	ns	0.71	ns	0.44	ns
2res happy interaction	46	0.10	ns	0.70	ns	0.47	ns	0.67	ns	0.07	ns	2.97	.09	0.04	ns
3res tired, fussy baby	46	0.38	ns	0.94	ns	0.03	ns	1.04	ns	0.21	ns	0.40	ns	0.25	ns
4res dull baby, picked up	46	2.76	.10	0.28	ns	0.49	ns	0.03	ns	0.00	ns	0.36	ns	2.49	ns
5res caretaker not mother	46	0.00	ns	3.78	.06	0.73	ns	0.38	ns	1.71	ns	0.84	ns	1.16	ns
6res quiet baby, social caretaker	46	6.61	.01	0.01	ns	0.07	ns	0.36	ns	0.01	ns	0.06	ns	4.57	.04
7res caretaker respond	46	3.17	.08	3.08	.09	1.49	ns	0.93	ns	7.18	.01	0.88	ns	0.01	ns
8res vocalization response	46	0.81	ns	1.48	ns	0.97	ns	0.28	ns	0.58	ns	0.13	ns	0.55	ns
9res smile response	46	1.24	ns	3.40	.07	0.39	ns	0.48	ns	0.96	ns	0.11	ns	2.83	.10

Slightly fewer than one-third of the infants were still breast-feeding at 8 months. The results of an analysis of variance on only these infants is included in Table 9.5. Effects of Maternal Education are less evident here than for the full sample. This may be partly due to the smaller number of subjects, but it certainly reflects the fact that the shift to nonmaternal caretaking by untutored mothers occurred primarily for weaned infants. Effects of Nutritional Supplementation, in contrast, become more visible. Nonsupplemented infants are seen on Scale 6 to be more quiet than the supplemented infants; while this might be interpreted in more than one way (see the effects of Education above), the results from Scale 1, positive activity, suggest that an important element is the babies' apathy: supplemented infants were more positively active. In addition, caretaker responsiveness was greater to supplemented males than to unsupplemented ones. These effects remain when scores are adjusted for the influence of setting (Table 9.6).

DISCUSSION

The results of the intervention programs are generally consistent with a broad range of prior research and theory. The home visiting program succeeded in altering the mothers' (and probably the sibling-caretakers') behavior. Tutored mothers were more responsive to the infants' vocal signals. At the younger age, they displayed more positive, playful behavior to the babies, and the babies responded in kind. Nutritional supplementation increased the infants' level of positive activity, social as well as nonsocial, as long as the babies were breast-fed. This was in part, initially, the result of being less tired and hungry (an interesting effect in its own right), but in addition the supplemented infants were better able to respond to the caretakers' level of stimulation even when the mediating state was statistically controlled.

There are two ways the present results add to our understanding of the consequences of nutritional deficit and the role of early interaction. First, the intervention design of this study permits a stronger causal interpretation than has been possible in the earlier correlational work, or in experimental models with less secure design and measures. Equally important, the results permit a preliminary differentiation of some of the pathways of behavioral mediation of moderate malnutrition. We have presented strong evidence for the hypothesized link between moderate malnutrition and lowered energy for participation in the social and physical environment. It remains for later reports to evaluate the consequences for competence, but unqualified demonstration of the behavioral effect is an advance.

The pattern of caretaker behavior and infant–caretaker interaction can be influenced through an education program directed at understanding the nature of infants and their needs for development. Although many mothers were initially reserved and doubtful of the educational program, they were quickly won over to the excitement and enjoyment of the more active, supportive, and responsive style of interacting with their babies. Their moment-to-moment behaviors were altered, and at the older age, the pattern of caretaking was too. Unlike the case in American folk and scientific theory, mothers in these barrios do not consider multiple caretaking to be potentially detrimental to the baby—mothers who indicated an interest in teaching their infants, in fact, were more likely than uninterested mothers to share the caretaking tasks. With the educational intervention, however, their interests and values shifted not only in content but also in structure; the highly motivated mothers now retained more exclusive care of their babies. The later cognitive consequences of this pattern, and the discrete behaviors that accompany it, are not evaluated here, but it is evident that maternal beliefs and values play a role in directing early experience. This role can be differentiated from the role of infant behavior and it can be addressed through separate interventions.

The mutual interplay of maternal and infant behavior, on the other hand, is attested to by several of the interaction effects reported here—that more active and responsive caretaking, for example, results in greater infant activity only under circumstances of adequate nutrition. Of more particular theoretical interest is the overlap of nutritional supplementation effects and caretaker behavior that begins to be visible at 8 months for the breast-fed babies: The greater activity of the better nourished infants coincided with more, and more responsive, caretaker interaction.

CONCLUSION

Human development does not proceed through isolated mechanisms. The emergence and shaping of social interaction involves a complex system of infant and parent behavior, guided in part by culturally defined values and expectations, and self-regulating in a context of resources for caretaking; there is a developmental course for the system as well as for the maturing individual (Super & Harkness, in press). Comparing existing cultural variations in early interaction has proven essential in revealing large scale features of the developmental system, such as the integration of social behavior and adult values, and in demonstrating common species characteristics. It is difficult however, to derive from static comparisons any firm understanding of the dynamics of early behavioral development and adaptation; yet the opportunities for experimental analysis are obviously rare. In addition to their programmatic implications, the results presented here are useful to theorists for their relatively straightforward causal interpretation concerning two points: moderate malnutrition in the first year does reduce infant activity, and direct intervention concerning maternal beliefs about infant development alters the mother's behavior. Both effects can be seen in immediate behavior, as well as in larger aspects of the systematic regulation of behavior such as assignment of caretaking responsibility and elicitation of response. There is also evidence for synergistic effects. The dynamics of interaction at this level present a challenge to the evaluation of intervention programs, but they also suggest a conceptual approach to understanding the pathways of influence of any single factor, whether naturally occurring or experimentally introduced.

ACKNOWLEDGMENTS

The research reported here was carried out as a collaborative project of the Colombian Institute of Family Welfare; the Department of Nutrition, Harvard School of Public Health; and the Institute of Nutrition, Justus Liebig University, Giessen, Germany. It was supported in part by the National Institute of Child Health and Human Development (USA) Grant RO1-HD06774-01A1; Ford Foundation grant 740-0348; The German Research Foundation; and the Fund for Research and Teaching, Department of Nutrition, Harvard School of Public Health. All views expressed and statements made are the sole responsibility of the authors.

REFERENCES

Brazelton, T. B., Tronick, E., Lechtig, A., Lasky, R., & Klein, R. The behavior of nutritionally deprived Guatemalan infants. *Developmental Medicine and Child Neurology*, 1977, *19*, 364-372.
Caudill, W., & Weinstein, H. Maternal care and infant behavior in Japan and America. *Psychiatry*, 1969, *32*, 12-43.
Chavez, A., Martinez, C., & Yaschine, T. The importance of nutrition and stimuli on child mental and social development. In J. Cravioto, L. Hambraeus, & B. Vahlquist (Eds.), *Early malnutrition and mental development*. Stockholm: Almquist & Wiksell, 1974.
Christiansen, N., Mora, J. O., & Herrera, M. G. Family social characteristics related to physical growth of young children. *British Journal of Preventive and Social Medicine*, 1975, *29*, 121-130.
Clarke-Stewart, K. A. Interactions between mothers and their young children: Characteristics and consequences. *Monographs of the Society for Research in Child Development*, 1973, *38* (6).
Dasen, P., Inhelder, B., Lavallée, M., & Retschitzki, J. *Naissance de l'intelligence chez l'enfant baoulé de Côte d'Ivoire*. Berne: Hans Huber, 1978.
Dobbing, J. Undernutrition and the developing brain: The relevance of animal models to the human problem. *American Journal of Diseases of Childhood*, 1970, *120*, 411-416.
Dobbing, J. Vulnerability of developing brain and behavior. *British Medical Journal*, 1974, *30*, 164-168.
Graves, P. L. Nutrition, infant behavior, and maternal characteristics: A pilot study in West Bengal, India. *American Journal of Clinical Nutrition*, 1976, *29*, 305-319.
Klein, R. E., Lasky, R. E., Yarbrough, C., Habicht, J.-P., & Sellers, M. J. Relationship of infant/caretaker interaction, social class and nutritional status to developmental test performance among Guatemalan infants. In P. H. Leiderman, S. R. Tulkin, & A. Rosenfeld (Eds.), *Culture and Infancy: Variations in the human experience*. New York: Academic Press, 1977.
Lambie, D. Z., Bond. J. T., & Weikart, D. P. *Home teaching with mothers and infants*. High/Scope Educational Research Foundation, Ypsilanti, Michigan, 1974.
Lester, B. M. A synergistic process approach to the study of prenatal malnutrition. *International Journal of Behavioral Development*. 1979, *2*, 377-393.
Lewis, M., & Ban, P. Variance and invariance in the mother-infant interaction: A cross-cultural study. In P. H. Leiderman, S. R. Tulkin, & A. Rosenfeld (Eds.), *Culture and infancy: Variations in the human experience*. New York: Academic Press, 1977.
Lewis, M., & Lee-Painter, S. An interactional approach to the mother-infant dyad. In M. Lewis & L. A. Rosenblum (Eds.), *The effect of the infant on its caregiver*. New York: Wiley, 1974.
Mora, J. O., de Navarro, L., Clement, J., Wagner, M., de Paredes, B., & Herrera, M. G. The effect of nutritional supplementation on calorie and protein intake of pregant women. *Nutrition Reports International*, 1978, *17*, 217-226.
Moss, H. A. Sex, age, and state as determinants of mother-infant interaction. *Merrill-Palmer Quarterly*, 1967, *13*, 19-36.
Ortiz, N., Florez, A., Clement, J., Mora, J. O., & Cuellar, E. *Investigación sobre desnutrición y desarrollo mental en Bogotá: Analisis de contenido del programa de estimulación temprana*. Unpublished manuscript. Available from M. G. Herrera, School of Public Health, Boston, Mass.
Piaget, J. *The origins of intelligence in children*. New York: International Universities Press, 1952 (originally published 1936).
Pollitt, E. Ecology, malnutrition, and mental development. *Psychosomatic Medicine*, 1969, *31*, 193.
Pollitt, E. Failure to thrive: Socioeconomic, dietary intake, and mother-child interaction data. *Federation Proceedings*, 1975, *34*, 1593-1597.
Super, C. M., & Harkness, S. The development of affect in infancy and early childhood. In H. Stevenson & D. Wagner (Eds.), *Cultural perspectives on child development*, San Francisco: Freeman, in press.

10 Early Interactions in the Marquesas Islands

Mary Martini
University of Chicago

John Kirkpatrick
Brown University

INTRODUCTION

In this chapter, ethnographic observations and a film study of caregiver–infant interactions on an island in the Marquesas Islands, French Polynesia, are reported.

In the Marquesas, infants have multiple caregivers and extensive social contact. Caregiver–infant interactions differ in notable ways from those reported in the bulk of mother–infant literature. Although the study of socialization in Polynesia is not new, studies of other Polynesian peoples (e.g., Howard, 1970, 1974; Levy, 1973; Ritchie, 1956; Ritchie & Ritchie, 1979) devote little attention to the details of early interactions. The authors of these studies argue that certain lessons are learned in infancy, but do not deal extensively with the infant's interactive experience or with the specific contributions of different caregivers. Hence they do not locate socialization processes as occurring with particular caregivers nor do they relate their account of Polynesian development to more general theories. Here we examine filmed interactions in order to identify components of early socialization developed in particular interactions. We draw on ethnographic knowledge to evaluate the film record, to identify other components, and to view Marquesan interactions with infants in the context of theories of early development.

ETHNOGRAPHIC BACKGROUND

The research was conducted on 'Ua Pou, where the first author worked in 1976–1977 and the second author worked in 1975–1977. Like the other islands of the Marquesas, 'Ua Pou is a high volcanic island, with rugged terrain. By 1977, it was the most populous island in the group, with 1563 inhabitants. The population is unevenly distributed in narrow valleys: one valley includes nearly eight hundred people whereas some contain less than one hundred. Valleys extend from the seashore toward the heights at the center of the island. People live toward the shore, going upland mainly for purposes of cultivation.

The populated area is a warm, rather dry zone with up to 33 persons per hectare. Infants come into proximity with a wide range of people when they are carried to church, movies, and other public events. (See Kirkpatrick, 1980a for further background information.)

Nowadays, Marquesans are Christians, and mainly Roman Catholic. Many people are literate in Marquesan as well as French or Tahitian. The local economy is mixed: subsistence horticulture and fishing, organized at the domestic level, provide basic resources; however, cash crop exports and wage labor are widespread. Marquesans value "progress" for their islands and shun practices that they consider to be "heathen."

In the two valleys in which extensive observations and filming were done, medical care was usually available from a trained paramedic or doctor. Both prenatal and postnatal medical services were well accepted. In accordance with Marquesan understandings of health a good deal of attention is given to keeping babies clean and well oiled. Though infant mortality has declined appreciably in recent decades, mothers continue to worry about the possibility of infant death during the first few months of life.

Marquesan households are often composed of one couple and their children: this pattern is seen as proper. However, with current levels of natality, these are not small groupings. In about half the households in the valleys studied, residential affiliation is complex due to the presence of fostered children, elderly dependents, adolescents boarding with a family while they attend school, or more than one couple residing in a household. The mean household population in the ethnographic sample is over seven persons per household (Kirkpatrick, 1980a: 79ff).

Marquesans marry far earlier in life than do many Protestant French Polynesians, for whom marriage seals an accomplished conjugal union, rather than initiating it. Immediate postmarital residence is often with the parents of one of the spouses. Consequently, first-born children are rarely the first-born in a household. Other children are available in the household as additional caregivers.

Whereas it is usually easy to identify a primary caregiver—the mother or foster mother—others have regular, extensive involvement with an infant, and even more people interact episodically with him. The primary caregiver need not, in fact, be the person most often found caring for the infant, especially after the baby's first few months. Children of 4- to 8-years are expected to take charge of infants for hours at a time. Older girls or elderly women may be regular daytime caregivers, who remain in the household while the mother goes to work elsewhere. The primary caregiver is not always socially distinctive in terms of her actions, but rather, in terms of authority. Culturally, the idea of nurturant care, of *hākai* "feeding," is focused on the mother, rather than elder siblings. Elder siblings may perform much of the job of child care, but they gain credit for this only when seen as mother substitutes (Kirkpatrick, 1980b). Thus we find one Marquesan referring to his older sister as "Mama" in his sentimental moments, "because she fed me and cared for me when I was young."

Once the cultural priority given to the mother as the ideal caregiver is noted, the treatment of others as "feeders" should also be recognized. Husbands are generally expected to "feed" by providing food for their households. More importantly in this context, many Marquesans recognize particular ascendants as their *tupuna hākai*, "feeding grandparents." A *tupuna hākai* may be an indulgent elder who gives a small child delicacies or who shelters the child from parents' irritation; the term is also used for fosterers, who care for children when natal parents do not. Marquesans expect, then, that the mother is the primary source of care and nurturance. Supplementary caregivers, however, who may be more indulgent or even more competent than the mother, are also expected to interact with the child and make valued contributions to his wellbeing.

MARQUESAN VIEWS OF DEVELOPMENT

Five broad stages of life are commonly distinguished in Marquesan speech: a person is an infant (*pēpē*), a child (*tō'iki*), a "wandering youth" (*taure'are'a*), a mature adult, and then an old person. Strictly speaking, these are moral stages, not age categories: maturity, for instance, may be incomplete or intermittent. The major indices Marquesans use to note people's life stage have to do with mobility, knowledge of the world, competence at everyday tasks, willingness to perform tasks, and styles of interpersonal relationship. With regard to all these criteria for distinguishing what sort of person one is, the infant is marked by minimal ability or performance.

Marquesans will say of a child of 3- to 5-years that he "has become a person" when a minimal interpersonal competence is attained. When seen as immobile and dependent, infants barely seem persons at all. Caregivers, however, view many infant behaviors as demands or reactions to bodily and environmental states. They note the acquisition of basic skills and interpersonal learning. Exploratory behavior is often seen as willful. Caregivers find evidence for a complex personality in these behaviors: *their* infant is viewed as a distinctive being in his own right.

Marquesan views of the life cycle are also relevant to an account of the infant's surroundings. Marquesans expect mature persons to be committed to an orderly and nurturant domestic life. The mature agent "recognizes what is to be done, and does it," by doing the job or delegating it to a dependent. Mature adults are characterized by *ka'oha* "concern" (cognate with the Hawaiian *aloha*), a combination of sensitive sympathy for others and willingness to ease others' difficulties. These expectations imply that adults take on valued identities in relation to infants and children not so much as interactants but as coordinators of activity and as facilitators of their children's attempts to act. Hence adults can be expected to be highly attentive to infants and to call on their adult "concern" and intelligence to provide a safe and supportive context for the infant's development. There is no expectation, however, that they set aside their maturity to engage in the "play" expected of children.

DESCRIPTIONS OF INFANCY

Seventeen mothers were interviewed concerning the developmental milestones, daily routines, and range and nature of social contacts of their infants and children. Questions were designed to elicit discussion of socialization goals and practices.

The mothers were in striking agreement as to a normative chronology of infant development, and noted regularly whether an infant was developing quickly or slowly. "Stocky" babies were believed to develop more quickly than "skinny" ones, but in making these observations the mothers were most concerned with the health and feeding patterns of the babies rather than with their motor or verbal skills. Mothers were particularly concerned if a baby was thin, did not nurse well, or did not easily accept canned milk or soft foods. Intestinal flu, fevers, diarrhea and dehydration were especially feared during the first two months of life. In spite of the fact that Marquesan babies are remarkably healthy, mothers gravitated toward topics of infant feeding and health, rather than motor or language development. They conveyed the sense that development occurs as a matter of course and requires little active teaching or attention by the mother, whereas optimal feeding occasionally does require sensitive maternal care. This parallels the cultural conception of the mother as "feeder."

Developmental stages in infancy were described in terms of the infant's physical maturation, the effects of this on changes in childcare practices, and the resultant expansion of the baby's social world. For example, when bottle feeding is introduced at 2 or 3 months, the infant can be left for longer periods with an alternate caregiver, such as the father or grandmother.

According to the reports, an infant is cared for almost exclusively by the mother for the first 2 or 3 months. The resident grandmother or adolescent daughter may be relied on for short periods of holding, but the infant is not yet entrusted to other women and children. This is a period of extensive contact between mother and infant. Mothers believe that even young infants visually attend or listen to them, and they spend much time holding and playing with their babies. They stress, however, that the young infant does not "really" understand language or know how to smile, talk, or play.

Typically, infants are breast-fed. Some mothers introduce bottle-feeding at 2- to 3-months, supplementing their own milk and gaining some freedom from constant infant care. While others tend the infant, they can go upland to work or to the shore to fish. By four months, when the baby can sit with minimal support, he is entrusted to the care of other children in the household and is passed around to other women at church or public events. The infant is handled somewhat more brusquely, and typically is cared for while facing away from the caregiver. For example, feeding is done from behind as the infant sits on a caregiver's lap. The undiapered baby is held away from the caregiver when the caregiver thinks he will urinate. All routine caregiving activities are performed while the baby faces outward.

By 5- or 6-months of age the infant is in the care of a number of people. Soft foods such as bananas and rice are introduced, freeing the mother of feeding duties. Older siblings often bathe and dress the infant, and young children carry the baby around the valley where they care for him while watching their friends play. In this situation, the infant is engaged in intensive face-to-face play with many of the valley children.

By 6- to 8-months Marquesan infants produce "easy" sounds such as *mama*, *papa*, and *nanā*, a quasi-French baby-talk greeting. They point to what they want, wave at people, and play games such as peek-a-boo, or look at so-and-so. Most baby games are socially complex, involving three or more people, e.g., one person holds the infant and directs him to look at, hit, push, kiss, wave at, or sit on the shoulders of another. The recipient of these actions is usually the 3- to 5-year-old sibling, who patiently tolerates the games. It is said that infants do not "really" know how to speak until 12 months of age when they can express their needs with words such as "food," "where's Papa?," "go to sea?," or "play ball." From 1 year on they are described regularly as "too noisy" and "too willful." By 24 months their command of pragmatically charged phrases—e.g., *umaha?*, which roughly means, "why in the world?" (should you ask/tell me that)—is noted and found amusing.

Initially infants creep on their stomachs, then crawl on hands and knees, and then creep on all fours, particularly on rough surfaces outside the house. A "stocky" baby may pull himself to stand and walk with support as early as 10 months. A "skinny" baby may walk as late as 18 months. Parents and child-caregivers delight in leading the baby around for his early steps and they toss objects for the child to fetch. In general, Marquesans delight in the incomplete development of infant skills and prompt the baby to perform imperfect sequences again and again while they laugh.

In many respects, 12 months is a major developmental turning point. The infant now stands and walks with support and is taken readily by siblings to the sea, stream, path and schoolyard to play. The baby becomes less bothersome because he no longer needs to be carried. On the other hand, the mother's job becomes increasingly difficult because the year-old infant constantly wanders into dangerous situations (e.g., onto the rocky hillside on which the houses are built) and also grabs at sharp household objects. Mothers do not restrict infant activities with strong "no's" but rather, try to distract them from dangerous or annoying behavior.

The 12- to 18-month-old eats solid foods and makes efforts to feed and dress himself. In addition, the child begins to understand to go outside to urinate and defecate. Weaning often occurs at this time, particularly if the mother is pregnant. An infant is always weaned before a new baby arrives. Similarly, the child is displaced from sleeping immediately next to his mother with the birth of a new baby. Children may continue to sleep near their parents, however, until 3- or 4-years-old, when they join the older sibling group in another area or room.

By 18- to 24-months, the toddler walks well and begins to leave the household area to play with peers on the nearby pathway. From this point on, independence and peer-group association increase steadily. Systematic observations of 2- to 4-year-olds in one Marquesan valley indicate that many toddlers spend a large part of the day in unsupervised peer groups of 3- to 6-children. While their older siblings are at school, these 2- to 4-year-olds play near the sea, in the boathouses, on the bridges, in the stream and in the schoolyard. Mothers worry that they will be swept up in the surf, and periodically chase them away from the sea, but the children quickly return. Preschool children are said to have "friends" who call on them to play. Adults draw a distinction between childhood friends (interchangeable companions) and personalized friends of adolescence and adulthood. Nonetheless, mothers report that children are very unhappy if forgotten by their peers, or if they are kept at home. Although young children are exuberant and daring with peers and siblings, they are generally afraid to leave the household area when alone.

Mothers mention the importance of the 2½- to 5-year-old child as companion, comforter, and instructor to the developing infant. These children are too young to attend school, yet they have the skill, interest, and patience to tend the infant and to engage him in play. Mothers note that 1½- to 2-year-olds may be "jealous" and "angry" at being displaced by a new baby, whereas the 3- to 4-year-old is rarely jealous and accepts caregiving responsibilities seriously and with pleasure. With these caregivers, the baby practices newly acquired skills. When adults are present, the child is often directed to put the baby through his paces, to the enjoyment of all.

The young child is routinely relied on to quiet the baby when adult attempts have failed. Also, the infant engages in face-to-face play most frequently with child caregivers and their peers. A great deal of early socialization, then, occurs in infant–child interactions that differ in important ways from infant–adult interactions.

Infant care by small children has important developmental implications for both the infant and the child. The infant learns motor, expressive, and cognitive skills from a child who is only recently and partially skilled. For the child, care of the new infant gives him a valued place in the domestic unit. He re-enters the day-to-day world of infancy, but as a responsible caregiver rather than as a dependent recipient of care. The child's relationship with his mother changes as they both direct attention to the infant. This practice seems to be an important step for the child's developmental move from infancy to childhood.

Mothers view development as a process that requires little active teaching. Infants and children are seen as moving from stage to stage easily and with minimal emotional upheaval. Processes such as weaning, toilet training, and sleeping away from the mother are said to happen as a matter of course: they are often described as occurring when the infant wants to practice more developmentally advanced behavior. Mothers discuss slightly older siblings as role-models for new forms of behavior for the infant, but view the infant's attempt to learn, rather than elders' teaching, as crucial for the acquisition of skills.

Throughout mothers' accounts of socialization practices is the belief that the infant, from birth, has a complex personality of his own. Complex motivations are ascribed to the infant in the first months, e.g., a mother asks her infant, "Why don't you want to look at me?" and caregivers interpret infant behaviors as indices of or attempts to deal with internal states: they infer that the infant is "fed up," "hot," "tired," or the like from his behavior. In describing situations in which babies acted in dangerous or disruptive ways, mothers emphasized the technique of redirecting the infant's attention rather than trying to deny or frustrate his will. (Infants can be tricked by distraction; they cannot, in this view, be persuaded.) In general, early training seems to be understood as a process of shaping the baby's behaviors in indirect ways, providing the situational framework in which he will do the proper thing as a matter of course.

FILM STUDY METHODOLOGY

Seventeen 3¼-minute-films were taken of nine infants ranging in age from 1½- to 12-months. (Details concerning the persons filmed are presented in Table 10.1.) The sample was limited by the availability of both infants and film. Filming was only begun after the researchers had acquired knowledge of domestic residence and work patterns, children's activities, and adult views of caregiving. Those adults filmed knew the filmmaker well and, although the film situation was certainly novel, they did not seem to view the filmmaker as a source of great discomfort.

Initially, the film project was planned as a naturalistic study of face-to-face interaction by mothers and other caregivers with infants. In pilot sessions, mothers were instructed to play with the baby in such a way that he or she would look at them. Face-to-face positioning was not selected spontaneously; the mothers in the pilot sessions were obviously strained and awkward. For the filming, caregivers were asked simply to play with the infant. The camera was positioned so that the caregiver and the infant could both be filmed in profile. The caregivers, however, invariably shifted position so as to face the filmmaker.

To approximate naturalistic conditions, dyads were filmed in relatively public parts of homes (e.g., in their yards, on house steps, or in cooking areas). Other residents and neighbors were normally present. In all but one film, other adults interacted with the filmed caregiver; in all but two films, up to four additional children were present. One infant was filmed only with his mother; the rest were filmed once with the mother and again with a major alternate adult caregiver, typically, one who lived in the same household.

The positions of the caregivers and infants approximated those of everyday activities. The presence of the camera, however, made the caregivers pay unusual attention to the personal appearance of the infant. Furthermore, the instruction that caregivers play with the infants raised questions for the mothers of the youngest infants, who said the babies were not capable of play.

The films were coded either with a frame-by-frame ($N = 9$) or an elapsed-time ($N = 8$) technique, in order to calculate the proportion of time each behavior occurred. To check the reliability of the coding, two additional trained coders examined five of the more significant behaviors in 5 to 7 films, using the elapsed-time technique. Intercoder reliability was 90% overall.

The modalities coded were: (1) position in which the infant was held relative to the caregiver; (2) closeness of the infant to the caregiver; (3) infant body orientation; (4) infant visual orientation in relation to the caregiver and others; (5) mutual gaze; (6) infant vocalization; (7) caregiver visual orientation; (8) caregiver vocalization; and (9) infant interaction with persons or objects other than the caregiver. These modalities and the classes of behaviors distinguished therein are presented in Table 10.2.

Finally, the sound track was taped and transcribed by one author, with the other collaborating when questions of interpretation arose. The record of utterances by caregivers, infants, and others was examined, and semantically meaningful utterances by the caregivers were counted and coded according to form (directives, questions or comments), topic (e.g., infant, off-camera person, events in general) and addressee. A simplified version of that coding will follow. As the verbal record was in Marquesan and French, the authors could not train independent coders.

On examining the data, we decided to treat the infants as within three distinct developmental stages and to apply analysis of variance. F-values were also calculated for mothers vs. other caregivers. Because of the limited sample size, the differences between mothers and caregivers with infants of each developmental stage were not treated in this manner.

PATTERNS OF INTERACTION

General Features

The naturalistic setting of the Marquesan interactions was socially complex. Others present (see Table 10.1) interacted with the caregiver–infant dyad. The

TABLE 10.1
Film Sample

Stage	Dyad	Infant			Caregiver		Others Present
		Age	Sex	Birth-Order	Relationship to Inf.	Age	
Stage I	DYAD 1	1½ mo.	F	6	Mother	34	2 adults; 1 child
(1½-to 3½-months old)	DYAD 2	1½ mo.	F	6	Sister	17	2 adults; 1 child
	DYAD 3	3½ mo.	F	3	Mother	22	1 adult; 1 child
	DYAD 4	3½ mo.	F	3	Grandmother	50	1 adult; 1 child
Stage II	DYAD 5	4½ mo.	F	8	Mother	34	1 adult; 4 children
(4½-to 9-months old)	DYAD 6	4½ mo.	F	8	Grandmother	75	1 adult; 4 children
	DYAD 7	5 mo.	M	13	Mother	36	1 adult; 2 children
	DYAD 8	5 mo.	M	13	Sister	17	
	DYAD 9	5 mo.	M	2	Mother	20	1 adult; 1 child
	DYAD 10	6 mo.	M	6	Mother	35	2 adults; 2 children
	DYAD 11	6 mo.	M	6	Aunt	34	1 adult; 1 child
	DYAD 12	9 mo.	M	9	Mother	37	1 adult; 1 child
	DYAD 13	9 mo.	M	9	Cousin	16	1 adult
Stage III	DYAD 14	12 mo.	F	2	Mother	21	1 adult; 1 child
(12 months old)	DYAD 15	12 mo.	F	2	Grandfather	69	1 adult; 1 child
	DYAD 16	12 mo.	M	15	Mother	43	1 adult; 1 child
	DYAD 17	12 mo.	M	15	Sister	20	1 adult; 1 child

TABLE 10.2
Interaction Behaviors By Stage of Infancy

	Stage I (N = 4)	Stage II (N = 9)	Stage III (N = 4)	Combined (N = 17)	F-Values (2,14 df)	p<
INFANT POSITION:						
SUPINE ON LAP	.65	0	0	.15	1.15	
SITS ON LAP, SUPPORTED	.32	.44	0	.31	2.39	.25
STANDS, SUPPORTED	.03	.37	.21	.25	.68	
SITS, UNSUPPORTED	0	.15	.36	.17	1.44	
STANDS, UNSUPPORTED, WALKS, CRAWLS, CREEPS	0	.04	.43	.11	5.05	.05
INFANT ORIENTATION:						
FACES CAREGIVER (315–45°)	.59	.16	.10	.25	9.09	.005
FACES HALF AWAY (45–135, 225–315°)	.28	.35	.28	.32	.10	
FACES AWAY (135–225°)	.13	.49	.62	.43	2.75	.10
INFANT CLOSENESS:						
HELD CLOSELY (more than two points of contact)	.41	.26	0	.23	2.29	.25
HELD DISTANTLY (2 or fewer points of contact)	.59	.54	.06	.44	3.57	.10
NOT HELD	0	.20	.94	.33	79.24	.001
INFANT VISUAL ORIENTATION:						
LOOKS AT CAREGIVER'S FACE	.30	.08	.04	.12	1.61	.25
LOOKS AT OTHER PERSON	.27	.27	.35	.29	.19	
LOOKS AT OBJECT	0	.22	.38	.21	5.84	.05
LOOKS AWAY, UNSPECIFIED	.44	.42	.13	.36	1.80	.25
INFANT VOCALIZATIONS:						
TOTAL VOCALIZATIONS	0	.25	.05	.15	5.33	.05
CRIES, SCREAMS (closed eye scream)	0	.11	.03	.06	1.43	
MUTUAL CAREGIVER-INFANT GAZE:	.26	.07	.03	.11	1.61	.25
CAREGIVER VISUAL ORIENTATION:						
AT INFANT	.84	.71	.55	.70	2.82	.10
AT OTHER	.15	.14	.30	.21	2.51	.25
AWAY, UNSPECIFIED	.01	.15	.15	.12	.81	
CAREGIVER VOCALIZATIONS:						
TO BABY	.70	.36	.08	.38	7.76	.01
TO OTHER	.10	.08	.21	.18	9.46	.005
INFANT INTERACTS WITH OTHER:	.02	.01	.40	.10	16.55	.001
INFANT ATTENDS TO OBJECT:	0	.22	.38	.21	5.84	.05

older infants (12 months) spent 40% of the time interacting with these additional people, sharing gaze as well as physical or object involvement (see Table 10.2). Mothers' visual and verbal involvement with other people increased as babies became older.

As indicated in Table 10.2, infants were not cradled or cuddled into the caregiver's body (infant held closely = 23%); instead, they were held in a sitting or standing position, if they were held at all (see Fig. 10.1). They were rarely held in a face-to-face position (25% of the time); they were faced outward 43% of the time and in a half-outward position 32% of the time.

Caregivers watched the infants carefully from behind (70% of the time) and followed and commented on the infants' direction of gaze. They vocalized to the infants 38% of the time, which is low compared to Field and Widmayer's (this volume) proportions for 4-month-olds (17% for black mothers; 53% for Puerto Rican mothers; 77% for South American mothers; and 82% for Cuban mothers.) It should be noted that these mothers were alone and in a face-to-face position with their infants, while the Marquesan adults were not.

In terms of general content of the interactions, the Marquesan caregivers spent much time calling the baby's name, directing him to look and wave at others, prompting him to perform motor skills, and directing the 3- to 6-year-old siblings to play with him. Major games consisted of directing the infant's gaze at others, placing him on his sibling's shoulders, and throwing objects for him to fetch. Intensive one-to-one games between adult and infant, such as tickling, singing, or tossing the infant in the air, were observed only three times in the 17 films. Instead, mothers and other caregivers were apt to set up complex, three-or-more-person interactions with the baby as focus.

Within this context, Marquesan infant behaviors were also distinctive. They looked at the faces of their caregivers 12% of the time, which is low in compari-

 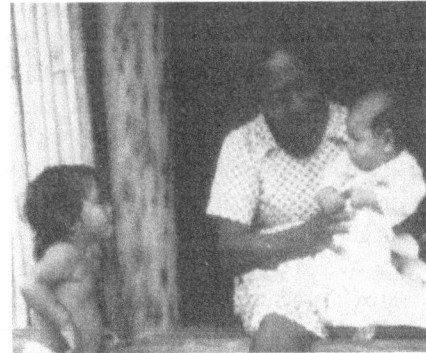

FIG. 10.1. A grandmother holds a 3½-month-old in a faced away position. The baby's attention is drawn by her 2-year-old sister, with whom she then interacts.

son to Stern's (1977) figure of 49% for American 5-month-olds in naturalistic settings, and to Field and Widmayer's (this volume) cross-ethnic sample for 4-month-olds (33% for Cuban infants; 50% for South Americans; 57% for blacks; 69% for Puerto Ricans). This yielded a low proportion of mutual mother–infant gaze (11%) for the Marquesan dyads.

The Marquesan infants were also remarkably quiet. The youngest babies (up to 3½ months) made few discernable sounds, and infants older than 4½ months vocalized only 15% of the time. Slightly less than half these vocalizations were bouts of loud, closed-eye crying. The 12-month-olds were particularly quiet, concentrating on physical activity that was unaccompanied by babbling. No maternal imitation of infant sounds was observed, though caregivers sometimes responded in rhythms similar to the infant vocalizations.

The Marquesan infants were particularly attentive to the surrounding social and object worlds from the first month onward. They watched other people 29% of the time, and attended to objects an additional 21% of the time. By 12 months they were interacting with siblings 40% of the time and playing with objects 38% of the time. In summary, although relatively uninvolved in intensive face-to-face play with their holding caregivers, the Marquesan infants either watched or actively engaged in play with others a mean of 64% of the time. In fact, whenever the infant sat and seemed visually uninvolved for more than a short period, his caregivers vigorously redirected him to either object play or interaction with others. They seemed to be trying to keep the infant minimally engaged, and to avoid infant self-absorption. Engagement, however, was not limited to face-to-face play with the mother or caregiver.

Developmental Trends

Significant variance was noted in caregiver–infant interactions across the stages of infancy. This was to be expected, given the mothers' reports of changing motor capacities, communication skills, social networks, and cultural expectations of infants at different ages. Analyses of the interaction data, revealed that the four films of very young infants and the four films of the oldest infants differed significantly from each other and from the nine films of an intermediate, more homogeneous set of infants. In view of this finding we decided to analyze the data in terms of stages. Stage I was comprised of infants aged 1½- to 3½-months; Stage II, of infants 4½- to 9-months, and Stage III of 1-year-old toddlers.

Across these stages, the caregiver–infant dyad became a less compact, exclusive interactional field. Caregivers gazed less often at the older infants and spent less time vocalizing to them. Infants were increasingly positioned away from the caregivers' faces and in postures that allowed diminished contact. By 12 months, the babies were held by the adult caregivers for only 6% of the time. (American viewers of the films have tended to overestimate the babies' ages, probably due to the postural evidence of motor ability and separateness of the infants.)

The infants' field of attention became increasingly complex and active across the stages. Objects took on increasing importance. Persons other than the holding caregiver were attended to, first visually and then interactionally as well. The wealth of interaction in the Stage III films resulted from both the increased interactive skills of the infant and increased activity of others. What is notable in these films is the high involvement of medial caregivers, i.e., children who interact with infants under the direction of adults. Adults encourage these children to help infants develop their less certain motor capacities. Through infancy, then, Marquesan babies deal with a social world; by the age of 12 months they have both the supervision of adults and extensive contact with child caregivers. Stage differences are noted in greater detail in the following section, and are summarized in Table 10.2.

Interaction Patterns at Different Stages of Infancy

Stage I (1½ to 3½ months). The youngest infants were held supine on the caregivers' laps, in a face-to-face position, about 60% of the time. In this position they looked at caregivers' faces 30% of the time, while mutual gaze was sustained 26% of the time, appreciably more than at the other stages. Stage I infants were held closely more often, were observed more intently, and were addressed verbally more than were older infants. Caregivers tried to elicit the youngest infants' visual attention by calling the infants by name; they engaged in repetitive vocalizations and semantically empty utterances more frequently at this stage than at others. Such utterances seemed to be attempts to win the babies' attention, and when this was accomplished the tone and sound of the utterances changed.

The mothers in particular engaged the infants in the most intense one-to-one interactions observed throughout the films. Other caregivers often pointed the baby toward his mother when engaging in talk with her. This finding meshes with mothers' reports that they are nearly exclusive caregivers for the newborn infants.

Stage II (4½ to 9 months). As described in the interviews, the 3- or 4-month-old baby can sit stably on a caregiver's lap and is often passed around to be held by others. In the films the Stage II infants were held in a sitting or standing position, facing outward most of the time. The infants looked at the caregivers only 8% of the time and mutual gaze was rare (7%). In contrast, they attended to objects and other people 49% of the time. These infants vocalized more than those at other stages (25%), but were also the most apt to scream and cry (11% of the time). The caregivers talked significantly less to infants, called less often for their attention, and repeated fewer nonsemantic utterances than with the younger infants. The caregivers continued to direct the infants' attention outward and directed them to perform: to pick up objects, stand up, stop screaming, and so forth. The "Where's so-and-so?" game mentioned earlier was common during this period as was stress on greeting behavior. In contrast to Stage I, the infant's attention was directed toward the outside world, rather than toward the mother's face.

The interactive styles of mothers and other caregivers differed less at this stage than at others. This parallels the tendency for others to share routinely in care of the baby after the first few months.

Stage III (12 months old). The 12-month-old infants appeared relatively independent of their adult caregivers. They stood or crawled 43% of the time, and sat unsupported 36% of the time. The rest of the time they stood with others' help. They were largely oriented away from their caregivers, and were rarely held. The infants gazed mainly at objects and third parties, looking at their caregivers only 4% of the time.

The Stage III infants were physically active and in contact with both objects and people, but the adult caregivers were less active than those caring for younger infants. Caregivers watched the infants for more than half the time, but tended to intervene by directing medial caregivers to interact with the infants, rather than by acting themselves. This was especially true of the mothers. One other adult caregiver, however, acted much like a medial caregiver, leading the infant by the hand as he took his early steps.

Verbal Data

In the verbal transcripts, the absence of an elaborated baby-talk vocabulary is striking. Many of the caregivers' vocalizations cannot be transcribed as Marquesan or French words, but these are largely repeated sounds such as /ku: ku:/ or /'a 'a 'a/. Croons, staccato sounds that accompany jiggling, expressions of attention to the infant, and attempts to gain the infant's attention can often be identified in the verbal record, but not on the basis of fixed phonetic forms. Two exceptions are worth noting.

A difference is audible between the sounds addressed to Stage I infants and to others. The former sounds often have supersegmental intonation patterns that exaggerate those of ordinary sentences. Using a 1 to 5 scale to model intonational level, we find in one case:

$$
\begin{array}{cccccc}
 & 5 & & & & 4 \\
2\ 2\ ^3 & 3\ 3\ _2 & & 3\ 3\ 3\ 3 & \\
 & & 1 & & & \\
/\ \text{ku sei} & \text{ku ku::} & \text{ku ku ku ku:}\ / \\
[\ \text{question} & \text{affirmative} & \text{comment} &] \\
 & \text{response} & &
\end{array}
$$

With older infants, caregivers do not use such intonational patterns for utterances lacking semantic value. Nonsense utterances, then, were not used for reciprocal vocalization with babies but, early on, to express communicative intent, using adult speech as a model, and later, to express particular directives with simple, repeated forms. Caregivers express other messages to older infants in short sentences and propositions across utterances (Ochs, Schieffelin & Platt, 1979), e.g., to a 6-month-old: *Bébé, où papa? a? ton papa... c'est papa. Voilà, regarde papa là bas!* ("Baby, where papa? a? Your papa?... it's papa. There, look at papa over there!")

Some baby talk vocabulary was heard, but only one term was often addressed to infants. With Stage I infants, *nanā* was combined with the name of a specific person, with the sense, roughly, of "look at X." Caregivers sometimes waved the baby's hand when saying *nanā*. With older infants, *nanā* was less clearly associated with the recognition of a specific other: the term was often said alone, and caregivers provided few or no clues to direct the infant's attention to one spot. In these cases, *nanā* seemed to be used to prompt the infant simply to attend to a social world.

A few utterances that we could not interpret may have been baby-talk specific to a particular household. These terms were exchanged with children age 3- or 4-years, not infants. The conclusion suggested by this pattern is that Marquesans develop baby-talk vocabularies only by mirroring children's semantically charged vocalizations, and these are absent when caregivers deal with infants deemed incapable of producing even malformed words. Caregivers, then, treat older infants as able to deal with shortened forms of ordinary speech and make little effort to develop a shared synthesis of adult speech and infant vocalizations.

The frequency of meaningful utterances by caregivers per film did not vary greatly across the stages. A mean of 34.8 caregivers' utterances/film was coded (irrespective of addressee). With Stage I infants a mean of 47.3 utterances/film was obtained; with Stage II, 21.7; and with Stage III, 40.3. It was possible to code these utterances for what we term focus, as shown in Table 10.3. Relying on semantic and pragmatic data, both visual and verbal, we sorted utterances as infant-focused (e.g., calling baby's name, directing the baby to recognize others or to perform, commenting on the activities of the baby), as focused on medical caregivers, small children actively engaged with the baby, or as focused on other persons or events. This provided an indication of the extent of caregivers' involvement with infants, complementing the measures of caregivers' gaze and vocalization directed at the infants (see Table 10.2).

Trends in the subcategory frequencies suggest a major shift in caregiving patterns over the first year. Talk to and about the infant diminishes, as do calls and attempts to get the baby to recognize others. Comments concerning the baby also decline in frequency. Table 10.3 does not, however, simply indicate a lessened

TABLE 10.3
Focus of Caregivers' Utterances for Infants of Different Ages

Focus On:	Stage I	Stage II	Stage III	All Stages	F-value
INFANT	.90	.63	.47	.66	4.10[c]
call	.37	.19	.06	.20	2.95
perform[a]	.02	.13	.35	.15	13.73[d]
look outward[a]	.31	.19	.02	.18	3.39
comment[b]	.19	.13	.05	.12	2.00
MEDIAL CAREGIVER	.02	.00	.40	.10	21.39[d]
OTHER	.08	.37	.13	.27	4.64[c]

All figures represent means for several caregivers of the percentage of the caregivers' utterances in a particular category.

[a] "Perform" and "Look outward" cover directives and interrogatives that direct the infant to act in particular ways or to recognize others.

[b] "Comments" are comments about the infant which may be directed to the infant or to others.

[c] p less than .05.

[d] p less than .001.

verbal attention to the infant. Attempts to stimulate the infant to act, shown in the *perform* row, increase, while the frequency of utterances to medial caregivers in Stage III includes many instructions to engage the infant in play. Also, focus on others, rather than on the infant, as measured in the *other* row—or, interpreting the data differently, in that row plus the *comment* row—do not show a simple trend. Caregivers are never exclusively attentive to infants, yet their talk is oriented elsewhere most frequently when dealing with Stage II infants.

Over the stages, there are other changes in the caregivers' talk to and about the infant that are not reflected in Table 10.3. With Stage I infants, caregivers mentioned the infant's inaction: "he doesn't play." They interpreted infant behavior as reactive to bodily states: "hot, Baby?," "(he'll) sleep soon," "defecate soon?" With older infants, caregivers said little about perceived bodily states; they were more apt to direct the infant to act and found less need to interpret the infant's behaviors. As infants grow older, it appears that caregivers see them as more capable of directed action schemes. Thus, "eat it" to a 9-month-old meant, in context, "go ahead and eat that filthy thing if you insist." Stage II and III infants were directed to stand or to play with objects, and they were even given information about their situation, e.g., "that's dirty" or "the European is not angry," conveying implicit, not explicit, directives.

Infant-focused talk, then, moves from a concern with the infant as an autonomous being on whom stimuli impinge to a concern with the infant's active participation in a larger social world. This trend parallels previous findings, that the caregiver-infant dyad becomes less exclusive over time, and that contact with others, via watching, then physical and object play, is increasingly encouraged by caregivers.

Most of the trends noted earlier hold for mothers and other caregivers alike. Mothers' attempts to elicit infant performance increased from Stage I to Stage II, but not in the next stage. This is understandable when the high frequency of their attempts to get medial caregivers to manage Stage III infant performance is noted.

Table 10.4 presents differences between mothers' and other caregivers' utterances. Mothers produced more codable utterances than others (with means of 34.8 utterances/film for mothers, 27.8 for other adults), although others were more voluble with the youngest infants. Much of this was due to their insistence that the babies notice other people, especially their mothers. Only 22% of the mothers' utterances to Stage I infants dealt with noticing other persons, versus 41% for the other caregivers. The mothers devoted 51% of their utterances to calls, versus 24% for the other caregivers.

At all stages, caregivers' talk was not exclusively directed to infants. Mothers of Stage I infants only talked about others 4% of the time; 21% of their talk consisted of comments: this presumed a comprehending audience. Other caregivers' talk varied less in focus from stage to stage; the decrease in infant-focused talk by mothers from Stage I to Stage II was precipitous. Although both mothers and other caregivers were more likely to talk of medial caregivers with Stage III infants, this talk occupied most of the mothers' utterances. Hence, from stage to stage, mothers' talk presented a far more complex pattern than the talk of other caregivers.

Mothers, Other Adult Caregivers, and Medial Caregivers

Overall, other caregivers tended to position infants further from their bodies than did mothers, and they were more apt not to hold the infants at all. Furthermore, several significant differences in the stages were more evident in mother–infant interactions than in those involving other caregivers (see Table 10.2).

In the Stage I filming, infants were more likely to be faced toward mothers than toward other caregivers. When held by mothers, these infants often gazed at the caregiver (56% of the time), however, they did so rarely (4% of the time) when held by others. Stage I infants held by other caregivers did not simply gaze away: they looked at persons other than the holding caregiver 53% of the time.

TABLE 10.4
Focus of Caregivers' Utterances, Broken Down by Infant Stage and Caregiver Type

Focus On:	Stage I		Stage II		Stage III		All Stages	
	Mothers	Others	Mothers	Others	Mothers	Others	Mothers	Others
Infant	.96	.84	.55	.73	.25	.69	.59	.75
Medial Caregiver	—	.04	—	—	.61	.19	.20	.08
Other	.04	.12	.45	.27	.14	.13	.21	.17

(When held by mothers, they did so only 1% of the time.) In brief, mothers established face-to-face contact with infants, whereas alternate caregivers often faced the infants toward others—especially toward mothers. With mothers, these infants were supine (81%); others were equally apt to place the infant in a supine or sitting posture.

In Stage II, differences between mothers and other caregivers were less noticeable. Mothers had infants sit on their laps (60% of the time) whereas others let the infants stand (23%) or sit unsupported (40% of the time).

The most striking aspect of Stage III, the interposition of medial caregivers who interact with the baby while adults supervise, was most prevalent while mothers were filmed. Mothers interacted with others more often, spent more time verbalizing to others, and made far more utterances to medial caregivers (61% of their utterances) than did other adult caregivers (19%).

Broadly speaking, other adult caregivers acted in relatively distant ways with infants of each stage, whereas mothers acted differently with infants of the first and last stages. A dyadic tie with the mother seemed to be established for the Stage I infants yet, by Stage III, mothers supervised and left interaction with their infants to others.

Viewed developmentally, these findings indicate that mothers do not simply interact in different ways from other caregivers. Rather, they assume different roles at different stages: first as the major interactive partners for infants, and later as the organizers of infants' interaction with others.

For example, in two film sequences mothers placed infants on the shoulders of other children. In one film, a mother chatted with her 4-year-old son. After a pause, she saw her 4½-month-old daughter reach toward the boy's head. The mother picked her up, set her on his shoulders, and held her in position, letting her grasp his head. The boy seemed stunned, then grinned and held the baby's legs. When the infant was secure, the mother engaged in smiling eye contact with her. When the infant reached toward her, she brought her back onto her lap. In this case, the mother attended to both the infant and the child. She acted responsively, treating their behaviors as cues and she aided the baby to hold onto the boy (see Fig. 10.2).

With older infants, mothers were more likely to supervise interaction than to move the infants about: children were directed to hold or bring objects to the infant. Mothers do not begin to direct their children only at this point, rather, in the films, they treated children as appropriate interactive partners only for Stage III infants.

With other adult caregivers, no similar change in interactive style was visible as infants developed. Instead, some younger adult caregivers acted much like medial caregivers, receiving directives from the mothers and commenting to them about the infants. Others, especially grandparents, did not attend to the mothers. The directed caregivers tended to interact more readily with infants than did older adults.

10. EARLY INTERACTIONS IN THE MARQUESAS ISLANDS 207

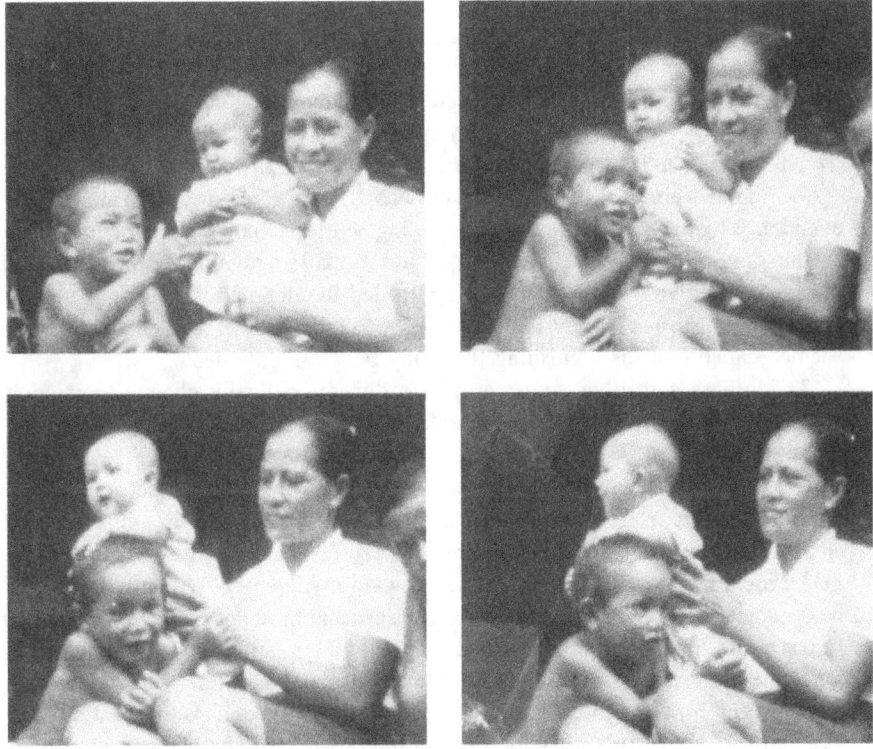

FIG. 10.2. The mother attends to her son's talk and then aids the baby in grasping his head. In this position the infant interacts with her older sister. The baby is eventually placed on the boy's shoulders.

In conclusion, the mothers' shift from dyadic interaction to the organization of the infants' environment was the major finding of this study. Medial caregivers and some adult caregivers followed mothers' directions, taking on a role distinct from that of these mothers, but with the mothers' approval. The films show caregivers acting in complementary ways, not opposed ones. They were collaborating in a single pattern of caregiving.

DISCUSSION

Patterns of Socialization

Recurrent themes in the filmed interactions indicate consistencies in the socialization of infants:

1. Marquesan infants were held, talked to, and played with as distinct beings with wills and motivations of their own. They were rarely cuddled, even if they tried to cling when distressed. Rather, adults tried to elicit the crying baby's attention by loudly calling his name and shaking him—actions that accentuate his separateness (see Fig. 10.3). Again, they talked to babies as if the babies' actions were motivated and, at times, as if babies' motivations ran counter to their own.

2. Babies were generally oriented outward. They were directed to attend, and eventually to interact, with the surrounding world. Complex interactions with surrounding others were set up. Marquesans did not engage in pseudo-dialogues in which caregivers act as if infants controlled the detailed turn-taking rules of conversation. Instead, they had infants "recognize" others, even before they seemed capable of distinguishing the many people mentioned.

3. Mothers and other adult caregivers did not radically change their adult behavioral style to play with the infant; baby talk and reciprocal games were rare.

On film, the caregivers can be seen as sharing patterned expectancies and goals for infant interaction, but as taking on different roles in implementing shared goals. From early on the infant is seen as an autonomous agent, and a major socialization goal is to direct him toward involvement with others, so that he does not become absorbed in his own wishes and thoughts. It is seen as proper to place him in regular contact with a range of others, and to provide contexts in which he can draw upon his motor and expressive skills to initiate his own social contact. The form in which caregivers implement these goals is affected by their evaluation of the baby's capacities and by their own participation in a set of roles for the organization of caregiving.

In the first months of life, the infant is engaged in social contact through visual attention to his mother. He is believed to be able to listen as well as

FIG. 10.3. A grandmother shakes and pats a 4½-month-old infant in an attempt to quell her crying. The 4-year-old brother arrives to assume his role in calming the baby.

10. EARLY INTERACTIONS IN THE MARQUESAS ISLANDS

visually attend to a nearby other, and his mother tries to maintain his attention by calling him, turning his head, or shaking or jiggling him. Mothers laugh and show mock disgust when the baby becomes self-absorbed. Other adult caregivers cooperate by directing the young infant to look at his mother.

With Stage II infants, the goal of keeping the baby socially involved is realized by facing him outward and helping him come into contact with others. Mothers are attentive to the baby's cues and the elaborate acts that the infant has initiated spontaneously. The interactive styles of mothers and other caregivers are similar at this stage: the dyadic bond with mother is extended to others.

The 12-month-old is expected to interact actively with others in physical or object play. Mothers structure social contexts for the infant: they sit back and instruct older siblings to play with him (see Fig. 10.4). Children become the infant's major interactive partners.

Over the stages, the mothers moved from being the active, prototypical social other for the baby, to being attentive organizers of the baby's interactive space. They consistently provided the infant with an interactively stimulating world, first by interacting, next by encouraging and making effective his attempts to make contact, and finally by directing others to interact with the infant. Caregivers in the films shaped the infants' attention towards others and objects, and shaped their movements towards effective contact and locomotion. By the end of the first year, infants were becoming interactants able to accompany and learn from older children in an environment supervised by adults.

Some American Comparisons

The early interaction patterns and inferred socialization goals in the Marquesan films are in marked contrast to American descriptions and theories of mother-

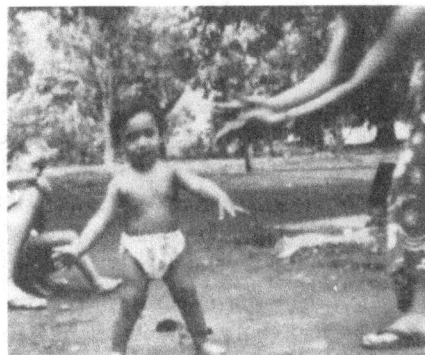

FIG. 10.4. A 12-month-old is put through his paces as he makes his first steps. The older sister throws objects for him to fetch, and then tries to break his concentration by clapping. The mother watches and laughs in the background.

infant interaction and its effects on psychological development. Most notably, American accounts center around an exclusive mother–infant dyad and emphasize reciprocal face-to-face play.

Kaye's (1977) description of early mother–infant interactions begins with the observation that infants are born with biological rhythms that assure regularity and hence predictability to their actions. Mothers are seen as trying to fit their behaviors into the infant's natural rhythms. According to Kaye (1977), the mother's attention "is not just to fit into the pattern, but to alter it, to prolong . . . her infant's attention and activity cycles and to generate in *him* a response to her [p. 198]." She behaves as if a true dialogue were occurring. She imitates the baby's vocalizations, facial expressions and limb movements. Her imitation, however, is "much more than a mirroring of her baby. She pulls him from where he is in the direction of her own agenda for him [p. 199]."

The mother is continuously engaged in structuring the details of the baby's interactive experience by varying her reactions to his minute expressive behaviors. The infant begins to acquire abilities to imitate, to adjust his timing and the like, and then mothers and infants can elaborate with complex, conventionalized games and shared vocabularies. In this extended play, the infant experiments with expressive forms, developing an individuated style. The American infant thus comes to participate appropriately in dialogue—which we take to be the culturally valorized mode of interaction—in which partners are held to understand each other's inner experience through its unfolding expression.

Theoretical accounts of the psychological development of the infant expand on two aspects of the mother–infant relationship: (1) the mother's role in imposing or "lending" structure to the infant's experience; and (2) the process by which the infant gradually internalizes or accepts this external structure as his own, and uses it to organize his behaviors and inner experience. Mahler (1968) and other psychoanalytically oriented theorists (Kohut, 1977; Winnicott, 1958) describe the mother as serving as a barrier against overwhelming stimuli. For example, by cuddling, rocking and cooing to a crying infant, she lends her rhythms and organizes the distressed baby. According to Mahler (1968), the infant develops psychologically by entering into a symbiotic union with his mother, in which the mother serves as an auxiliary ego. The infant eventually individuates from the mother by differentiating his structures from hers. Only gradually does the mother become a distinctive other for the infant.

Several points of contrast are evident between these accounts and the Marquesan findings. First, the filmed interactions are strikingly lacking in the micro-structuring of baby actions described by Kaye (1977). Marquesan mothers are attentive to their infants and do mold their behaviors in certain directions, but they do not respond with continuous mirroring of the infant's behavior. Even in face-to-face positions, the caregivers tended to gaze at and comment on the baby's autonomous functioning.

Again, Marquesan adults typically reacted to an infant's distress with an attempt to distract him with calls, and vigorous jiggling. They treated distress as a problem manageable through an intrusive change in stimuli, not a reduction of stimuli.

Were only the film record available, the argument could be made that Marquesan infants reach their second year with little experience of the interactions discussed above. From this, it might be extrapolated that the development of both their psychological structures and expressive skills is limited.

The film record, however, is incomplete in scope. On the basis of more general observations, we can state that Marquesan infants experience a much wider range of interaction. For example, much face-to-face play occurs between the infant seated on his mother's lap and older siblings. Older children play games with infants carried by child-caregivers. When adults' actions do not end an infant's distress, child-caregivers provide rhythmic soothing. In addition, parents report playing face-to-face games such as peek-a-boo with their infants in their homes at night. Cuddling is probably also extended to older infants and children at night.

Behaviors similar to those stressed by Western theorists are, then, not absent in the Marquesas, although they rarely appeared in the film study. Such behaviors involve child caregivers or mothers acting in ways quite distinct from the major patterns of socialization found in the films. Such behaviors may, we believe, be understood as necessary for the learning of particular skills, but not for the larger patterns associated with them in Western accounts. Child caregivers offer examples of expressive behavior and vocalization that can serve as models for the infant, using simpler forms than adults do. In these interactions, which are peripheral to mother–child interaction, we can recognize learning experiences, but not the psychological birth of the Marquesan infant.

We can suggest a tentative answer to the problem of where and how self development begins in the Marquesas. It is clear that mothers do not engage in the mimicking activity that instantiates their theorized role as auxiliary egos. Instead, they serve as prototypical social others, and the brief interactive routines developed in the mother–infant dyad are quickly generalized to interaction with others. Rather than mirroring the infant's expression, mothers shape the infant's movements into engaged and effective ones, converting what may be little more than a groping motion into a grasp. They insist on and abet social involvement. The suggestion here is that mothers' structuring of the infants' world augments the infants' efficacy in dealing with both social others and objects. The infant does not find control over others in elaborate mirroring play but perhaps in the ability to initiate or participate in simpler interactive sequences with many other persons. Marquesan adults largely succeed in creating a world in which the infant can experience pleasure through effective motor coordination and simple interactions with others. Such experiences prepare the infant well for more extensive motor and expressive training in later infant–child interactions. Similarly, Marquesans' expectation that small children treat any person willing to play as their friend seems an appropriate outcome of a socialization pattern in which effective motor activity and a safe, accepting social world are valued.

In infants' experiences, we suggest, various interactions combine to contribute to the development of the infant's self in relation to others. Mothers and those they direct provide a coherent set of messages concerning interaction, namely that persons are autonomous beings who present and negotiate aspects of will within a complex social world. Child-caregivers provide other messages, i.e., that there is a population of similar, supportive others, ready to engage in unarticulate but concerned interaction. Adult–infant interactions, then, repeatedly convey messages about the infant's autonomy; infant–child interactions are far more flexible, carrying greater potentials for both complex, reciprocal interchanges and close, physical sharing.

The presence of multiple caregivers allows for the elaboration of differentiated contacts in which distinct messages can be transmitted. This seems to enhance the complexity of the infant's social experience, rather than dulling or stereotyping his learning by spreading it thinly over a number of caregivers. We suggest that the communicative potential of early socialization messages may be increased by their allocation to distinctive others who reiterate them in repeated interactions.

CONCLUSION

The film record included interactions appropriate for public view. Much activity important for infant socialization was not apparent because it fit poorly with Marquesan ideas of proper social behavior. The camera effect was an accentuation of culturally valorized patterns, not disorganization.

A theoretical point is implicit in this finding: Early socialization is structured by cultural expectations as a combination of differentially valued messages. Caregivers act on standard expectancies and hence impress on infants rule systems associated with these. Socialization processes that are not easily accommodated by the dominant expectations are accomplished, but only at moments when these expectations are set aside. We stress, then, that early socialization is strongly shaped by adults' attempts to make interactants out of infants according to *their* ideas of interactive propriety. Although infant potentials that do not fit with such ideas are realized, they are developed only partially or at the margins of social life.

ACKNOWLEDGMENTS

This research was made possible in part by financial support from the National Institutes of Health (fellowship PHS 1-F31-MH05154) and the National Science Foundation (grant

SOC 75-13983) through the University of Chicago. Professor Daniel G. Freedman provided funds for some of the film. In French Polynesia, we benefitted from the permission to conduct research and the cooperation extended by the Territorial government, the officials and people of 'Ua Pou, and the Centre O.R.S.T.O.M. on Tahiti. We also thank Nancy Bradney and Bonnie Urciuoli for help in the analysis of the data.

REFERENCES

Howard, A. *Learning to be Rotuman.* New York: Teachers College Press, 1970.
Howard, A. *Ain't no big thing: Coping strategies in a Hawaiian–American community.* Honolulu: University Press of Hawaii, 1974.
Kaye, K. Thickening thin data: The maternal role in developing communication and language. In M. Bullowa (Ed.), *Before speech.* Cambridge: Cambridge University Press, 1977.
Kirkpatrick, J. *The Marquesan notion of the person.* Unpublished Doctoral dissertation. Department of Anthropology, University of Chicago, 1980. (a)
Kirkpatrick, J. Meanings of siblingship in Marquesan society. In M. Marshall (Ed.), *Siblingship in Oceania: Studies in the meaning of kin relations,* ASAO Monographs, No. 8, Ann Arbor: University of Michigan Press, 1980. (b)
Kohut, H. *The restoration of the self.* New York: International Universities Press, 1977.
Levy, R. *Tahitians: Mind and experience in the Society Islands.* Chicago: University of Chicago Press, 1973.
Mahler, M. *On human symbiosis and the vicissitudes of individuation: Infantile psychosis.* New York: International Universities Press, 1968.
Ochs, E., Schieffelin, B., & Platt, M. Propositions across utterances and speakers. In E. Ochs & B. Schieffelin (Eds.), *Developmental Pragmatics.* New York: Academic Press, 1979.
Ritchie, J. *Basic personality in Rakau.* Wellington, New Zealand: Department of Psychology, Victoria University, 1956.
Ritchie, J. & Ritchie, J. *Growing up in Polynesia.* Sydney: George Allen & Unwin, 1979.
Stern, D. *The first relationship: Mother and infant.* Cambridge: Harvard University Press, 1977.
Winnicott, D. Primary maternal preoccupations. *Collected papers.* New York: Basic Books, 1958.

11 Age-Related Changes in Attachment Behavior in Polymatrically Reared Infants: The Kenyan Gusii

Guy Reed
P. Herbert Leiderman
Stanford University

INTRODUCTION

Attachment was a construct introduced by Bowlby in 1958 to describe the mother–infant relationship. It was first empirically studied by observing the behavior of infants upon separation from their mothers (Ainsworth, 1967). Because of this research on attachment behavior, we understand a fair amount about its expression, especially in the first year of life, and particularly among infants in Western monomatric societies.

For instance, it is widely accepted that the infant does not differentiate between figures in his expression of attachment behaviors until about the 3rd quarter of his first year of life; after this time his behavioral display is increasingly figure-specific (Ainsworth, 1979; Schaffer & Emerson, 1964; and others). In addition, there are data from Western and non-Western societies which suggest that constituent attachment behaviors (cf. separation distress), increase in frequency to a maximum at about 13- 15-months-of-age, and decline thereafter (Kagan, Kearsley, & Zelazo, 1978).

Yet there are many questions that remain unanswered about the development and expression of attachment behaviors:

1. For instance, it has been hypothesized (Ainsworth, 1973) that an infant expresses different types of attachment behavior as he or she matures. That is, a transformation occurs in the type of attachment behavior shown. It has been thought that such a change reflects a maturation in the affective components of the relationship. This has been described as "goal corrected partnership."

2. In general, we know only a small amount about the manifestation of attachment behavior in non-Western, non-monomatric societies (Marvin, Van Devender, Iwanaga, LeVine & LeVine, 1977). Yet the study of attachment behavior, in societies with different caretaking patterns, should help to elucidate the importance of social context in its expression. As such, the polymatric (Leiderman, Thiemann, Reed, manuscript in preparation) Gusii Society represents a "natural experiment" whereby we may reexamine attachment behavior under different social conditions.

3. The studies that have observed age-related differences in the expression of attachment behavior have been largely cross-sectional. Because of this it remains uncertain whether the differences seen merely reflect individual dissimilarities or represent age-related (developmental) changes. Consequently, a longitudinal analysis of individual changes in attachment behavior may be of some help in resolving this question.

In conclusion then, we sought to test the following hypotheses in a polymatric African society.

1. Is there a transformation in the type of attachment behavior expressed with increasing age?
2. Do infants reared in a polymatric, non-Western society replicate, cross-sectionally and longitudinally, the age related, maternally directed, attachment behavior change seen in other cultures?
3. What is the age-related pattern of attachment behavior for other caregiving figures?

SELECTION OF ATTACHMENT BEHAVIOR INDICES

Attachment behavior has been quantified in a multitude of ways (for overview see Ainsworth, Blehar, Waters & Wall, 1978; Coates, Anderson, & Hartup, 1972a; & Gewirtz, 1972). Many early studies used different discrete behaviors as indices of attachment. However, dissatisfaction with these indices arose when independent studies failed to replicate each other (cf. Coates, Anderson, & Hartup, 1972b; Feldman & Ingham, 1975). These contradictory results have been ascribed to a number of empirical problems: lack of similarity among experimental contexts and situations (Ainsworth et al., 1978; Waters, 1978), failure to consider individual differences, the instability of correlational analyses of small samples (Masters & Wellman, 1974) and, in general, differences between studies in the level of data analyses (Waters, 1978).

In selecting a quantitative measure of the amount of attachment behavior expressed, we have sought to answer these criticisms. Though arrived at independently, we have adopted a system of "functional equivalence" in the scoring of attachment behaviors (cf. Waters, 1978), using the categories of behaviors suggested by (Ainsworth, 1973, pp. 12, 13; Ainsworth et al., 1978, pp. 42, 276; see Table 11.1).[1] By this scheme, all behaviors are scored equally for their occurrence and weighted only for their duration. As such, each type of behavior is quantitatively equal, and individual differences in the pattern of behavior expressed are not considered. The advantage to this type of analysis is greater interexperiment stability (Waters, 1978). In addition, this approach more closely retains the original structure of the data, because it does not demand a priori assumptions about the relative salience of specific attachment behaviors.

Given the effect of context in determining the significance of the behavior expressed (or the type of behavioral system operating), we have restricted our analysis to a separation episode.[2] This was done to insure that "infant attachment system" was stressed and that the behaviors observed reflected the perturbation. In addition, only the first 20 seconds of the departure sequence was analyzed to allow a standardized temporal comparison of one caregiver with another. This obviated the need to consider caregiver interactions in weighting behavioral scores.

Much like ethologists, we have been looking for overall age-related patterns in the display of attachment behaviors. As a result, our analysis differs somewhat from previous studies. This is because we have sought a phenomenological description of general age-related changes in attachment behavior: one which, with the fewest assumptions and abstractions (e.g., about individual behavioral differences) most closely measured the quantity of attachment behavior expressed. Consequently, previous analytic approaches, which ranked behaviors among each other, according to a priori notions such as relative "intensity," would be inappropriate. Also unsuited for these purposes, would be the widely employed Ainsworth "Strange Situation," which has been used to study individual and maternal categorical differences in the affective quality of attachment relationships (e.g., "secure," "avoidant," etc.).

---

[1]However, "eye contact" and "looks at person" behaviors were excluded from the analysis. Apparently the meaning of these behaviors is different in this society: Children are trained from an early age not to look directly at a person of higher status (R. LeVine to P. H. Leiderman, personal communication, 1974). This cultural training confounds the consideration of looking as an attachment behavior.

[2]In this paper we have chosen to use the term attachment behavior rather than the more general expression "social responsiveness." In fact, the behaviors examined in this study are ones thought by Ainsworth and others to indicate infant attachment. Yet these same behaviors may have different meaning in a nonattachment context. We also recognize that the behaviors chosen to reflect attachment may be only a subset of a larger group of social behaviors, unexamined in this study, which may or may not be related to attachment behavior.

SOCIAL AND CULTURAL CONTEXT

This study was conducted among the agricultural Gusii people of Kenya, East Africa (see LeVine & Levine, 1963). In this society women are responsible for subsistence farming. Because of this, they require additional help with infant and neonate caregiving. As a result, older children and family members also serve as the infant's caregivers.

A typical household consists of a husband, wife, and their children, living on the husband's father's land. Because this same land is sometimes shared with the husband's brothers, several such households might be in close proximity to one another, thereby providing considerable contact between groups of children and adults of all ages. Women, as wives and mothers (S. LeVine, 1979), reside in the homestead and are responsible for maintaining the household and raising subsistence crops for food. Sometimes the male family members remain at home and occasionally help their wives with chores. More frequently they have intermittent local jobs, or rarely, jobs in distant communities. Consequently they may visit their families only once or twice a year. As a result, the older male family members do not participate in child caregiving.

Primary schools are readily available in the community through seventh grade. However, because of the fee system, attendance at school depends on the family income, and the family's attitude toward education. Nevertheless, school attendance affects the child caregiving system. It means that children approximately 7- to 12-years-old are not available as child caregivers. Consequently, younger children must increasingly assume that role.

Methods

Sample. Twenty-eight Gusii infants ranging from 6.1 to 30.3 months of age participated in the study. The sample was equally divided between boys and girls. The children were selected because of their age, willingness of their mother to participate, and geographically proximity to the town center. They also were chosen with certainty of variability in clan and religious affiliations. The same infants and their families had participated in a larger intensive anthropological, psychological, and medical study of a Gusii village adapting to modern social and economic conditions (LeVine, Brazelton, & Leiderman, manuscript in preparation).

Experimental Protocol. According to a previously defined experimental scheme (Leiderman & Leiderman, 1974), infants were sequentially exposed to their mother, child caregiver, and an unfamiliar local adult (who was usually female). Each stimulus figure was to spend approximately 5 minutes with the (infant) child: She was to approach and greet the child, spend approximately 2 minutes playing with him or her, depart from the child (out of sight), return after approximately 2 minutes and remain with the child for about 90 seconds. This situation enabled us to observe and measure the infant's responses to the *approach* by his caregiver, to being *with* her, *separated* from her, *alone* without her, and then experiencing her *return*.

The child's reaction to this entire sequence of interaction was videotaped outdoors in front of the infant's homestead. The videotaping occurred about 2 hours after feeding when the infant was alert. Each infant in the sample completed the protocol twice, the unfamiliar adult figure being different in the second session. The order of stimulus figure presentation was varied to allow each figure to be first, second, or third an equal number of times.

The mean age of the children at the first session (Time 1) was 15.1 months (range 6.1 to 27.2 months). Approximately 3 months later, when this same sequence was repeated, the mean sample age was 18.3 months (range 9.0 to 30.3 months). This second session (Time 2) was to provide a replication of the cross-sectional group observations made at Time 1. It also afforded information about individual longitudinal changes in behavior from Time 1 to Time 2.

Behavior Codes and Data Analyses. Videotapes of the experimental situation were analyzed by two observers unfamiliar with the hypotheses of the study. After a training period, these observers independently coded attachment behaviors for five experimental sequences. The Kappa for interobserver reliability, based on these sequences, was .81. Subsequently, each observer coded every other experimental sequence. Periodic independent codings of the same sequences indicated that the same level of reliability was being maintained throughout the analyses.

The first 20 seconds of the separation sequences was used to quantify attachment behavior. The separation sequence was chosen because, as others have pointed out (Ainsworth, 1977), it is the situation most likely to elicit such behaviors. The coded attachment behaviors are listed in Table 11.1. An attach-

TABLE 11.1
Categories of Attachment Behaviors[a]

Vocalizing/Signaling Behaviors	*Contact Seeking/Maintains Behaviors*	*Proximity Promoting (Locomotor) Behaviors*
CRIES	REACHES	MOVES TOWARD
WHINES	REACHES FOR BREAST	LEANS TOWARD
SMILES	LIFTS ARMS TO BE HELD	TURNS BODY TOWARD
VOCALIZES	TOUCHES PERSON	MOVES AFTER
WAVES HANDS	CLIMBS ON PERSON	
	CLINGS	

[a]cf. Ainsworth, 1973, p. 2; Ainsworth et al., 1978, p. 42

ment behavior score was computed for the amount of attachment behavior an infant displayed with each of three stimulus figures—his mother, his caregiver, and an unfamiliar figure. This a priori score was determined by counting the number of occurrences of an attachment behavior and weighting for duration. Specifically stated, when an attachment behavior occurred and lasted 6- to 10-seconds, it was assigned a 2; if it lasted 11- to 15-seconds, it was counted as a 3 and, if it endured for 16- to 20-seconds, it received a 4. This procedure was reiterated for every new occurrence of an attachment behavior in the 20-second separation interval. The sum of these numbers constituted the infant's attachment score for a given figure (mother, child, caregiver or unfamiliar figure). We considered this a measure of the quantity of attachment behavior shown for that figure during the separation episode.

Before computing the attachment behavior scores, all nonstandard separation sequences (those with durations less than 20 seconds or those not following the protocol), were rejected.[3] The rejected sequences did not show any systematic similarity in age, sex, or behavior exhibited.

Graphs of the amount of attachment behavior versus age were smoothed, first by running medians of three (Tukey, 1977) and then by local least squares straight line fitting.[4] The bandwidth selected for this latter procedure was designed to visually minimize local variability without increasing systematic error. Unfortunately, there is currently no widely accepted statistical model for precisely assessing the uncertainty of the estimation (e.g., variance) made using these graphical techniques.

Results

Age-Related Changes in Attachment Behavior: Amount of Attachment Behavior as a Function of Age

Figures 11.1, 11.2, 11.3, and 11.4, show how attachment behavior varies by child's age for each of the three figures. They are cross-sectional and display values for Time 1 and Time 2. Figures 11.5 and 11.6 are longitudinal and show

---

[3]The number of sequences rejected was, Time 1: Mother (4), Child Caregiver (3), Unfamiliar Figure (6); Time 2: Mother (3), Child Caregiver (5), Unfamiliar Figure (5). Thus the total number of sequences available for cross-sectional analysis varied according to caregiving figure and Time (1 or 2). The number of sequences available for longitudinal analysis was always less than or equal to the number available for cross-sectional interpretation. This is because to perform a longitudinal analysis, an infant had to have a standard sequence *both* Time 1 and Time 2.

[4]The statistical assumption behind smoothing procedures is that the observed (ordinate) values are decomposable into a function and random error. In smoothing a graph one attempts to perform this decomposition, eliminating the random error and exposing the assumed underlying function. Such a technique helps to elucidate the relationship between two variables—particularly a dependent (e.g., attachment behavior) and an independent one (such as age).

how an individual child's scores change from Time 1 to Time 2. Specifically, they plot the child's attachment score and age at Time 1 with a line connecting the coordinate of his age and score at Time 2. Thereby it shows the direction and magnitude of the longitudinal individual changes in attachment behavior.

Age-Related Attachment Behavior for Mother. Figure 11.1 shows cross-sectionally how the children's attachment behaviors for mother varied as a function of age at Time 1 and Time 2. Other than some differences in magnitude and a slight disparity in phase, the figures display striking similarities. They indicate that attachment behavior increases as a function of age until approximately 11 months. It then drops to a nadir between 14- and 16-months of age. Again it increases with age to a peak at 18- to 21-months, when it subsequently declines to a minimum at approximately 25 months of age. It shows no significant oscillation after this time as we approach the limit of our sample's ages—30 months. Thus, we are unable to say whether or not this oscillatory pattern of attachment behavior continues beyond this age.

Age-Related Attachment Behavior for the Child Caregiver. Figure 11.2 demonstrates how the attachment behavior score varies with age for the child's caregiver. Again, despite some differences in magnitude, and a slight shift in phase, the age-related pattern of attachment behavior at Time 1 shows striking similarities to that of Time 2. The infants at Time 1 show an early peak in the amount of attachment behavior expressed at about 8 months of age. This peak is seen later, Time 2, at approximately 12.5 months. But after this interval both curves decline to a minimum near 16 months of age. From this nadir they again

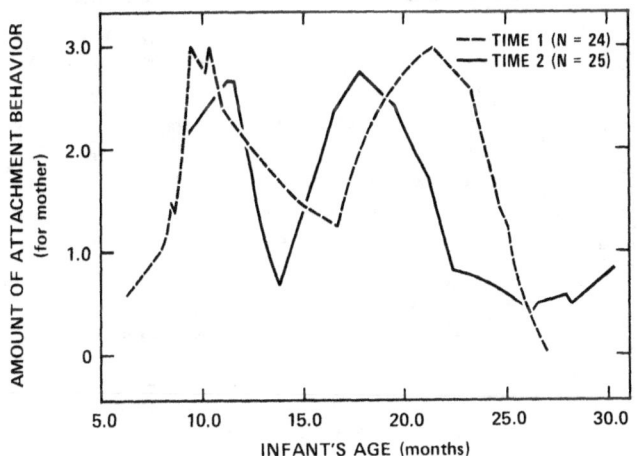

FIG. 11.1. Infant attachment behavior for mother.

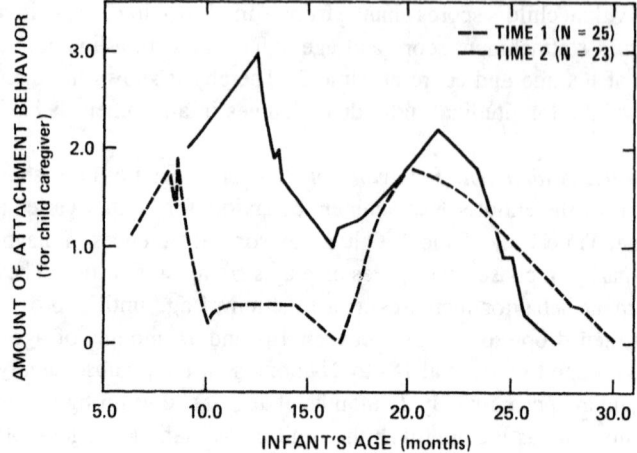

FIG. 11.2. Infant attachment behavior for child caregiver.

rise to peaks at 20- to 22-months of age only to decline to zero around 27 months (Time 2) or 30 months (Time 1). Again we are unable to extrapolate about attachment behavior beyond this interval because of our limited sample.

Age-Related Attachment Behavior for the Unfamiliar Figure. Figure 11.3 displays how attachment behavior varies as a function of age for the unfamiliar figure. Time 1 again shows striking similarities in overall pattern to Time 2. The data for the group at Time 1 suggest that attachment behavior increases from 6- to 8-months of age when it is the highest, as it was for the other familiar figures.

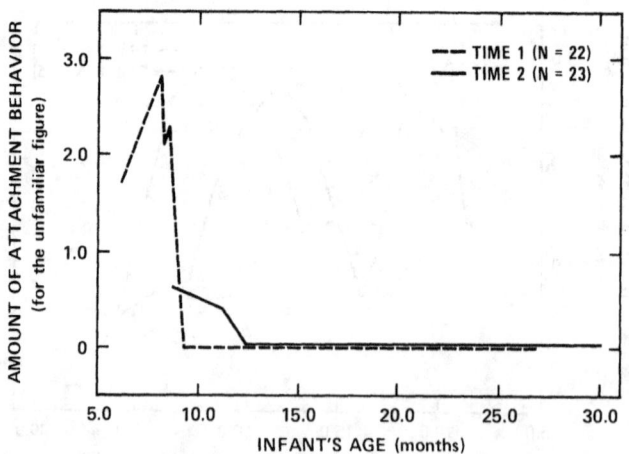

FIG. 11.3. Infant attachment behavior for unfamiliar adult.

This is echoed, though incompletely, by the plot of Time 2. Thereafter, both plots decline smoothly, though slightly out of phase, to a nadir at 9 months after Time 1, or 12 months after Time 2. From that point on, attachment behavior for the unfamiliar figure is essentially nonexistent both Time 1 and Time 2. These results indicate that in infants up to 9- to 11-months of age, the display of attachment behavior is nonspecific even though it is obvious that they can recognize different figures. The attachment behavior that is expressed after 10- to 12-months appears to be reserved largely for specific familiar figures. This finding substantiates the research done in Western cultures, which places the age of figure-specific attachment behavior in the last quarter of the first year.

In summary then, there are clear similarities between the age-related pattern of attachment behavior for a given figure, both Time 1 and Time 2. And, as we shall see, the general pattern of attachment behavior is similar for both mother and child caregiver.

That is not to say there are not differences between the Time 1 and Time 2 figures. In fact, they differ in both phase and magnitude. Some of these dissimilarities may be due to repetition of the experiment Time 2. In addition, other differences may be a result of limited sampling from an underlying curve that has its own distribution. If this were the case, we would expect that our estimates of this "true" curve would be similar in pattern, but different in phase and magnitude.

On the other hand, what is the explanation for the similarities between graphs in the age related pattern in attachment behavior? One interpretation is, that we are merely detecting individual differences in the amount of attachment behavior expressed. This would mean that the children who expressed high amounts of attachment behavior just happened to be between 8- to 12-, and 19- to 22-months of age. Likewise, those children who showed small amounts of attachment behavior were, by chance, between 15- to 16, or older than 25 months. However, this hypothesis, that the observed age-related pattern of attachment behavior is due to individual differences, is less likely because of the consistency among Figs. 11.1, 11.2 and 11.3. Nevertheless, we shall examine this possibility by looking at the age-related, individual, longitudinal changes in attachment behavior.

One other interpretation of this phenomenon is that it represents an age related change in the expression of one constituent attachment behavior or type of behavior. This question too will be addressed in a later section.

Cross-Sectional Comparison Among Different Figures for Age-Related Changes in Attachment Behavior. Figure 11.4 is a summary graph for Time 1. There are striking similarities in the structure of the plots. For instance, all three plots show increasing attachment as measured by separation situation in the age range of 6- to 8-months. There is some difference among the curves in the age at which maximum attachment behavior is displayed for each figure. Specifically,

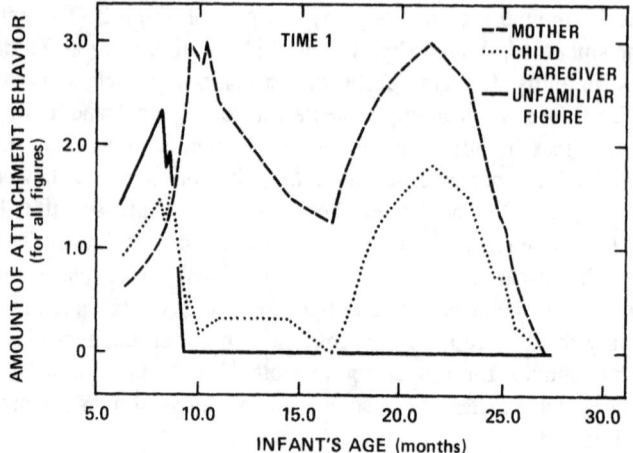

FIG. 11.4. Comparison of infant attachment behavior among the different figures.

the children show maximum attachment behavior with their mother at about 11 months, with their caretaker at about 9 months, and with the unfamiliar figure at 8- to 9-months. After those ages, the amount of attachment decreases to a nadir of about 16 months for mother and caretaker, and about 9 months for the unfamiliar figure.

Thus, there are interesting similarities between the amount of attachment behavior expressed for each of the three stimulus figures, as a function of age. It may be said, that to the limits of accuracy of our measurements, the curves for mother and caretaker oscillate in a similar age-related manner. The same appears to be true of attachment behavior displayed for the unfamiliar figure up to the age of 11 months. After that time there is a striking dissociation between this plot (for the unfamiliar figure) and that of the child caretaker and mother. This is a clear indication of the onset of figure specific or differential attachment behavior.

Longitudinal Changes in Attachment Behavior as a Function of Age

It could be argued that the observed periodicity of attachment behavior with age is an artifact produced by individual differences in the expression of behavior. If this were the case, we would expect that a longitudinal plot, of individual development changes in attachment behavior, would fail to recapitulate the cross-sectional curves.

Figures 11.5 and 11.6 are longitudinal plots of the amount of attachment behavior displayed vs. age, both Time 1 and Time 2. The amount and direction of each individual change, is denoted by a line connecting the two points, for Time 1 and Time 2. As such, a line segment with a positive slope, indicates that

11. AGE-RELATED CHANGES IN ATTACHMENT BEHAVIOR 225

the amount of attachment behavior that infant displayed, increased with age. A negative slope, of course, denotes the converse.

Longitudinal Changes in Attachment Behavior for Mother. The plot of longitudinal changes in infant attachment behavior for mother (Fig. 11.5) displays some striking similarities to the corresponding sectional graph (Fig. 11.1). Like Fig. 11.1, Fig. 11.5 shows that the predominant individual change in attachment behavior, for infants up to about 11 months (Time 2) is to show increasing attachment behavior with age. This corresponds to the upward rise to peak attachment behavior seen in Fig. 11.1.

After 11 months, to about 16 months of age, the change with age is to show increasingly less attachment behavior. Again, this alteration with age recapitulates that seen cross-sectionally in Fig. 11.1, where the attachment behavior declines to a nadir between 14- to 16-months of age.

Figure 11.5 shows that from 16- to 21-months, individual infants tend to display increasing amounts of attachment behavior. After about 21 months, the tendency is for each child to show less behavior with increasing age until 25 months. From this point on, like Fig. 1, the modal change with age is not clear: two children show an increase, and another two show a decline, in the amount of behavior displayed with age.

In summary then the longitudinal plot of individual changes in attachment behavior largely replicates the cross-sectional patterns seen in Fig. 11.1. Nevertheless there are a few individual deviations from this cross-sectional pattern.

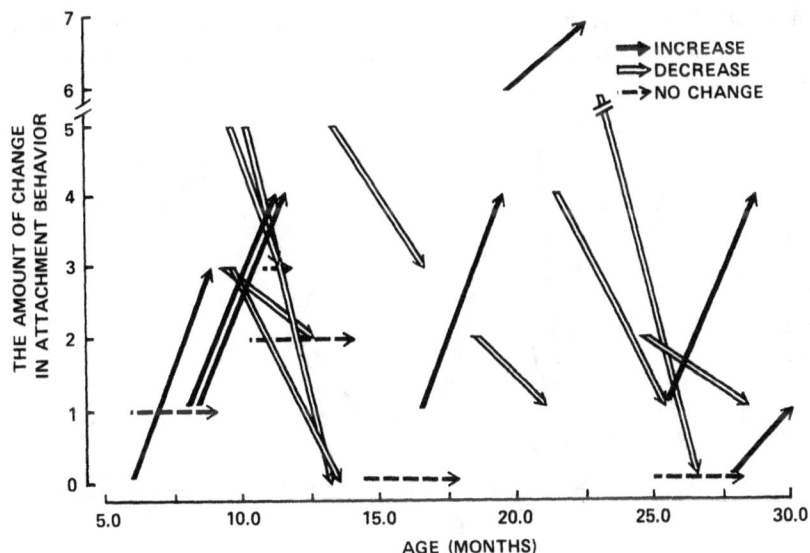

FIG. 11.5. Longitudinal changes in infant attachment behavior for mother.

One plausible explanation is that, like any developmental sequence, these changes may be delayed for some children. Yet overall, the striking similarities between the cross-sectional and longitudinal graphs, are strong evidence that this pattern is developmental, and not merely indicative of individual differences in behavior.

Longitudinal Changes in Attachment Behavior for the Child Caregiver. Comparing Fig. 11.6 with Fig. 11.2 suggests that the individual longitudinal changes in attachment behavior for the child caregiver also reiterate the cross-sectional patterns discussed earlier. However, the replication is less striking than that observed for the child's mother.

From 6- to approximately 13-months most children show an increasing or constant amount of attachment behavior. This is similar to the cross sectional changes observed in Fig. 11.2 where peaks were seen at 8 (Time 1) to 12.5 (Time 2) months. After this time and until about 16 months, individual children show a decrease or consistent nadir in the amount of behavior with age. However, the longitudinal data for this period is based on only two subjects, and thus we are reluctant to draw any inferences about this interval.

After 16 months, until approximately 22 months, the individual changes in behavior again tend to reiterate the pattern seen cross-sectionally. Specifically, there is a modal increase in the amount of behavior expressed with increasing age. Unfortunately, after this period, until about 25 months, we have no information on longitudinal changes. Beyond this time, from 25 to 30 months, all four children fail to show any change in the general low level of attachment behavior expressed. This roughly corresponds to the changes seen cross-sectionally, which indicate that attachment behavior declines to a nadir during this period.

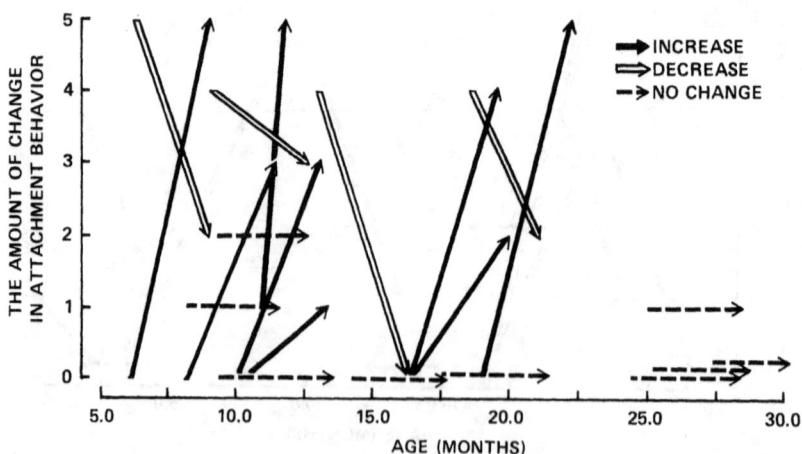

FIG. 11.6. Longitudinal changes in infant attachment behavior for child caregiver.

TABLE 11.2
Direction of Longitudinal Changes
in Infant Attachment Behavior
By Age Group (N = 21)

*Number of children showing a change with
age in the amount of attachment
behavior for:*

	Mother[1]				Child-Caregiver[2]		
Mean Age Months	↑	→	↓	Mean Age Months	↑	→	↓
6–11	3	1	0	6 –12.5	5	3	2
11–15	0	2	5	12.5–15	0	0	1
15–21	2	1	1	16 –21	3	2	1
21–26	0	0	2	21 –30	0	4	0
26–30	2	1	1				

[1] $p < 0.0001$
[2] $p < 0.017$ (Wilcoxon signed rank tests, one tailed)

On the whole, the longitudinal plots of individual changes, in attachment behavior for child caregiver, only approximately recapitulate the cross-sectional ones observed in Fig. 11.2. Like the age related alterations in behavior for the mother, they argue, though less strongly, that the pattern observed is developmental and not only due to individual differences.

Cross-Sectional Predictions of Longitudinal Changes in Attachment Behavior. Table 11.2 is a summary of how well the cross-sectional changes in attachment behavior for both mother and child caregiver, predict the individual longitudinal ones. For example, Fig. 11.1 suggests that children between 6 and 11 months show increasing amounts of attachment behavior with age. Table 11.2 indicates, that of the four children with a mean age (Time 1 and Time 2) between 6–11 months, three showed an increase in the amount of behavior with age, and one showed no change. Continuing in this fashion, using the cross-sectional graphs to predict the individual longitudinal changes in behavior, we find that it does so in a statistically significant way. That is, the cross-sectional graph correctly predicts the direction of longitudinal changes in maternal attachment behavior, in 12 of 13 children (with mean Time 1 and Time 2 ages from 6- to 26-months[5]). The probability of this relationship arising by chance alone is $p < 0.0001$ (Wilcoxon signed rank test, one tailed).

---

[5]The cross-sectional pattern for the change in attachment behavior with age after 26 months was, it will be recalled, not clear.

Table 11.2 also performs the same analysis of attachment behavior expressed for the child caregiver. Again, the age intervals listed here are derived from the cross-sectional data in Fig. 11.2. For example, Fig. 11.2 indicates that attachment behavior continues to increase with age up to approximately 12.5 months (Time 2), that it declines to a minimum at about 15 months, to again increase to a peak at approximately 21 months; thereafter it declines to a minimum at about 30 months (Time 1). How well do these cross-sectional changes with age correspond to the longitudinal ones? Again, using the cross-sectional age intervals above, Table 11.2 indicates whether children with a mean age in these epochs, showed an increase, decrease, or no change, in the amount of attachment behavior with age. Here too, the cross-sectional changes correctly foretell the longitudinal ones in 9 of 12 infants: $p < .015$ (Wilcoxon signed rank test, one tailed).

In conclusion then, this is strong evidence that the age-related changes in attachment behavior may be developmental. Nevertheless, the pattern of behavior with age, for the child caregiver, is less clear-cut than that for mother. In addition, there are significant individual deviations from the predicted age-related pattern of behavior. This suggests that other factors (environment, temperament, etc.) do have some influence on the pattern of individual changes. It also indicates that these factors, may, for most individuals, have more influence on the pattern of attachment to nonmaternal caregivers, than they do for maternal ones.

Age-Related Changes in Attachment Behavior: Changes in the "Type" of Attachment Behavior Exhibited as a Function of Age

Having observed that the amount of attachment behavior oscillates in an age-related manner, it is natural to wonder if these fluctuations reflect changes in the kind of attachment behavior shown. In fact, previous investigators have predicted such developmental alterations in attachment behavior. As noted earlier, Ainsworth's (1973) speculations have been most explicit. She has predicted changes, in the earliest year, in the relative frequencies of contact maintaining and seeking, proximity promoting (locomotor), and vocalizing/signaling attachment behaviors, as the child matures.

Grouping the attachment behaviors as suggested by Ainsworth, we have tested this assertion both longitudinally (Table 11.3) and cross-sectionally, (Table 11.4). In the latter test (Table 11.4) we grouped children by age cohort. Doing so, we found no meaningful change with increasing age in the relative amount of each type of attachment behavior.

We also analyzed the data longitudinally (Table 11.3) by noting any individual change in the type of attachment behavior expressed from Time 1 to Time

TABLE 11.3
Longitudinal Changes in the Type of Attachment Behavior Expressed[a]

Person for Whom This Behavior Expressed		Type of Behavior			
		Vocalizing/ Signaling	Contact Maintaining/Seeking	Proximity Promoting	
Mother	Increase	4	3	2	9
	No Δ	11	12	13	36
	Decrease	6	6	6	18
Child Caregiver	Increase	7	1	4	12
	No Δ	11	19	17	47
	Decrease	5	3	2	10
Unfamiliar Adult	Increase	4	0	0	4
	No Δ	12	19	20	51
	Decrease	4	1	0	5

[a] No. of children showing a change in the amount of a given type of attachment behavior expressed at Time 1 compared to Time 2

2. The entire sample was studied together and was broken down into age cohorts. Again, no meaningful change in the relative frequency of each type of behavior was seen.

This finding argues that the observed oscillation, in the *amount* of attachment behavior expressed as a function of age, does not reflect an underlying fluctuation or developmental change in the *type* of attachment behavior shown. It also lends further weight to the notion of functional equivalence among attachment behaviors.

TABLE 11.4
Mean Percentage Attachment Score by Behavioral Category for Infants Younger and Older than 15 Months

		Type of Behavior					
		Vocal/Signaling		Contact Promoting		Proximity Promoting	
	Age	<15 mo.	>15 mo.	<15 mo.	>15 mo.	<15 mo.	>15 mo.
Mother	Time 1	68	65	16	13	16	22
	Time 2	85	50	0	33	15	16
Caregiver	Time 1	85	62	10	8	5	31
	Time 2	74	74	3	0	22	26
Unfamiliar Figure	Time 1	79	52	14	48	7	0
	Time 2	100	(100) 0	0	(100) 0	0	(100) 0

DISCUSSION

In this study we have been concerned with a quantitative measure of the amount of attachment behavior expressed during separation. As such, we did not measure the "intensity" of attachment behavior shown, because all attachment behaviors were regarded as "functionally equivalent"; viz., there was no ranking of these behaviors among each other in any dimension. Nor did we attempt to measure the "quality" of individual attachment relationships, (for which assessment the Ainsworth Strange Situation is often used). And, in particular, in this study, we have not assessed individual differences in the expression of attachment behavior. Rather, we have examined the attachment behavior pattern of a group of children as it relates to their ages.

Nevertheless, the age-related changes in the expression of attachment behavior which we have observed suggest some further hypotheses about the attachment construct. The most conservative of these hypotheses relate to attachment behavior itself. These results suggest that it unfolds in an age-related fashion.

Specifically, our results confirm that in this polymatric society, as in Western monomatric ones, the modal expression of attachment behavior is not figure specific until after the third quarter of the first year of life. After that time most infants discriminate among figures in their display of this behavior, showing increasingly less attachment behavior for an unfamiliar figure.

To some perhaps, it is anomalous to say that an infant expresses attachment behavior for an unfamiliar figure. Yet, it is our view that, in the infant's first year, it is reasonable to assume that these behaviors reflect early social bonding or attachment, even to such a figure. In fact, "attachment" to unfamiliar figures has been shown previously (Feldman & Ingham, 1975). The evidence suggests that, under stressful conditions, such as separation, the infant under 10 months of age may direct attachment behavior to any potential caretaking figure. Possibly as a result of further cognitive development, the infant under the stress of separation, will make a finer discrimination between these individuals. Thus he will not respond to the separation from an unfamiliar figure as he would to separation from his mother. Nevertheless, the survival value to the infant of an attachment response to "category," rather than a single individual, should be obvious enough. Perhaps after the infant has achieved finer discrimination of individuals (beyond 10 months of age) then attachment behavior directed towards a single, specific figure, further ensures survival in a more complex environment.

Nevertheless, after they have become figure specific or discriminating in their display of attachment behavior, they still continue to show an age-related pattern that is similar for both maternal and nonmaternal caregivers. That is, they tend to show an increasing amount of behavior from approximately 10- to 12-months, a decreasing quantity from approximately 12- to 15- or 16-months, an increasing amount to 20- to 24-months, with a precipitious decline thereafter to 26 months, and beyond. And, as we have seen, this change in the amount of attachment behaviors expressed is not merely due to an alteration in the type, and frequency, of constituent behaviors being exhibited (cf. Kagan, Kearsley & Zelazo, 1978).

This finding of an oscillatory pattern in the expression of attachment behavior may have some implication for the issue of continuity and discontinuity in human development (Kagan, 1980). Specifically, if the underlying pattern of the behavior to be studied is nonlinear, sampling must be done at a frequency which is consonant with that function. For example, taking only two points (ages, measurements, etc.) from a parabola would cause one to assume that the function is monotonic or linear. Or sampling any number of times, each time, at a rate equal to the frequency of the underlying function again would cause one to hypothesize a linear relationship when the real one was cyclic. In another way, by taking measurements only during the declining phase of a function, one might be convinced that the quantity measured was discontinuous.

Consequently, this finding of an oscillatory pattern in behavioral display, suggests caution in estimating a pattern on the basis of only a few sample points—especially when the underlying pattern has not been estimated previously. This does not argue that discontinuous developmental processes do not exist, but merely that procedures for estimating them must consider nonlinearity. In addition, these findings indicate that using absolute attachment scores for different aged children is an inappropriate measure of the "quality of attachment."

What might be of significance of this observed oscillation in attachment behavior with age? One hypothesis is that it represents an age-related process of formation and consolidation of an attachment relationship (see hypothesized Fig. 11.7). As such, the maxima in attachment for all figures prior to approximately 10 months of age may be regarded as indicating nonspecific attachment behavior. After that time, there appears to be an age-related increase in the amount of

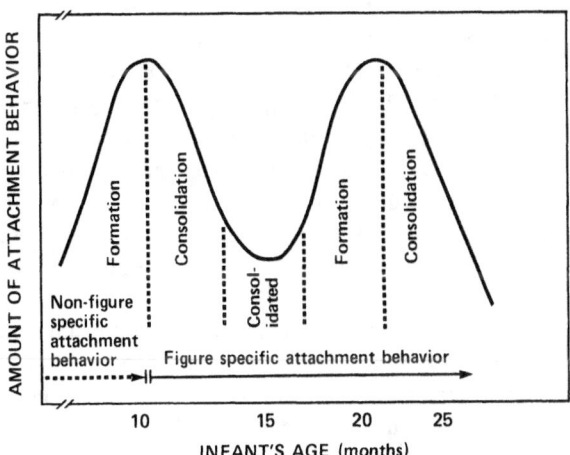

FIG. 11.7. Hypothesized relationship of infant attachment behavior with age.

attachment behavior for the mother (and less so for the child caretaker). Since the relationship is most tenuous for this time, the child may be expected to react most vigorously (show most attachment behavior), when the attachment figure departs. However, as the attachment relationship matures, we would expect that separation attachment behavior gradually decreases to a minimum. It is during this period that we would think that the child would be most certain of the security of the relationship and more tolerant of separations.

In fact, a similar finding has been described (Ainsworth et al., 1978, p. 178; citing Bell, 1978) among 'Group B' (securely attached) infants in the Ainsworth Strange Situation at approximately 15-months of age. During this period, these children, who had shown positive behavior toward mother, and positive affect, at 11- and 24-months of age, failed to do so at 15 months. In addition, Schaffer and Emerson (1964) also noted an "unexplained dip [in the amount of attachment behavior] in the last lunar month of the first year [p. 38]." This occurred during what was regarded as the most stressful attachment situation: "outside house" and "outside shop." Unfortunately, they did not assess the amount of attachment behavior again until the infants were 18 months of age. By that time, as in our sample, the amount of behavior had increased to previous levels. Nevertheless, this too is suggestive evidence, for the existence of an oscillatory pattern in the age-related expression of attachment behavior.

After an attachment relationship is consolidated or secure, it is hypothesized that infants re-experience an age-related period of receptivity for the formation and consolidation of a new attachment relationship. During this interval from approximately 18- to 22-months, the child shows anew the tendency to form another attachment relationship. Again, during this process of formation of the bond, the child is least secure with separation from the new attachment figure. In fact, it appears as if this insecurity generalizes even to the older attachment relationship, so that in effect, with the formation of this new bond, the older one is recast. Thus when the new attachment relationship is consolidated, the older bond also emerges reintegrated within the new affective network.

As such, this oscillation would represent possibly a biologically driven, (though socially modulated), phase of receptivity for the formation of attachment relationships. It would be developmental, in that we would expect that the type of attachment figure, to whom one is receptive, to vary as a function of age and previous bonds. It may not be developmental in the sense that, with the formation of each new attachment relationship, one experiences a recrudescence of insecurity, or anxiety, with separation from the new, and probably older attachment figures.

What then would be the purpose behind this oscillation in attachment relationships? Though Bowlby (1969) and others originally conceived of attachment as having the function of protecting the species from predation, one might expect that its purpose is larger than this, and that it changes with the individual's maturation. Thus, while attachment may cause the infant to seek the protection of a caregiver, it may later prompt the young child to seek the company of same-age peers. With these peers he or she may begin the process of socialization and integration into the species group. It may, still later, spur the adolescent or young adult to seek a mate (a same-age attachment figure) and bring about the continuation of the species. Thus, the original child becomes caregiver and renews the cycle.

Summary and Conclusions

1. The development of figure specific or differential attachment behavior for polymatric infants is similar to that observed in monomatric societies. This similarity in the pattern of infant attachment behaviors across cultures, and between caregiving figures, suggests that this behavior is less culturally or socially influenced, and more developmentally determined.

2. There is an oscillatory pattern to attachment behavior (with age) which is similar for primary (maternal) or secondary attachment figures. Within this pattern, peaks occur at approximately 9- to 11-months, and 20- to 22-months. Nadirs appear at 15- to 16, and 24- to 26-months.

3. The nadir of attachment behavior at approximately 15 months, and at about 24 months, may indicate that a secure attachment relationship has been formed.

4. The oscillatory nature of attachment behavior suggests that social relationships are more dynamic than is generally appreciated.

5. Controversies regarding continuity and discontinuity in certain phenomena may be due to inadequate estimation of an underlying possibly nonlinear pattern.

6. Nonlinearity of behavioral phenomena may be more widely extant than heretofore appreciated.

7. There was no transformation in the type of infant attachment behavior expressed with increasing age.

ACKNOWLEDGMENTS

The field work portion of this study was supported by a grant to Professor Robert LeVine of Harvard University from the National Science Foundation in 1976–78. Aspects of the data analysis were supported by the Spencer Foundation, Chicago, the Grant Foundation, New York, and the Boys Town Center, Stanford University, and a gift to Professor P. H. Leiderman from Mr. D. P. Booth, Jr., of San Francisco. Portions of data analyses were supported by the Computation Center of Stanford University.

We want to express our appreciation to Dr. Gloria Leiderman, Dr. T. Berry Brazelton, Dr. Constance Keefer and Dr. Edward Tronick for help in initial planning, to Dr. David Feigal for collection of the data in the field, Mr. Paul Amato and Ms. Erica Leiderman for coding of behavior, to Ms. Sue Thiemann and Ms. Rowena Hardin for data analyses and Ms. Joan Wolfe for typing of the manuscript. Particularly, we want to express our thanks to the participants in this research and their families, to our Gusii research assistants, and our colleagues in the field, Professor Robert LeVine, Ms. Sarah LeVine, Dr. Suzanne Dixon, without whom this research could not have been accomplished.

REFERENCES

Ainsworth, M. D. S. *Infancy in Uganda: Infant care and growth of love.* Baltimore: Johns Hopkins Press, 1967.

Ainsworth, M. D. S. The development of infant-mother attachment. In B. M. Caldwell & H. N. Ricciuti (Eds.), *Review of Child Development Research,* (Vol. 3). Chicago: University of Chicago Press, 1973.

Ainsworth, M. D. S. Attachment theory and its utility in cross-cultural research. In P. H. Leiderman, S. R. Tulkin, & A. Rosenfeld (Eds.), *Culture and infancy: Variations in human experience.* New York: Academic Press, 1977.

Ainsworth, M. D. S. *Attachment: Retrospect and prospect.* Paper submitted for publication, 1979.

Ainsworth, M. D. S., Blehar, M. C., Waters, E., & Wall, S. *Patterns of attachment: A psychological study of the strange situation.* Hillsdale, N.J.: Lawrence Erlbaum Associates, 1978.

Bowlby, J. The nature of the child's tie to his mother. *International Journal of Psychoanalysis,* 1958, *39,* 350-373.

Bowlby, J. *Attachment and loss: (Vol. I) Attachment.* New York: Basic Books, 1969.

Coates, B., Anderson, E. P., & Hartup, W. W. Interrelations in the attachment behavior of human infants. *Developmental Psychology,* 1972, *6,* 218-230. (a)

Coates, B., Anderson, E. P., & Hartup, W. W. The stability of attachment behaviors in the human infant. *Developmental Psychology,* 1972, *6,* 231-237. (b)

Feldman, S., & Ingham, M. Attachment behavior: A validation study in two age groups. *Child Development,* 1975, *46,* 319-330.

Gewirtz, J. L. On the selection and use of attachment and dependence indices. In J. L. Gewirtz (Ed.), *Attachment and dependency,* New York: Winston, 1972.

Kagan, J. Perspective in continuity. In O. G. Brim, & J. Kagan (Eds.), *Constancy and change in human development.* Cambridge: Harvard University Press, 1980.

Kagan, J., Kearsley, R., & Zelazo, P. *Infancy: Its place in human development.* Cambridge, Mass.: Harvard University Press, 1978.

Leiderman, P. H., & Leiderman, G. F. Affective and cognitive consequences of the polymatric infant care in the East African highlands. *Minnesota Symposium on Child Psychology,* 1974, 81-109.

Leiderman, P. H., Thiemann, S., Reed, G. *Maternal and child caregiver behavior and cognitive development.* Manuscript in preparation.

LeVine, R. A., Brazelton, T. B., & Leiderman, P. H. Study of a Gusii village. Manuscript in preparation.

LeVine, R. A., & Levine, B. B. Nyansongo: Gusii community in Kenya. In B. Whiting (Ed.), *Six cultures—studies of child rearing.* New York: Wiley, 1963.

LeVine, S. *Mother and wives: Gusii women of East Africa,* Chicago: University of Chicago Press, 1979.

Marvin, R. S., Van Devender, T. L., Iwanga, M. I., LeVine, S., & LeVine, R. A. Infant-caregiver attachment among the Hausa of Nigeria. In H. McGurk (Ed.), *Ecological factors in human development.* Amsterdam: North-Holland Publishing Company, 1977.

Masters, J. C., & Wellman, H. M. The study of human infant attachment: A procedural critique. *Psychological Bulletin,* 1974, *81,* 218-237.

Schaffer, H. R., & Emerson, P. E. The development of social attachments in infancy. *Monographs of the Society for Research in Child Development,* 1964, *29* (Serial No. 94).

Tukey, J. *Exploratory data analysis,* Reading, Mass.: Addison Wesley, 1977.

Waters, E. The reliability and stability of individual differences in infant-mother attachment. *Child Development,* 1978, *49,* 483-494.

V METHODOLOGICAL CONSIDERATIONS

12 The Cross-Cultural Study of Early Interaction: Implications from Research On Culture and Cognition

Martha Zaslow
National Institute of Child Health and Human Development

Barbara Rogoff
University of Utah

A major contribution of cross-cultural research to the field of developmental psychology has been in the area of methodology (Laboratory of Comparative Human Cognition, 1979). Research in a foreign culture tends to throw into sharp relief methodological problems that are present but less apparent in a home culture. Cross-cultural work has increased the awareness of such issues as the complex nature of apparently straightforward independent variables (e.g., social class, culture, age; Whiting, 1976) and of problems in making inferences from restricted samples of behavior (as in laboratory tests) to more general competencies or behavioral tendencies (LCHC, 1979; Price-Williams, 1975; Scribner, 1976).

The concern with methodological issues which has characterized cross-cultural psychology for at least a decade has centered largely in the area of cognitive research. With the important exception of the publications of the Six Cultures Study, (Whiting, 1966; Whiting, Child, & Lambert, 1966; Whiting & Whiting, 1975), there have been few methodological discussions specific to the topic of this book—the study of early social interaction in varying cultural contexts. In this chapter we will summarize the methodological concerns that have been raised in cross-cultural studies of cognition to provide a starting point for consideration of the analogous and contrasting methodological issues in cross-cultural studies of early interaction.

Building from concerns expressed in cross-cultural cognitive research, we will identify three issues with relevance to studies of social interaction: (1) questions about the equivalence of situations compared across cultures (including comparability of stimuli, behaviors, procedures, and settings); (2) the impact of the observational context itself upon behavior; and (3) the relationship between the behavior sampled in the observational context (laboratory or field) and behavior in other settings in the culture.

In both cognitive and social cross-cultural research, the underlying issue is the need to obtain sufficient information about the cultural context to allow a culturally coherent interpretation of the behavior observed; to determine equivalence of the situations that are being compared cross-culturally; and to determine the extent to which sampled behavior generalizes to other settings within each culture. As will be seen, the increasing concern with contextual factors in cross-cultural research has not only methodological but theoretical implications as well.

METHODOLOGICAL ISSUES IN CROSS-CULTURAL STUDIES OF COGNITION

> ... if Australian aborigines fail a Piagetian conservation test, or Central Asian peasants draw conclusions from logical syllogisms on the basis of their concrete experiences, overriding the logic of the problem ... there is the lurking suspicion that the instructions may have been poorly understood, the stimuli meaningless, the subjects bored or frightened. In short, rather than indicating crucial differences in psychological makeup, such research may do little more than rediscover problems in the conduct of developmental research [LCHC, 1979, p. 827].

Methodological discussions in cross-cultural studies of cognition have consistently voiced concern about laboratory tasks and experimental situations as sources of information about cognitive activity. More specifically, questions have been raised concerning the use of identical stimuli and procedures in cultures in which familiarity and connotations differ; the assumption that the experimental context is understood in the same way in different cultures; and more fundamentally, whether experimental tasks accurately reflect cognitive activity outside of the laboratory.

Comparability of Materials and Procedures

The earliest point of criticism in cross-cultural studies of cognition was the potential unfairness of stimuli and procedures used in laboratory tasks. Researchers have frequently questioned the use of literally identical materials and procedures in two or more cultures, as opposed to materials and procedures of comparable familiarity, salience, and importance within each (Cole & Bruner, 1971; Cole, Gay, Glick & Sharp, 1971; Cole & Scribner, 1974, 1975; Frijda & Jahoda, 1966; Glick, 1975; LCHC, 1979; Price-Williams, 1962, 1975; Scribner, 1976).

There have been striking demonstrations of differences in cognitive performance according to the familiarity of materials used in a task (Deregowski & Serpell, 1971; Irwin & McLaughlin, 1970; Okonji, 1971). Irwin, Schafer and Feiden (1974) report that American undergraduates responded to requests to sort bowls of rice with the same hesitance and bewilderment shown by Liberian nonliterates when asked to sort cards decorated with squares and triangles. Both groups, when tested with unfamiliar materials, sorted in a fashion considered less advanced.

In addition to familiarity of materials, familiarity of activities performed on the materials must also be considered (Cole, Sharp, & Lave, 1976; Greenfield, 1974; Lave, 1977). Serpell (1979) contrasted Zambian and English children's ability to copy visual displays in four activities differing in familiarity for the two cultures. The Zambian children performed better when asked to copy two-dimensional figures formed of strips of wire (an activity that Serpell had observed Zambian children engage in frequently) whereas the English children surpassed the Zambian in copying two-dimensional figures with paper and pencil (a common activity of English but not Zambian children). No differences were found in activities to which the two groups had similar exposure: copying positions of adults' hands, and modeling figures out of clay. The results support the conclusion that differences reflect varying exposure to particular activities, rather than a general perceptual difference between groups. Other studies making use of indigenous concepts (Greenfield & Childs, 1977; Kelly, 1977) have found impressive performance by non-Western groups.

Findings such as these have made researchers more concerned with ecological validity: the match between their measures and their subjects' everyday experiences. The findings also raise questions about "the basic assumption that it is possible, in principle and in fact, to examine memory processes [and other cognitive processes] across diverse social groups with relatively little concern for the content of what is being remembered [Cole & Scribner, 1975, p. 254]."

Response to the Experimental Situation

Experimental situations are contexts that create reactions. Yet "they have been carried from the West to the non-West... without being studied as a phenomenon themselves [Edgerton, 1974, p. 63]." Differences in performance on a cognitive task may derive, not from differences in underlying cognitive competence, but in variation in the readiness with which individuals in a culture enter into the subject role (Cole & Scribner, 1975); differences in the subjects' understanding of the experimenter-subject relationship (Frijda & Jahoda, 1966; Scribner, 1976); differences in subjects' hypotheses about what problem is under investigation and what methods are proper for solving it (Goodnow, 1976; LCHC, 1979; Scribner, 1976); and finally, the subjects' assumptions about what behavior is appropriate in the presence of the experimenter and in this particular setting (Scribner, 1976; Rogoff, in press).

An anecdote reported by Glick (1975) illustrates the possibility that the subjects' conception of a task may differ from the experimenter's. Kpelle subjects sorted twenty objects into functional groups (e.g., knife with orange, potato with hoe) rather than categorical groups, and would often volunteer, upon being further questioned, that this is the way a wise man would do things. "When an exasperated experimenter asked finally, 'How would a fool do it,' he was given back sorts of the type that were initially expected—four neat piles with food in one, tools in another, and so on [p. 636]."

The social aspects of the experimental situation may be rapidly grasped by Western children familiar with testing in school, but highly discrepant for non-Western children and adults. In many cultures it is unusual for a high status adult, who already knows the answer to the question, to request information of a lower status person, such as a child. Engaging in conversation with an adult; being tested at an arbitrary point in the learning process rather than participating in an activity when competent; and performing a task alone rather than in a group may all be unfamiliar social situations though they are essential components of experimental settings (Cazden & John, 1971; Harkness & Super, 1977; Rogoff, in press).

The importance of attention to the social features inherent in an experimental setting is indicated by Irvine (1978). According to Irvine, previous findings of Piagetian nonconservation by nonschooled Wolof adolescents and adults (Greenfield, 1966) might be due to the test-like quality of the experimental setting. For a Wolof adult to ask another adult or a child to answer a question to which it is clear that the questioner already knows the response implies a challenge or trick-riddle. Further, Irvine notes that reticence to talk in the experimental situation, e.g., to explain responses to the conservation task, would be related to cultural attitudes concerning talk for high status Wolof, the majority in the village studied by both Irvine and Greenfield. In formal situations it is customary for high status persons to be taciturn.

Irvine (1978) informally investigated adults' conservation responses by modifying the setting of examination. Her subjects were informants who dropped in to visit her in the familiar setting of a village household. She presented the task in the context of questions about language (explain to the ignorant language-learner words like "more" and "the same" using water and beakers for illustration), rather than as a test. Irvine paused and waited for elaborations of initial respones, or indicated that she did not understand word meanings. Several of the informants' initial responses suggested nonconservation, with responses strikingly similar to the ones recorded by Greenfield. However each informant subsequently elaborated with a response clearly reflecting conservation (e.g., "The glasses are not the same, but the waters are the same" p. 306). Although discrepancies between Irvine's and Greenfield's observations are not resolved (see Greenfield, 1979), the work clearly illustrates the importance of considering the impact of the social context for interpretation of the cognitive skills displayed.

Cognitive Performance in Laboratory Tasks Versus Tasks in Everyday Life

Whereas cross-cultural psychologists have thus looked *within* laboratory tasks, questioning the comparability of materials, procedures, and expectations aroused by them in different cultures, they are increasingly looking *beyond* the laboratory task, questioning the extent to which cognitive activity manifested in the laboratory is operative in the same fashion in everyday situations (Cole & Bruner, 1971; Cole & Scribner, 1975; LCHC, 1979; Scribner, 1976). Doubts about generalizing from samples of behavior in experimental situations to everyday cognitive activity have been generated by observations, like those of Scribner, that often subjects who perform poorly on cognitive tests use elegant reasoning outside of the experiment.

Increasingly, cross-cultural cognitive researchers are urging the systematic study of cognitive activity as it naturally occurs (Cole & Bruner, 1971; Cole, Gay, Glick & Sharp, 1971; Cole, Hood & McDermott, 1978; Cole & Scribner, 1975; LCHC, 1979; Scribner, 1976). They note that describing behavior indicative of cognitive activity as it normally occurs (an "ethnographic psychology" of cognitive activity) is not a simple matter:

> It turns out that once we move beyond the highly constrained confines of our laboratory tasks and standardized tests, not only do we lose the technology for making statements about psychological processes, we also lose the framework within which we are accustomed to describe intellectual behavior [LCHC, 1979, p. 830].

It is important to note that what is being proposed is not a rejection of experimental studies, but rather the development of a new field-lab balance. These researchers advocate starting with a period of intensive observation and description of a particular activity as it naturally occurs in a culture, and then moving to quantitative methods. However, rather than relying on a single standardized task carried out in multiple cultures, these researchers propose systematically varying aspects of the task within each culture to gain insight into the specific determinants of behavior. Similarly Price-Williams (1975) proposes a sequence of research including (1) ethnographic description of the particular activity under study; (2) examination of cognitive performance as it occurs on a familiar task, in the usual context, and with familiar materials; and (3) examination of performance when the familiarity of task, material, and context are varied separately and in combination.

The increasing focus on the naturally occuring contexts of cognitive activity has raised important theoretical questions about the situational specificity of cognitive activity (Cole, Hood & McDermott, 1978; Kessel, 1979; LCHC, 1979, 1980; Mehan, 1976; Rogoff, 1978 and in press). Three views on this issue may be contrasted. The most general view holds that performance in one situation (e.g., a test) is indicative of a unitary cognitive ability (like a trait) characteristic of all of the individual's cognitive activity. An intermediate position views cognitive activity as divided into several sub-abilities rather than one general one, with consistency of performance across situations for each sub-ability. A more specific view is emerging from consideration of the generality of laboratory vs. everyday cognitive activity. According to this view cognitive activities cannot be separated from their uses in particular situations. Performance does not represent an underlying ability but rather a learned skill in handling a particular problem situation, and transfer from one situation to another is limited. Cross-cultural differences may reside not so much in different underlying competencies but in "the situations to which different cultural groups apply their skills [Cole & Bruner, 1971, p. 874]." Cole and Scribner (1975) note that most psychologists think that it is possible to examine cognitive processes without concern for the content of what is being processed; i.e., that it is possible to neutralize the task so that performance reflects "pure process." These authors question the feasibility of ever separating process from context.

COMPARABLE ISSUES IN CROSS-CULTURAL STUDIES OF EARLY INTERACTION

The focal point of criticism in studies of culture and cognition is the structured laboratory task: it may be so structured as to miss entirely the way in which a group of people actually utilizes thought processes in daily tasks. Cross-cultural differences may originate in response to characteristics of the task rather than cognitive processes used within a culture. The heavy reliance on laboratory tasks stems from the fact that cognitive activities are not directly observable but must be inferred from behavior or verbal report. The tasks provoke cognitive activity under controlled circumstances. As Cole, Hood and McDermott (1978) note, when studies of cognitive activity move from the laboratory to the field the researcher is faced with the problem of how to be certain when a task is actually being engaged in. Any intrusion into the naturalistic situation by the experimenter to determine (e.g., by asking) what cognitive problem is being tackled violates the ecological validity of the situation.

By contrast, studies of early interaction like those reported in this book aim directly at recording overt behavior. Whereas inference is still involved in interpreting what is observed, the process of interest is more accessible than in cognitive research. As such, studies of early interaction do not require researcher-structured situations or laboratory tasks, and indeed many studies have been carried out in the contexts in which infants and their social partners are normally found. Studies based on observation of social behavior in the field are free of the methodological concerns of cultural differences in subjects' reactions to task materials or procedures, or to unfamiliar laboratory settings. By sampling behavior from everyday life, these studies are free from the criticism that the data reflect what the subjects can do in a strange situation rather than what they actually do in the situations in which they are normally found.

Despite these important differences, cross-cultural studies of early interaction are faced with methodological problems that are quite similar to those of cognitive research. The concerns fall into three categories, closely corresponding to the issues in cross-cultural cognitive research reviewed earlier. First, even when observations have been carried out in naturalistic contexts, researchers have expressed concern about cultural variations in reactions to the observational context. Second, though no task materials or procedures are involved, issues of comparability in sampling and interpreting behavior arise in cross-cultural studies of social behavior. Third, researchers have voiced concern about the relationship between restricted samples of behavior and the broader cultural context.

Culture and Reactions to the Observational Context

Evidence has been presented that in cross-cultural studies of cognition, individuals use cultural information to interpret what is expected of them in an experimental situation. In American research on social interaction, strong arguments have been made for increasing the ecological validity of data by relying on direct observations in naturalistic contexts rather than observing behavior in unfamiliar situations (Bronfenbrenner, 1977, 1979; Gibbs, 1979; McCall, 1977; Willems, 1977). Although naturalistic observations may come closer to documenting interactions that occur normally, it is not clear that this method is entirely free of problems associated with subjects' interpretations of the situation (Pedersen, 1980). In particular "it seems likely that one influence of the observer on parents is to produce a heightened frequency of behavior that the participants judge to be more socially desirable and inhibit behavior considered socially undesirable [p. 181]." Pedersen notes however that the impact of the observer's presence in naturalistic contexts has not been systematically studied. The limited research in this area focuses on laboratory studies.

In the United States, a study by Graves and Glick (1978), although carried out in a laboratory setting, suggests how American middle-class mothers interpret what is expected of them when being observed. Graves and Glick contrasted behaviors of mothers with their 18- to 25-month-old children when the mothers thought they were being observed (video equipment was conspicuously running) and when they thought they were simply waiting in an observation room (repairs were "being made" on the video equipment; in fact observations were done throughout from behind a one-way mirror). The mothers' behavior when they thought they were being observed seemed to reflect their concept of "good mothering." Speech to the children doubled when the mothers thought they were being observed; mothers used more indirect directives, produced more test questions, engaged in more naming and action routines, made more evaluative comments, asked more questions and spent more time in joint interactive focus with their children, than when they thought they were not being observed. This study has been replicated recently among lower income mothers (Field & Ignatoff, in preparation).

The reports of researchers observing early interaction in other cultures provide fascinating indications that the presence of an observer leads to changes in behavior as well, and further that subjects interpret the observational context differently in diverse cultures. Among the Zinacantecos, a group of Mayan Indians living in Mexico, Brazelton (1977) describes fear of the observer in both adults and infants:

> We were automatically endowed with 'the evil eye' until I assured mothers that I was a 'curer' and could counteract it if I had it. However the effects of stranger anxiety in the baby were powerfully reinforced by his parents' constant anxiety about out presence. We were unable to relate to babies after nine months of age because the effect was so powerful [p. 174].

Brazelton expresses concern about the impact on the data of such an intense reaction to the observer.

On the other hand, the appearance of an observer may produce great interest rather than fear, which nevertheless disrupts the naturalness of the observation. Munroe and Munroe (1971) report that in Logoli households, as soon as the observer arrived, the infant was readied for display. It was picked up and brought to the observer for inspection. This cooperation on the part of the Logoli mothers made for difficulty in observing the usual caretaking of the infants. The Munroes changed their observational procedure to a "spot observation" which relied on data taken from a first glance (a "snapshot") of the infant and its surroundings, before the observer's presence was noticed and disrupted the ongoing activity.

Several authors have noted the necessity to choose socially appropriate times of day to observe (to avoid private times or intrusions on the mother's work, etc.) and the subjects' insistence on limiting the duration of the observation (Ainsworth, 1977; Lusk & Lewis, 1972). These limits reflect the subjects' views of the observer's intentions and roles. For example, Ainsworth (1977) reports an apparent categorization of observer as visitor among the Ganda. The mothers insisted that she observe during the afternoon, a time generally allocated to leisure and entertaining visitors.

Like the experimenter, the observer plays a social role which must be taken into account when considering the constraints on the interaction observed. The observer may be regarded as an intruder, a visitor, or a strange alien whose behavior must be tolerated, but it is not likely that the observer's presence is ignored. Cross-cultural comparisons may involve contrasting the observed behavior of two groups whose responses to, or even tolerance for, the presence of an observer differ substantially.

The impact of the observer's presence on subjects' behavior may be diminished in at least two ways: (1) spending a sustained period of time establishing rapport before carrying out observations; and (2) training native observers, whose presence will be less discrepant (though still not unobtrusive). At a minimum, it is important that research reports state the apparent impact of observer presence on behavior, so that this can be taken into account in interpreting cross-cultural differences.

Comparability in Behavioral Observations

In addition to considering the impact of their own presence on interactions, observers of early social interaction are faced with decisions regarding the choice of settings in which to observe, the particular behaviors to observe, and how to interpret observed behavior. In experimental studies of cognition the issue of using comparable as opposed to identical research procedures arose primarily in regard to materials and tasks, however, in cross-cultural studies of early interaction, comparability is an issue with respect to how to sample and interpret behavior:

> Although an ideal study would use identical methods with both or all societies being compared, this ideal is perhaps both unrealistic and in some instances mistaken, if, for example, techniques and methods developed in observing one society provide a distorting filter for viewing and assessing practices in another [Ainsworth, 1977, p. 143].

Choice of Settings

Drawing on an extensive body of cross-cultural data, B. B. Whiting (1980) has recently presented evidence that different contexts elicit different social behaviors from children, and further that habits of interpersonal behavior are shaped by the settings to which children are accustomed. According to Whiting (1980) the most important feature of a setting is its cast of characters. There is substantial cross-cultural variation in the usual cast of characters with which infants find themselves. Given this variation, on what basis is a researcher to choose settings in which to observe interaction that are comparable in two or more cultures?

An illustration of the difficulties in situational sampling is provided by the research of Sostek et al. reported in this volume. Caregivers and infants in the Micronesian Island of Fais are rarely found alone as a dyad. The large majority of filmed sequences on Fais showed caregiver and baby in the presence of a small group or surrounded by a larger group. In collecting comparative data of American caretakers and infants, it was necessary to choose between sampling the most prevalent social context in which caregivers and infants are found (i.e., alone), or holding social context constant in the two cultures, filming American caregivers and infants in the presence of others. In short, it was necessary to decide between sampling identical social contexts, or contexts that were comparable in the sense of being most prevalent in each society.

Chapter 2 lays out the decision: behavior was sampled when caregivers and infants were both alone and in the presence of others in both cultures, and the impact of context on interaction was examined. As Whiting's (1980) discussion would predict, social context proved to be an important determinant of caregiver-infant interaction in each culture. The possibility must be considered that cross-cultural differences in infants' experiences are attributable at least in part to differences in the settings in which infants and their caregivers are most often found. (See also chapters by Chisholm and by Martini and Kirkpatrick, this volume.)

In this study the researchers started with the prevalent social context in a non-Western culture and worked backward to consider what situations to sample in the United States. However, it is far more typical for research to begin with the context most frequently found in the home culture and to hold this constant in observing in a second culture. A major concern here has been the sampling of mother and infant time together, to the exclusion of other caregiving and social situations.

Leiderman and Leiderman (1974) note the wide variation in caretaking arrangements for infants. They cite evidence that while in the United States 92% of mothers usually or always cared for their infants, in an East African agricultural society 38% of mothers were the usual caregivers. Despite the fact that mothers in this and other societies are not their infants' primary social companions or caregivers, researchers have tended to sample mother-infant time exclusively. Following identical procedures in two cultures, in this case observing only mother-infant interaction, may function as a "distorting filter" for understanding infants' experiences in cultures in which mother-infant isolation is not the predominant pattern.

Contexts may differ on dimensions other than the number and type of people present. Substantial ethnographic work may be necessary to detect a culture's own delineation of contexts so as to sample them adequately or interpret behavior in any one context. For example, Price-Williams (1975) notes that "among Hausa mothers, the custom is not to show affection for their infants in public. Now those psychologists who are concerned with nurturance and dependency will go astray on their frequency counts if they do not realize this. A casual ethnographer is likely to witness only public interaction; only when much further inquiry is made is the absence of the event put into its proper perspective [p. 17]."

Decisions about which contexts are sampled will depend heavily on the research question being asked. For example, if the question concerns cross-cultural differences in the mother-infant relationship, then sampling mother-infant settings in both cultures may be "comparable." However, if the aim is to understand infants' experiences in different cultures, then limiting observations to times when mothers and infants are alone will provide an inaccurate view of infants' social interactions in many cultures. If the aim of the research is to describe the range of infants' social experiences, then observing behavior across whole days (Gewirtz & Gewirtz, 1968; Greenbaum & Landau, 1977, 1979) may be desirable (where it is accepted by the subjects). Alternately, spot observations (Munroe & Munroe, 1971; Rogoff, 1978) can be used to determine prevalence of social contexts, and more extended observations can then be carried out in chosen contexts.

Before concluding the discussion of the comparability of observational contexts in cross-cultural research we must note that in some discussions, serious doubts are raised as to whether situations are ever comparable in cross-cultural studies. In a recent reevaluation of culture and personality theory, Schweder (1979b) concludes that they are not:

> To talk of personality differences one must observe behavior differences in equivalent situations. . . . The crucial question then becomes, How are we to decide that the differential responses we observe are in fact differential responses to an equivalent set of stimuli. . . . *With respect to which particular descriptive components must stimuli (situations, contexts, environments) be shown to be equivalent?* . . . a situation (environment, context, setting) is more than its physical properties as defined by an outside observer. . . . It is a situated activity defined in part by its goal *from the point of view of the actor.* 'What any rational person would do under the circumstances' depends upon what the person is trying to accomplish [pp. 282-284].

Schweder (1979b) makes the argument that since we must write conventions and norms for the appropriate means of reaching a goal into the very definition of the behavioral situation, "two actors are in 'comparable' or 'equivalent' situations *only to the extent that they are members of the same culture!* [p. 285]"—that is, they share conventions and norms.

Choice and Interpretation of Behaviors

Perhaps the most crucial methodological issues in cross-cultural studies of interaction are in deciding on the level of behavior to record, choosing which behaviors to document, and ascertaining the meaning within each culture of the behaviors observed. These decisions have a bearing on the comparability of the data across cultures.

The importance of choice and interpretation of behaviors for observation is illustrated in a study of native Hawaiian and Caucasian children in Hawaiian classrooms by Gallimore, Boggs and Jordan (1974; cited by Price-Williams, 1975, and recently explored further by McKessar & Thomas, 1978, and Thomas, 1978). These researchers were interested in help-seeking behaviors as contributors to differences in school performance. They found fewer verbal requests for help among the native Hawaiian children, who showed poorer school performance in general. However, before concluding that this group was making fewer requests for assistance, the researchers considered the possibility that requests for help were being made in a different modality. They discovered that the Hawaiian children were requesting assistance through nonverbal behaviors: steadily watching the teacher from a distance; approaching the teacher; standing near the teacher or briefly touching her. Further, these behaviors could be directly related to the cultural background of the children, in which verbal requests for help from adults are considered inappropriate but nonverbal requests acceptable. This study suggests that in two or more cultures it cannot be assumed that the same behavior is endowed with identical meaning, and that careful consideration must be given to the range of behaviors to be included in an observational study.

Even within cultures, topographically identical behaviors may have multiple purposes or be interpreted in different ways by participants according to the immediate interactional context. For example, visual contact between a mother and her child in an instructional interaction may signal a number of different messages: "Are you sure that's right?" "Now it's your turn to do it," etc. The researcher faces the choice of simply recording eye contact, a more reliable but less interesting way of representing the interaction, or attempting in some way to interpret the interaction by incorporating information from the immediate context. The problem of how to reliably use contextual information in the interpretation of behavioral interactions is currently under examination (see for example, McDermott, Gospodinoff & Aron, 1978).

There has been widespread discussion of the problem that identical behaviors may have differing connotations and functions in two cultures:

> Obviously, if similar activities have different functions in different societies, these parameters cannot be used for comparative purposes. It is a problem which constantly plagues comparative research, and which emerges at all levels of investigation [Frijda & Jahoda, 1966, p. 116].

Ways of overcoming this problem have been suggested by several authors. Sears (1961) and Berry (1969) both proposed choice of behavioral variables at a level at which cross-cultural comparisons could legitimately be made. Sears argued for distinguishing between goal responses, reflective of the motivational system (e.g. help seeking in the Gallimore et al. (1974) study) and instrumental acts used in the service of goal responses (e.g., the Hawaiian children's verbal and nonverbal requests for assistance). In his view, although instrumental acts vary from culture to culture, the goal responses could be considered transcultural variables. Berry proposed that aspects of behavior be compared "only when they can be shown to be *functionally equivalent*, in the sense that the aspect of behavior in question is an attempted solution" to a recurrent problem shared by two or more groups [p. 122]. Essentially, these authors propose basing cross-cultural work on comparable instead of identical, and higher order rather than discrete variables.

In cross-cultural studies of cognition as well as of interaction, the proposal to use comparable as opposed to identical procedures solves one set of problems but raises another. At what point can researchers be certain that behaviors or procedures are comparable (Berrien, 1967)? Further, leaving comparisons at the level of "goal responses" might in many cases fail to reveal interesting cultural differences in means to goals. For example, referring again to the Hawaiian study, it would be unfortunate to report simply a lack of difference in overall help-seeking, and ignore the differences between the cultural groups in means of requesting help.

Researchers have expressed concern not only about the interpretation of identical behaviors in different cultures, but also about the selection of specific behaviors for observation. According to Tulkin (1977):

> We tend to see social interaction as including behaviors such as face-to-face looking and talking, whereas the more passive physical presence and availability of a parent or caretaker who holds a child or lets a young child climb over him might not be scored as social interaction [p. 569].

Using a range of behaviors appropriate to one culture does not assure that we are taking into account the full range of social behaviors in a second.

To summarize, although studies of early social interaction do not necessarily involve introducing unfamiliar materials, tasks, or contexts, the fact that these studies involve *sampling* behavior makes it necessary to consider comparability of the situation (social and otherwise) sampled, and of the behaviors selected for observation. Identical contexts (e.g., mother-infant interaction without others present) may not sample equally representative proportions of the infant's experience in different cultures. Behaviors chosen for observation on the grounds that they sample the range of social interactions in one culture may sample behaviors incompletely in another, providing a distorted view of interaction. Identical behaviors need not have the same connotations in different cultures.

Relating Sampled Behavior to the Broader Cultural Context

A major concern in the recent reevaluation of methodology in cross-cultural studies of cognition is the need to understand the relationship between behavior sampled in a structured task and cognitive activity occurring outside of the experimental setting.

In cross-cultural studies of early interaction there has also been widespread concern that restricting research to the collection of quantitative data, using formats designed for research in a home culture, has serious consequences for understanding what segments of an infant's experience have been sampled, and for interpreting findings of behavioral differences between cultures. Researchers returning from the field have repeatedly called for a period of descriptive, ethnographic work focusing on caregiving practices, attitudes, and the daily experiences of infants, prior to the collection of quantitative data. Unfortunately in many instances the quantitative work continues to stand alone, and the implications of quantitative differences in observed behavior continue to be interpreted in terms of plausible, rather than carefully explored hypotheses (LeVine, 1970). Further, hypotheses have tended to be derived from work in the home culture, rather than from a "discovery phase" in a new culture (Strodtbeck, 1964).

As in cognitive cross-cultural work, social interaction researchers have suggested starting with descriptive ethnographic work and moving to more quantitative methods. The eloquent statements of researchers speak for themselves:

> The use of quantitative methods alone (lab situations, standardized tests, checklists of behavior) confines one to preconceived variables, and leaves little possibility of discovering new and important behavioral relationships between these and the variables one had set out to observe . . . Let us not blind ourselves to the unusual features of the unfamiliar society by limiting ourselves to variables or to procedures based on the familiar society—our own [Ainsworth, 1977, p. 145].

> The most important aspect of the work, I thought then (and still think), was to get into the home and look. . . . While experimental methods were, I thought, inappropriate at the outset, I hoped that the outcome of observational work would point to some questions that could be answered experimentally. . . . What is lost when an investigator spends a few months administering tests to a rarely tested sample and calls it a study is the most valuable part of comparative work in another culture: the chance to be shaken by it, and the experience of struggling to understand it [Goldberg, 1977, pp. 215, 239].

> Any findings of group differences, can open up a Pandora's box of competing explanations, and it is only the investigator with intensive knowledge of characteristics differentiating the populations involved who can generate plausible alternative hypotheses that fit the data at hand and deserve more controlled research. Ethnographic ignorance can lure the researcher into false conclusions [LeVine, 1970, p. 569].

LeVine (1970) notes that there are multiple paths to basing a cross-cultural study on ethnographic information: The investigator can collect background information on relevant variables; he or she can rely on native informants for such information; or the investigator can collaborate with anthropologists specializing in the culture and knowlegable about the particular issue under study (for an excellent example and discussion of collaborative research, see Konner, 1977).

Berry (1969) proposes a series of steps for coordinating ethnographic and quantitative methods in a study. According to Berry, ethnographic background information ("emic") should be used to inform the quantitative system brought from the home culture ("imposed etic") to achieve a quantitative system faithful to the visited culture ("derived etic"). Price-Williams also argues for the importance of a coordination of methods: "a truly cross-cultural study is logically contingent on an intracultural study [1975, p. 38]." The study of *Children of Six Cultures* (Whiting, 1966; Whiting & Whiting, 1975) was explicitly based on the assumption that two phases of field work were necessary: a period aimed at describing child rearing practices and beliefs in each culture, and a phase of collection of quantitative data.

Given these precedents, and the strong feelings of psychologists returning from periods of study in different cultures, why hasn't the practice of using complementary descriptive and quantitative procedures become more widespread? Certainly practical factors are involved. A two-phase study requires more time and more resources, as well as an array of skills. However, this issue is not restricted to cross-cultural research, but is now widely discussed in developmental psychology in general. The heart of the issue is a distinction between "rigorous" and "authentic" data collection procedures (Bronfenbrenner, 1977, 1979; Gibbs, 1979) and the tradition in developmental psychology, to favor and respect the rigorous exclusively. Recently, concern has been expressed that the accumulating body of research at the so-called "rigorous" end of the continuum has serious limitations, and there have been repeated calls for new research designs that reflect a synthesis of the two poles.

Ecological psychologists have encouraged movement away from "context stripping" (Mishler, 1979) studies of interaction, especially studies of interaction in strange places with unfamiliar people for very brief periods (Bronfenbrenner, 1977, 1979), and towards studies of behavior in naturally occurring contexts. The major concerns have been with the limitations of laboratory and experimental studies of interaction. However many of the same considerations can be seen to apply to quantitative studies carried out in naturalistic contexts in different cultures, when they are unsupported by descriptive information about the contexts of behavior.

Speaking to developmental psychologists, McCall (1977) suggests looking carefully before choosing which behaviors, variables, contexts, and groups of subjects to study. His statement is very close to the statements of the cross-cultural researchers quoted earlier:

> We rarely take the time to keep our experimental hands off a behavior long enough to make systematic descriptive observations in naturalistic settings of the several dimensions and circumstances of the behavior we wish to study [p. 336].

Researchers have rejected the assumed incompatibility between studies that are rigorous in methodology on the one hand or relevant in their implications on the other. Bronfenbrenner (1977, 1979) calls for experimental designs in naturalistic contexts rather than in the lab. Others (Parke, 1979; Weisz, 1978) call for integrative designs drawing on the strengths of both laboratory and field work. Parke, for example, suggests a multistep strategy, starting with a "search phase" for the generation of hypotheses and isolation of meaningful variables, followed by tests of the hypotheses with more systematic manipulation of variables.

There is striking agreement between the two phase approach proposed by Parke and recent proposals in cross-cultural studies of cognition. Thus, in developmental psychology in general, there is movement toward methodologies that start with exploration and hypothesis generation in naturalistic contexts, complemented by more controlled and quantitative methods. Whereas the need for a "search" or ethnographic phase may be particularly noticeable in cross-cultural research, it is equally essential in the home culture.

CONCLUSION

Despite substantial differences in the aims and procedures used in cross-cultural studies of cognition and social interaction, we have found analogous methodological concerns in the two areas. In both cognitive and social research, concern is voiced over comparability of research procedures; cultural variation in subjects' reactions to the research setting; and the need for coordination of ethnographic and quantitative methods. Of particular interest, in both areas, we have noted a growing concern with understanding the relationship between observed behavior and the cultural context in which it is embedded.

While we have approached the issue of context as a methodological concern for the purposes of this paper, this issue has theoretical implications as well. Several authors are developing theoretical statements that consider the contextual specificity of social and cognitive activity (Chisholm, this volume; LCHC, 1980; Schweder, 1979a, 1979b; Whiting, 1980). The theoretical shift involves placing context foremost, either as a determinant of behavior or as an integral aspect of observed activity, and considering the participants' active construction of their own interpersonal contexts. Further, as we have noted, researchers in both cognitive and social spheres have raised the possibility that cross-cultural differences may originate not so much in underlying competencies or behavioral propensities, but rather in the contexts in which individuals in a culture spend their time, or in the contexts in which specific skills are manifested.

These developments in cross-cultural research suggest that in the future, increasing attention will be paid to context, not only as a variable that requires control in cross-cultural studies, but as a topic deserving study in its own right. We see two research strategies emerging in studies of culture and social interaction that focus explicitly on context:

1. A "macro" approach to context, in which the aim is to describe the range of settings in which infants or children in a culture spend their time, i.e., where, with whom, and in what activities. For example, researchers might address the hypotheses that first- and later-born infants experience different social contexts in their daily lives, and that observed differences in behavior between these groups are related to the differences in social context. Cross-cultural research might find that whereas in the United States first- and later-born infants experienced major differences in daily social contexts, in a culture with extended family residences, the discrepancy might be smaller.

2. In a "micro" approach to context, the aim of research is to select a circumscribed context of particular interest and describe interaction within it in detail. McDermott et al. (1978) chose the elementary school reading group for intensive study, making use of the rich immediate interactional context to interpret the observed behavior. An example of a context of possible interest to cross-cultural researchers of early interaction is the time infants spend with their sibling caregivers. Focusing on a limited context would begin to make possible the interpretation of specific interactive events and the incorporation of contextual information into the recording of behavior from moment to moment.

Overall, we see growing concern in cross-cultural studies of early interaction with using information about the cultural context in deriving research hypotheses and strategies, and in interpreting findings.

REFERENCES

Ainsworth, M. D. S. Infant development and mother-infant interaction among Ganda and American families. In P. H. Leiderman, S. R. Tulkin, & A. Rosenfeld (Eds.), *Culture and infancy*. New York: Academic Press, 1977.

Berrien, F. K. Methodological and related problems in cross-cultural research. *International Journal of Psychology*, 1967, *2*, 33–43.

Berry, J. W. On cross-cultural comparability. *International Journal of Psychology*, 1969, *4*, 119–128.

Brazelton, T. B. Implications of infant development among the Mayan Indians of Mexico. In P. H. Leiderman, S. R. Tulkin, & A. Rosenfeld (Eds.), *Culture and infancy*. New York: Academic Press, 1977.

Bronfenbrenner, U. Toward an experimental ecology of human development. *American Psychologist*, 1977, *32*, 513–531.

Bronfenbrenner, U. *The ecology of human development*. Cambridge: Harvard University Press, 1979.

Cazden, C. B., & John, V. P. Learning in American Indian children. In M. L. Wax, S. Diamond, & F. O. Gearing (Eds.), *Anthropological perspectives in education.* New York: Basic Books, 1971.

Cole, M. & Bruner, J. S. Cultural differences and inferences about psychological processes. *American Psychologist,* 1971, *26,* 867-876.

Cole, M., Gay, J., Glick, J. A., & Sharp, D. W. *The cultural context of learning and thinking.* New York: Basic Books, 1971.

Cole, M., Hood, L., & McDermott, R. P. Concepts of ecological validity: Their differing implications for comparative cognitive research. *Institute for Comparative Human Development Newsletter,* 1978, *2,* 34-37.

Cole, M., & Scribner, S. *Culture and thought.* New York: Wiley, 1974.

Cole, M., & Scribner, S. Theorizing about social cognition. *Ethos,* 1975, *3,* 250-268.

Cole, M., Sharp, D. W., & Lave, C. The cognitive consequences of education. *Urban Review,* 1976, *9,* 218-233.

Deregowski, J. B. & Serpell, R. Performance on a sorting task: A cross-cultural experiment. *International Journal of Psychology,* 1971, *6,* 273-281.

Edgerton, R. B. Cross-cultural psychology and psychological anthropology: One paradigm or two? *Reviews in Anthropology,* 1974, *1,* 52-65.

Field, T., & Ignatoff, E. *Effects of videotaping on interactions of lower income mothers and infants.* In preparation.

Frijda, N., & Jahoda, G. On the scope and methods of cross-cultural research. *International Journal of Psychology,* 1966, *1,* 109-127.

Gallimore, R., Boggs, J., & Jordan, C. *Culture, behavior and education: A study of Hawaiian-Americans.* Beverly Hills: Sage, 1974.

Gewirtz, H. B., & Gewirtz, J. L. Caretaking settings, background events, and behavioral differences in four Israeli child-rearing environments: Some preliminary trends. In B. M. Foss (Ed.), *Determinants of infant behavior* (Vol. 4). London: Methuen, 1968.

Gibbs, J. C. The meaning of ecologically oriented inquiry in contemporary psychology. *American Psychologist,* 1979, *34,* 127-140.

Glick, J. Cognitive development in cross-cultural perspective. In F. Horowitz et al. (Eds.), *Review of child development research* (Vol. 4). Chicago: University of Chicago Press, 1975.

Goldberg, S. Infant development and mother-infant interaction in urban Zambia. In P. H. Leiderman, S. R. Tulkin, & A. Rosenfeld (Eds.), *Culture and infancy.* New York: Academic Press, 1977.

Goodnow, J. J. The nature of intelligent behavior: Questions raised by cross-cultural studies. In L. B. Resnick (Ed.), *The nature of intelligence.* Hillsdale, New Jersey: Lawrence Erlbaum Associates, 1976.

Graves, Z. R., & Glick, J. The effect of context on mother-child interaction. *The Quarterly Newsletter of the Institute for Comparative Human Development,* 1978, *2,* 41-46.

Greenbaum, C. W., & Landau, R. L. Mothers' speech and the early development of vocal behavior: Findings from a cross-cultural observation study in Israel. In P. H. Leiderman, S. R. Tulkin, & A. Rosenfeld (Eds.), *Culture and infancy.* New York: Academic Press, 1977.

Greenbaum, C. W., & Landau, R. L. The infant's exposure to talk by familiar people: Mothers, fathers, and siblings in different environments. In M. Lewis & L. A. Rosenblum (Eds.), *The child and its family.* New York: Plenum, 1979.

Greenfield, P. M. On culture and conservation. In J. S. Bruner, R. R. Olver, & P. M. Greenfield (Eds.), *Studies in cognitive growth.* New York: Wiley, 1966.

Greenfield, P. M. Comparing dimensional categorization in natural and artificial contexts: A developmental study among the Zincantecos of Mexico. *Journal of Social Psychology,* 1974, *93,* 157-171.

Greenfield, P. M. Response to "Wolof 'magical thinking': Culture and conservation revisited" by Judith T. Irvine. *Journal of Cross-Cultural Psychology,* 1979, *10,* 251-256.

Greenfield, P. M., & Childs, C. P. Understanding sibling concepts: A developmental study of kin terms in Zinacantan. In P. R. Dasen (Ed.), *Piagetian psychology: Cross-cultural contributions*. New York: Gardner Press, 1977.

Harkness, S., & Super, C. M. Why African children are so hard to test. In L. L. Adler (Ed.), *Issues in cross-cultural research. Annals of the New York Academy of Sciences*, 1977, 285, 326-331.

Irvine, J. T. Wolof "magical thinking": Culture and conservation revisited. *Journal of Cross-Cultural Psychology*, 1978, 9, 300-310.

Irwin, M. H., & McLaughlin, D. H. Ability and preference in category sorting by Mano schoolchildren and adults. *Journal of Social Psychology*, 1970, 82, 15-24.

Irwin, M. H., Schafer, G. N., & Feiden, C. P. Emic and unfamiliar category sorting of Mano farmers and U.S. undergraduates. *Journal of Cross-Cultural Psychology*, 1974, 5, 407-423.

Kelly, M. Papau New Guinea and Piaget—An eight-year study. In P. R. Dasen (Ed.), *Piagetian psychology: Cross-cultural contributions*. New York: Gardner Press, 1977.

Kessel, F. S. Research in action settings: A sketch of emerging perspectives. *International Journal of Behavioral Development*, 1979, 2, 185-205.

Konner, M. Infancy among the Kalahari Desert San. In P. H. Leiderman, S. R. Tulkin, & A. Rosenfeld (Eds.), *Culture and infancy*. New York: Academic Press, 1977.

Laboratory of Comparative Human Cognition. Cross-cultural psychology's challenges to our ideas of children and development. *American Psychologist*, 1979, 34, 827-833.

Laboratory of Comparative Human Cognition. *Intelligence as cultural practice*. Unpublished manuscript, 1980.

Lave, J. Tailor-made experiments and evaluating the intellectual consequences of apprenticeship training. *The Quarterly Newsletter of the Institute for Comparative Human Development*, 1977, 1, 1-3.

Leiderman, P. H., & Leiderman, G. F. Affective and cognitive consequences of polymatric infant care in the East African highlands. In A. D. Pick (Ed.), *Minnesota symposia on child psychology* (Vol. 8). Minneapolis: University of Minnesota Press, 1974.

LeVine, R. A. Cross-cultural study in child psychology. In P. H. Mussen (Ed.), *Carmichael's manual of child psychology* (Third edition). New York: Wiley, 1970.

Lusk, D., & Lewis, M. Mother-infant interaction and infant development among the Wolof of Senegal. *Human Development*, 1972, 15, 58-69.

McCall, R. B. Challenges to a science of developmental psychology. *Child Development*, 1977, 48, 333-344.

McDermott, R. P., Gospodinoff, K., & Aron, J. Criteria for an ethnographically adequate description of concerted activities and their contexts. *Semiotica*, 1978, 24, 245-275.

McKessar, C. J., & Thomas, D. R. Verbal and non-verbal help-seeking among urban Maori and Pakeha children. *New Zealand Journal of Educational Studies*, 1978, 13, 29-39.

Mehan, H. Assessing children's school performance. In J. Beck, C. Jenks, N. Keddie, & M. F. D. Young (Eds.), *Worlds Apart*. London: Collier Macmillan, 1976.

Mishler, E. Meaning in context: Is there any other kind? *Harvard Educational Review*, 1979, 49, 1-19.

Munroe, R. H., & Munroe, R. L. Household density and infant care in an East African society. *The Journal of Social Psychology*, 1971, 83, 3-13.

Okonji, M. O. The effects of familiarity on classification. *Journal of Cross-Cultural Psychology*, 1971, 2, 29-49.

Parke, R. D. Interactional designs. In R. B. Cairns (Eds.), *The analysis of social interactions*. Hillsdale, New Jersey: Lawrence Erlbaum Associates, 1979.

Pedersen, F. A. *The father-infant relationship: Observational studies in the family setting*. New York: Praeger, 1980.

Price-Williams, D. R. Abstract and concrete modes of classification in a primitive society. *British Journal of Educational Psychology*, 1962, 32, 50-61.

Price-Williams, D. R. *Explorations in cross-cultural psychology.* San Francisco: Chandler and Sharp, 1975.

Rogoff, B. Spot observations: An introduction and examination. *Institute for Comparative Human Development Newsletter,* 1978, *2,* 21-26.

Rogoff, B. Schooling and the development of cognitive skills. In H. C. Triandis & A. Heron (Eds.), *Handbook of cross-cultural psychology* (Vol. 4) Rockleigh, New Jersey: Allyn & Bacon, in press.

Schweder, R. A. Rethinking culture and personality theory part I: A critical examination of two classical postulates. *Ethos,* 1979, *7,* 255-278. (a)

Schweder, R. A. Rethinking culture and personality theory part II: A critical examination of two more classical postulates. *Ethos,* 1979, *7,* 279-311. (b)

Scribner, S. Situating the experiment in cross-cultural research. In K. F. Riegel & J. A. Meacham (Eds.), *The developing individual in a changing world.* Chicago: Aldine, 1976.

Sears, R. Transcultural variables and conceptual equivalence. In B. Kaplan (Ed.), *Studying personality cross-culturally.* Evanston: Row, Peterson & Company, 1961.

Serpell, R. How specific are perceptual skills? A cross-cultural study of pattern reproduction. *British Journal of Psychology,* 1979, *70,* 365-380.

Strodtbeck, R. L. Considerations of meta-method in cross-cultural studies. In A. K. Romney & R. G. D'Andrade (Eds.), *Transcultural studies in cognition.* Special publication of *American Psychologist,* 1964, *66,* 223-229.

Thomas, D. R. Communication patterns among Pakeha and Polynesian mother-child pairs: The effects of class and culture. *New Zealand Journal of Educational Studies,* 1978, *13,* 125-132.

Tulkin, S. R. Dimensions of multicultural research in infancy and early childhood. In P. H. Leiderman, S. R. Tulkin, & A. Rosenfeld (Eds.), *Culture and infancy.* New York: Academic Press, 1977.

Weisz, J. R. Transcontextual validity in developmental research. *Child Development,* 1978, *49,* 1-12.

Whiting, B. B. (Ed.) *Six Cultures Series.* Volumes I-VII. New York: Wiley, 1966.

Whiting, B. B. The problem of the packaged variable. In K. F. Riegel & J. A. Meacham (Eds.), *The developing individual in a changing world.* Chicago: Aldine, 1976.

Whiting, B. B. Culture and social behavior: A model for the development of social behavior. *Ethos,* 1980, *8,* 95-116.

Whiting, J. W. M., Child, I. L., & Lambert, W. W. *Field guide for a study of socialization.* (Written with the field teams for the *Six Cultures Series.*) New York: Wiley, 1966.

Whiting, B. B., & Whiting, J. W. M. *Children of six cultures: A psychocultural analysis.* Cambridge: Harvard University Press, 1975.

Willems, E. P. Relations of models to methods in behavioral ecology. In H. McGurk (Ed.), *Ecological factors in human development.* Amsterdam: North-Holland, 1977.

Author Index

Italics denote pages with bibliographic information

A

Adamson, 134, *146*, 150, *167, 168*
Ainsworth, M. D. S., 4, *18*, 98, *111*, 215, 216, 217, 219, 228, 232, *234*, 244, 245, 250, *253*
Als, H., 134, *146*, 150, 156, *167, 168*
Anderson, B. J., 27, 34, *36, 37*
Anderson, E. P., 216, *234*
Arnold, R., 100, *111*
Aron, J., 248, *255*
Ashe, M. L., 27, *36*

B

Balikci, A., 33, *37*
Ban, P., 43, *61*, 83, 88, *90*, 171, *188*
Basso, K., 7, *18*
Bayley, N., 65, 87, *89*
Bear, R. M., 64, *90*
Beckwith, L., 41, 57, *60, 61*
Bee, H. L., 53, 57, *60*
Beebe, B., 134, *147*
Bell, R. Q., 67, 80, *89*
Bennett, S. L., 134, *147*
Benson, J., 47, *62*
Berrien, F. K., 249, *253*
Berry, J. W., 248, 251, *253*

Birns, B., 66, 67, 87, 88, *90*
Blehar, M. C., 98, *111*, 216, *234*
Blurton Jones, N. G., 5, 6, *18*
Bobbitt, R. A., 34, *37*
Boggs, J., 248, *254*
Bond, J. T., 175, *188*
Bowlby, J., 232, *234*
Brazelton, T. B., 35, *36*, 41, 59, *60, 61*, 115, 128, 129, *131*, 134, *146*, 149, 150, 155, 156, 163, 164, *167, 168*, 172, *188*, 218, *234*, 244, *253*
Bronfenbrenner, U., 33, *36*, 96, 97, 98, *111*, 243, 251, 252, *253*
Bronson, G. W., 16, *18*
Brophy, J. E., 64, *90*
Brown, R., 86, *90*
Bruner, J. S., 238, 241, 242, *254*
Bulatao, R., 100, *111*
Buripakdi, R., 100, *111*

C

Cain, R. L., 34, *37*
Callaghan, J. W., 136, *146*
Campbell, E. R., 66, *90*
Caudill, W., 35, *36*, 41, *60*, 102, *111*, 149, 166, *167*, 171, *188*

258   AUTHOR INDEX

Cazden, C. B., 240, *254*
Chavez, A., 171, 172, 173, *188*
Child, I. L., 6, *19*, 237, *256*
Childs, C. P., 239, *255*
Chisholm, J. S., 7, 8, 14, *18*
Christiansen, N., 173, *188*
Chung, B. J., 100, *111*
Clarke-Stewart, K. A., 34, *36*, 153, *167*, 175, *188*
Clement, J., 174, 175, *188*
Coates, B., 216, *234*
Coates, D., 88, *90*
Cohen, E. S., 41, 57, *60*, *61*
Cole, M., 238, 239, 241, 242, *254*
Coleman, J. S., 66, *90*
Coombs, C. H., 100, *111*
Coombs, L. C., 100, *111*
Crocker, W. H., 33, *37*
Crosignani, P. G., 9, *18*
Cuellar, E., 175, *188*

D

Danzger, B., 101, *112*
Dasen, P., 172, *188*
Dave, R. H., 64, *90*
Day, R. D., 101, *112*
DeBoer, M., 139, *147*
de Navarro, L., 174, *188*
de Paredes, B., 174, *188*
Deregowski, J. B., 239, *254*
Deutsch, M., 63, 86, *90*
Devereux, E., 96, 97, *111*
Dixon, S., 150, *167*
Dobbing, J., 171, *188*
DuBois, W. E. B., 48, *61*

E

Edel, A., 64, *90*
Edgerton, R. B., 239, *254*
Ember, C., 4, *18*
Emerson, P. E., 215, 232, *234*

F

Faulstich, G., 27, *36*
Fawcett, J. T., 100, *111*
Feiden, C. P., 239, *255*
Feldman, S., 216, 230, *234*

Field, T. M., 43, 52, 53, 55, 57, 58, 59, *61*, 127, *131*, 134, 146, *147*, 244, *254*
Finger, S., 55, *61*
Fishman, C., 65, *90*
Florez, A., 175, *188*
Fraiberg, S., 21, *36*
Freedle, R., 67, *90*
Freedman, D. G., 59, 61, 115, *128*, *131*, 136, *138*, 139, *145*, *147*
Freedman, N., 59, *61*
Frijda, N., 238, 248, *254*

G

Gallimore, R., 5, *19*, 248, 249, *254*
Gay, J., 238, 241, *254*
Gewirtz, H. B., 101, *111*, 247, *254*
Gewirtz, J. L., 101, *111*, 216, *234*, 247, *254*
Gibbons, J., 134, *147*
Gibbs, J. C., 243, 251, *254*
Glick, J. A., 238, 240, 241, 243, *254*
Goldberg, S., 34, *36*, 150, *167*, 250, *254*
Golden, M., 66, 67, 87, 88, *90*
Goodnow, J. J., 239, *254*
Gospodinoff, K., 248, *255*
Graves, P. L., 172, *188*
Graves, Z. R., 243, *254*
Greenbaum, C. W., 247, *254*
Greenberg, M., 99, *111*
Greenfield, P. M., 239, 240, 241, *254*, *255*
Grossman, K. E., 98, 101, 110, *111*
Gurri, I., 45, 46, *61*

H

Habicht, J. P., 41, *61*, 172, *188*
Harkness, S., 187, *188*, 240, *255*
Harrington, M., 49, *61*
Hartup, W. W., 216, *234*
Herrera, M. G., 173, 174, *188*
Hess, R. D., 64, 66, 86, *90*
Hinde, R., 34, *36*
Hitchcock, J., 153, *167*
Hobson, C. J., 66, *90*
Hoffman, H. S., 16, *18*
Hoffman, L. W., 100, *112*
Hood, L., 241, 242, *254*
Hopkins, B., 145, *147*
Howard, A., 189, *213*
Huck, S. W., 104, *112*
Hunt, J. McV., 65, *91*

AUTHOR INDEX

I

Ignatoff, E., 244, *254*
Ingham, M., 216, 230, *234*
Inhelder, B., 172, *188*
Iritani, T., 100, *111*
Irvine, J. T., 240, *255*
Irwin, M. H., 239, *255*
Iwanga, M. I., 216, *234*

J

Jacobs, B. A., 57, *61*
Jaffe, J., 134, *147*
Jahoda, G., 238, 248, *254*
Jensen, G. D., 34, *37*
John, V. P., 240, *254*
Johnson, D. C., 53, *61*
Jones, S. J., 102, *112*
Jordan, C., 248, *254*

K

Kagan, J., 16, *18*, 53, 57, *62*, 65, *90*, 215, 231, *234*
Kaplan, J., 34, *36*
Kaye, K., 59, *61*, 116, *131*, 210, *213*
Kearsley, R., 215, 231, *234*
Kelly, M., 239, *255*
Kessel, F. S., 242, *255*
Kestenberg, J., 134, *147*
Kilbride, M. W., 53, 57, *61*
Kirkpatrick, J., 190, 191, *213*
Klein, R. E., 41, *61*, 172, *188*
Kohn, M. C., 43, *61*
Kohn, M. L., 102, *112*
Kohut, H., 149, 166, *167*, 210, *213*
Konner, M. J., 9, 14, 16, *19*, 22, 34, *36*, 101, *113*, 150, *167*, 251, *255*
Koslowski, B., 41, *60*, 128, *131*, 134, *146*, 149, *167*
Kotelchuck, M., 101, *112*

L

Lamb, M. E., 34, *36*
Lambert, W. W., 5, *19*, 237, *256*
Lambie, D. Z., 175, *188*
Landau, R. L., 247, *254*
Lasky, R. E., 41, *61*, 172, *188*
Lavallee, M., 172, *188*

Lave, C., 239, *254*
Lave, J., 239, *255*
Lechtig, A., 172, *188*
Lee, S. J., 100, *111*
Lee-Painter, S., 175, *188*
Lefley, H., 42, *61*
Leiderman, G. F., 5, *19*, 216, 218, *234*, 246, *255*
Leiderman, P. H., 5, 17, *19*, 21, *36*, 101, *113*, 217, 218, *234*, 246, *255*
Lester, B. M., 173, *188*
Levin, H., 6, *19*
LeVine, B., 151, *167*, 218, *234*
Levine, J., 65, *90*
LeVine, R. A., 95, 112, 151, 152, 153, 166, *167*, 216, 217, 218, *234*, 250, 251, *255*
LeVine, S., 151, 152, *167*, 216, 218, *234*
Levy, R., 189, *213*
Lewis, M., 43, *61*, 65, 66, 67, 78, 83, 88, *90*, *91*, 171, 175, *188*, 244, *255*
Light, R. J., 64, *90*
Lockie, M. S., 53, *60*
Luria, Z., 100, *113*
Lusk, D., 244, *255*

M

Maccoby, E. E., 5, 6, *19*
Mackey, W. C., 101, *112*
Mahler, M., 210, *213*
Main, M., 41, *60*, 128, *131*, 134, *146*, 149, *167*
Maloney, M. M., 33, *37*
Martinez, C., 171, *188*
Marvin, R. S., 216, *234*
Masters, J. C., 216, *234*
Mayer, P., 151, *167*
McCall, R. B., 243, 251, *255*
McClelland, G. H., 100, *111*
McDermott, R. P., 241, 242, 248, 253, *254*, *255*
McGranahan, D. V., 95, *112*
McGurk, H., 66, *90*
McKessar, C. J., 248, *255*
McLaughlin, D. H., 239, *255*
McLean, R. A., 104, *112*
McPartland, J., 66, *90*
Mead, M., 35, *37*
Mehan, H., 242, *255*
Messer, S. G., 65, *91*
Metraux, R., 96, *112*

Minturn, L., 5, *19*
Mishler, E., 251, *255*
Modell, A., 135, *147*
Monroe, R. H., 34, *37*
Monroe, R. L., 34, *37*
Mood, A. M., 66, *90*
Moore, T., 66, *91*
Mora, J. O., 173, 174, 175, *188*
Morris, J. L., 98, *111*
Moss, H. A., 57, *61,* 102, *112,* 175, 178, *188*
Munroe, R. H., 4, 14, *19*
Munroe, R. L., 4, 14, *19*
Myers, J. L., 52, *61*

N

New, R., 152, 153, *168*
Nyman, B. A., 53, *60*

O

Ochs, E., 203, *213*
Okonji, M. O., 239, *255*
O'Leary, S. E., 99, 100, 110, *112*
Olson, J. P., 101, *113*
Ortiz, N., 175, *188*
Osofsky, J. D., 101, *112*

P

Palmer, F. H., 66, *91*
Parke, R. D., 34, *37,* 99, 100, 101, 110, *112,* 252, *255*
Parmelee, A. H., 41, *60*
Pavenstedt, E., 64, *91*
Pawlby, S., 42, 43, 58, 59, *61*
Pearlin, L. I., 43, *61*
Pedersen, F. A., 34, *37,* 83, 85, *91,* 243, *255*
Piaget, J., 172, *188*
Pinkney, A., 48, *61*
Platt, M., 203, *213*
Poffenberger, S. B., 100, *112*
Poffenberger, T., 100, *112*
Pollitt, E., 171, 172, *188*
Price-Williams, D. R., 237, 238, 241, 246, 248, 251, *255, 256*
Provenzano, F. J., 100, *113*

R

Rainwater, L., 96, 97, *112*
Rao, C. R., 52, *61*

Raphael, D., 9, *19*
Rapp, D. W., 97, *112*
Reed, G., 216, *234*
Retschitzki, J., 172, *188*
Rheingold, H., 16, *19*
Richards, J. L., 55, *61*
Richards, M. P. M., 7, *18*
Ritchie, J., 189, *213*
Robyn, C., 9, *18*
Rogg, E. M., 44, 45, *61*
Rogoff, B., 240, 242, 247, *256*
Rohner, R. P., 95, *112*
Rosenblum, L., 67, 80, *90*
Rosenfeld, A., 21, *36*
Rubensten, J. L., 83, 85, *91*
Rubin, J. Z., 100, *113*
Rubinstein, D. H., 22, 26, 34, *37*

S

Salk, L., 55, *61*
Sawin, D. B., 100, 101, *112*
Schaefer, E. S., 64, *91*
Schafer, G. N., 239, *255*
Schaffer, H. R., 215, 232, *234*
Schaffner, B., 96, *113*
Schecter, S., 33, *37*
Schieffelin, B., 203, *213*
Schweder, R. A., 247, 252, *256*
Scott, K., 45, *61*
Scribner, S., 237, 238, 239, 240, 241, 242, 254, *256*
Sears, R. R., 5, *19,* 248, *256*
Sellers, M. J., 41, *61,* 172, *188*
Senior, C., 44, 46, *61*
Serpell, R., 239, *254, 256*
Sharp, D. W., 238, 239, 241, *254*
Shipman, V. C., 64, 66, 86, 89, *91*
Sigman, M., 41, *60*
Smith, P. V., 64, *90*
Sorenson, E. R., 32, 35, *37*
Spencer-Booth, Y., 34, *36*
Stern, D. N., 41, *61,* 134, *147,* 149, 157, *168,* 200, *213*
Streissguth, A. P., 53, *60, 61*
Strodtbeck, R. L., 250, *256*
Suci, G., 96, 97, *111*
Super, C. M., 187, *188,* 240, *255*

T

Thane, K., 101, *111*
Thiemann, S., 216, *234*

Thoman, E. B., 101, *113*
Thomas, D. R., 248, *255, 256*
Tronick, E., 134, *146*, 150, 157, 164, *167, 168*, 172, *188*
Truss, C., 47, *62*
Tukey, J., 220, *234*
Tulkin, S., 21, *36*, 42, 53, 57, *62*, 64, 65, *91*, 249, *256*

U

Uzgiris, I. C., 65, *91*

V

Van Devender, T. L., 216, *234*
Van Egeren, L. F., 53, *60*
Vietze, P. M., 27, *36*

W

Wachs, T. D., 65, *91*
Wagner, M., 174, *188*
Wall, S., 98, *111*, 216, 234
Waters, E., 98, *111*, 216, 217, *234*
Weidman, H. H., 44, 45, 46, 47, 50, 57, *62*
Weikart, D. P., 175, *188*
Weiland, I. H., 55, *62*
Weinfeld, F. D., 66, *90*
Weinstein, H., 35, *36*, 102, *111*, 149, 166, *167*, 171, *188*

Weise, S., 134, *146*
Weisner, T. S., 5, *19*
Weisz, J. R., 252, *256*
Wellman, H. M., 216, *234*
West, M. M., 101, *113*
West, S., 99, *112*
White, B., 66, *91*
Whiting, B. B., 3, 4, 5, *17, 19*, 149, 153, *168*, 237, 245, 246, 251, 252, *256*
Whiting, J. W. M., 3, 4, 5, 6, *19*, 149, 153, *168*, 237, 251, *256*
Willems, E. P., 243, *256*
Wilson, C. D., 65, *90*
Wilson, E. O., 66, *91*
Winnicott, D., 210, *213*
Wise, S., 150, *167*
Wolff, P. H., 42, *62*
Wolfheim, J. H., 34, *37*
Woodson, R. H., 5, 6, *18*
Worthman, C., 9, *19*
Wu, T. S., 100, *111*

Y, Z

Yarbrough, C., 41, *61*, 172, *188*
Yarrow, L. J., 83, 85, 87, 88, *91*
Yaschine, T., 172, *188*
Yogman, M. W., 150, *167, 168*
York, R. L., 66, *90*
Zelazo, P., 215, 231, *234*
Zigler, E. I., 64, *91*

Subject Index

A

Activity level of infants, 172-173, 186
  intervention effects on, 179-185
  measurement of, 176-177
Adoption, 25-26
Attachment, 215-233
  age-related changes, 220-230
  behavioral indices, 216-220
  changes in receptivity for, 232
  formation and consolidation of, 231
  group "b" babies, 232
  hypotheses about, 231-232
  in Western infants, 215
Attachment behavior
  categories of, 219
  change with age, 215, 216
  child caregiver, for, 221, 224
  cross sectional vs. longitudinal, 216, 224, 225, 227
  continuity, discontinuity, 231
  development of, 215
  differential expression, 215
  hypotheses about, 216
  individual differences, 230
  measures of indices of, 216, 217, 230
  nadir of, 233
  non-Western societies, in, 215
  oscillatory pattern of, 231
  polymatric societies in, 230
  scores, 220
  separation, 217, 219
  stability between experiments, 216
  transformation in type of, 215, 228, 229
  unfamiliar figure, for an, 223, 224, 226

B

Baby talk, 203
Birth interval, 9
Breast-feeding, 9, 184, 185

C

Caregiver behavior, 192-207
  holding infants, 192, 193, 195, 198-202
  social involvement, 196, 198, 209
  visual orientation, 198-199
  vocalizations, 195, 198, 201
Child caregivers, 21, 27
Child care practices, 95-98
Coding, 117-118
Cognitive performance, 71, 72, 75-77, 80-85
Columbus project, 116
Coronary heart disease, 41, 49
Cross-cultural comparisons, 95-98, 101
  German-American comparisons 95-98, 106-107, 109-110
Cultures
  Bahamian, 48

SUBJECT INDEX

Cultures (continued)
 Brazilian, 47
 British, 43
 Chilean, 43, 47
 Colombian, 43, 47, 171-188
 Cuban, 43, 47
 Fais, 22-27
 German, 95-98, 106-107, 109-110
 Guatemalan, 47
 Gusii people of Kenya, 151-166, 215-234
 Haitian, 48
 Honduran, 43
 Hopi indian, 115-130
 Indian, 42
 Italian, 43
 Japanese, 41
 Marquesan Islands, 189-213
 Mexican, 41
 Navajo Indians, 10, 11, 138, 141, 144
 Peruvean, 47
 Puerto Rican, 41, 46, 50-56
 South American, 47, 50-56
 Southern Black, 48-56
 Venezuelan, 47
 Yugoslavian, 43

E

Early interactions, 3-17, 41-60, 134-146, 151-166
 age/sex/kinship identity of interactors, 3, 4, 5, 9, 17
 cradleboard use, 6, 7, 14
 effects of residence patterns on, 11-14
 effects of Navajo-Anglo differences, 11-14
 feeding, 42, 51, 55-60
 generalization of, 4
 methodology, 5-7, 9, 14-15
  among the Navajo, 6, 7, 9
  assessing the social context, 5, 6
  ethological, 5, 6
  fear of strangers, 14-15
  reliability and validity, 6
  spot observations, 7, 9
 social opportunity, 9, 16-17
Ethnographic film, 22, 27, 25-26

F

Face-to-face interaction between infants and adults, 41-60, 134-144, 149-166
 Black dyads, 139, 141, 144
 Caucasian dyads, 139, 141, 144
 culture specific elements of, 49, 164-166
 Gusii infant-mother, 151-166
 importance in infancy, 150
 monadic phase scoring system of, 155-157
 mutual cuing, 136, 142-144
 Navajo dyads, 138, 141, 144
 structure of, 149-150, 163-164
  among the Gusii of Kenya, 159-163
  monadic phase analysis, 155-157, 159-160, 161-162
  transitions in, 160, 162-163
Fais, 22-27
 description of, 22-23
 demography of, 23-25
 socialization in, 26-27
Fathers, 95-113
 child care practices, 95-98
 cross-cultural comparisons, 95-98, 101
  German-American comparisons, 95-98, 106-107, 109-110
 relationships with infants, 98-111
 sex of infant, 100-101, 106-107, 110
Fear of strangers, 14-15
 cradleboard effects, 14
 Navajo-Anglo differences, 14-15
 Navajo nuclear-extended family differences, 14-15
Feeding,
 interactions, 42, 51, 55-60
 practices, 192-193
Filming,
 effects of, 127
Friendship,
 children's, 194, 212

G

Gusii people of Kenya, 151-166, 216-218
 childrearing practices among, 152-153, 218
  structured observations of, 153
 customs and rituals among, 151-152, 218
 ethnographic background, 151, 218
 face-to-face interaction among, 151-166
  individual variation in adult-infant interaction, 158-159
  method of study, 154-155
  naturalistic observations of adult-adult interactions, 151-152

SUBJECT INDEX   265

naturalistic observations of adult-child interactions, 152-153
structured observations of adult-infant interactions, 157-163

H

Hopi Indians, 115-130
  infant behavior, 120, 122-124, 127-130
  maternal behavior, 124-130

I

Infant behavior, 192-207
  play, 194
  position and posture, 193, 198-201
  social awareness, 198-200
  visual orientation, 198-200
  vocalization, 193, 198-201
Infant development, 192-195, 200-202
Infant health, 171-173, 192
Infant socialization patterns, 207-209, 211
Interactions, 27-33, 177-184
  coding of, 27-28
  head orientation, 28, 29, 33
  mutual regard, 28, 29, 33
Intervention, 173, 175, 178-187

M

Malnutrition, 171-173, 186, 187
Marquesan society, 190-192
Maternal stimulation
  distal, 83, 84, 88
  deviant, 135, 136, 146
  optimal, 139, 145
  proximal, 78, 83, 84, 87, 88
  rhythmicity, 135, 140, 143-144
  vocalization, 65, 80, 88, 136
Methodology, cross-cultural, 237-256
  cognition, cross-cultural studies of, 238-242
    comparability of materials and procedures, 238-239
    comparability of response to experimental situation, 239-241
    laboratory tasks versus everyday activity, 241-242
  context, importance of in cross-cultural studies, 252, 253
  social interaction, cross-cultural studies of, 242-252

comparability in behavioral observations, 245-249
reactions to being observed, 243-245
sampled behavior and the cultural context, 250-252
Mother-infant interactions, 3-17, 41-50, 63-91, 134-146, 151-160
  face-to-face, 41-60, 134-144, 149-166
  feeding, 32, 51, 55-60
  floor play, 71, 72, 75, 76, 80-89
Mothers, 95-113
  child care practices, 95-98
  cross-cultural comparisons, 95-98, 101
    German-American comparisons, 95-98, 106-107, 109-110
  mothering skills, 133, 145
Mutual gaze, 119-121, 127, 129-130

N

Navajo Indians, 115-130
  infant behavior, 120, 122-124, 127-130
  maternal behavior, 124-130
Newborn behavior, 115, 128

R

Relationships with infants, 98-111
  sex of infant, 100-101, 106-107, 110
Residence groups, 3, 7-16
  change in Navajo, 8
  effects on Anglo early interaction, 11-14
  effects on mother, 11
  effects on Navajo early interaction, 11-14
  extended family, 7-11, 11-14
  household size, 4, 13-14
  housing, 11
  Navajo-Anglo compared, 10-11
  Navajo nuclear-extended families compared, 8-11
  neolocal, 7-11, 11-14
  nuclear family, 7-11, 11-14
  social opportunity, 9, 16-17
  strangers, 9, 11, 14-15

S

Sibling caregivers, 190-191, 193-194, 201, 206-207
  as medial caregivers, 201, 206-207

Social context, 22, 29, 31–35
Socioeconomic status, 41–60
 education, 68, 69, 87–89
 lower income groups, 41–60
 middle income groups, 63–89
 occupation, 68, 69, 89

T

Teenage pregnancy, 49
"Unpacking" culture, 17